LEN - THANK

HUNT!

JIM MORRELL - 1998

36" DALL SHEEP

Clare Abbott

SHEEP & SHEEP HUNTING

by Jack O'Connor

SHEEP & SHEEP HUNTING

by Jack O'Connor

SAFARI PRESS, INC

P.O. Box 3095, Long Beach, CA 90803, U.S.A.

O'Connor, Jack

ISBN 0-940143-73-9

1992

10 9 8 7 6 5 4 3 2 1

Dedication

For old-time sheep hunters who have gone to their reward:

Charles Sheldon, N. Myles Brown, Col. Harry Snyder, William J. Morden, James Clark, Carrington Weems, Richard K. Mellon, Julio Estrada, Grancel Fitz, Ernie Miller, Sir George Littledale, E. Demidoff (Prince San Danato), Col. Wilson Potter, Herb Klein

For sheep guides and outfitters who have gone on to the Happy Hunting Ground, where all the rams have heavy horns and curls of at least 40 inches, where all the dudes can climb, and where they never get buck fever and blow easy shots:

Charlie Ren, Bert Rigall, Ned Frost, Roy Hargreaves, Eugene and Louis Jacquot, Isaac Plante, Field Johnson, Frank Golata, Alex Davis, Jim Ross, Stanley Clark, Bryan Williams, John Creake-Dennis, Buck Dickson, Jack Brewster, Jim Simpson, George Ball, Jack Walters

And for guides and outfitters who are still with us:

Sam Williams, Frank Cooke and Frank Cooke, Jr., Bruce Creake-Dennis, Lynn Ross, Moose Johnson, Les Bowman, "Skook" Davidson, Harold Chambers, John Keller, "Dal" Dalzill, Alex Van Bibber, Bob Housholder

And for notable living sheep hunters:

Donald S. Hopkins, Oscar Brooks, George Parker, Elgin Gates, H.I.H. Prince Abdorreza Pahlavi, Yar Mohammed Shadloo, Jim Rikhoff, Jay Mellon, Bradford O'Connor, George Landreth, General Jimmy Doolittle, John Batten, Rashid Jamsheed, Miguel Alesio Robles, Felipe Wells, Dr. Loren L. Lutz, Victor O'Farrill, Bert and Chris Kleinberger, Jack Atcheson, Allen High

And for the hard-working, long-suffering biologists who have added to our knowledge of sheep, who have patiently endured the wise guys among the public, and many of whom have patiently answered my questions:

Dr. Valerius Geist, John Russo, Lyman Nichols, John Stelfox, Bill Helms, Allen Cooperrider, Jim Morgan, George Post, and many others

And for the organizations that are working to preserve the mountain sheep:

The Desert Bighorn Council, the Society for the Conservation of Bighorn Sheep, the Fraternity of the Desert Bighorn, the Arizona Desert Bighorn Society

And let us not forget the many officers and members of the various state wildlife organizations who support the game departments and good game management, who try to educate the ill-informed, who defend the biologists and the land against the forces of shortsighted and predatory greed!

Contents

Foreword

I did my first sheep hunting in Sonora just forty years ago. As I write this in the spring of 1974, at least half the time since then I have been toying with the notion of writing a book on North American sheep and sheep hunting. Back in 1957 I had actually put a couple of chapters on paper, but a bad automobile accident put me in traction, on crutches, and finally flanked by canes for several months, and when I could get back to a typewriter, economic necessity and the demands of a job on a magazine made me put the manuscript aside. When I got to it again I did not like what I had written. I might add that exactly a year to the day after I had been carried into a hospital in Spokane, Washington, with a broken pelvis, a dislocated hip, a great gash in my forehead through an encounter with the windshield, and numerous contusions, abrasions, and edemas, I climbed a rocky hill in the southern Sahara Desert in what is now the Chad Republic and shot a Barbary ram. Such is the sheep hunter!

I must confess that I have had a hell of a time with this book. In the first place, I had difficulty deciding how to divide it up and organize it so it would not be too repetitious, and yet make each chapter relatively complete for those readers who skip chapters on subjects that don't interest them. In the second, I had to decide whether I was to make it a research job and plow through everything that had been written on North American sheep for the past fifty years or rely largely on my own reasonably extensive experience. I decided to quote enough from the biologists to keep me on the track but otherwise to depend pretty largely on my own experience and observations.

I do not think that there is any doubt but that a large *old* ram of any North American sheep species carries more prestige than any other. The good ram is relatively rare, and securing one requires hard work, judgment, and self-control. Many an Alaskan brown bear has been shot by fat old men with emphysema and fallen arches after a short stalk along a level beach. Many a grizzly has been collected when he has come to dine on a dead horse used for bait. Those great cats, the lion and the tiger, have been baited and driven and shot by old men who wouldn't walk a mile if their lives depended upon it. But the wild ram is found in high and generally rough country. Sometimes ram country is so high and so rough that the hunting is dangerous. I have come close to breaking my neck in the low but very rough mountains in Sonora, and once in Iran I took a tumble and broke and cracked a half-dozen ribs. Hunting at 11,000 feet in Wyoming, I once made a scramble up a steep ridge that left me so short of wind that for a moment I wondered if I was having a heart attack.

Today much sheep hunting is done for prestige, but one of the things about it that fascinated the old-timers (and many present-day hunters) was sheep country itself. From the high pastures under the glaciers in the Yukon to the hot dry ranges of Sonora with cactus-clad flanks and feet thrust into the purple sea, the country where wild sheep are found is the most spectacular part of this continent. I have been on many sheep hunts where I did not fire a shot, but I have never been on a sheep hunt from which I did not return refreshed and invigorated.

Oddly enough, there is no book in existence solely devoted to the wild sheep of North America. Valerius Geist's *Mountain Sheep: A Study in Behavior and Evolution* is the nearest thing to it, but Dr. Geist has nothing to say on the desert sheep. This is a real scientific work, a genuine contribution to the knowledge of North American sheep. Some of the book is heavy going for the nonprofessional, but Dr. Geist writes better than most biologists and the more thoughtful sheep hunter will find the book full of information that is not too difficult to dig out.

Among excellent monographs on North American sheep are Lawson G. Sugden's *The California Bighorn Sheep in British Columbia,* John Russo's *The Desert Bighorn Sheep in Arizona,* Dwight R. Smith's *The Bighorn Sheep in Idaho,* and Adolph Murie's *The Wolves of Mount McKinley,* which has largely to do with the wolf–Dall sheep relationship. Helmut K. Buechner's *The Bighorn Sheep of the United States, Its Past, Present, and Future* came out in 1960 and is necessarily somewhat outdated but it concentrates more material on the bighorn in the United States than any book I know of. Many short articles by biologists have appeared, but most of them are of interest mostly to other biologists.

W. T. Hornaday's *Campfires on Desert and Lava* has long been out of print, but it gives an excellent picture of desert sheep hunting under primitive conditions. Charles Sheldon's *The Wilderness of the Upper Yukon* is also long out of print, and for this reason Sheldon's map of the distribution of the Stone and Dall sheep is being reproduced in this volume. Sheldon's *The Wilderness of the Denali,* which is about the Dall sheep of the Mount McKinley region, was reprinted about twenty years ago.

Those are my primary written sources, and I will be mentioning them again and again. Since my other source is my own experiences—which I'll also be mentioning again and again—I'll say a word here about them too.

I am not a biologist but a sheep hunter, and although some of the observations in this book may be of interest to biologists the audience for which it is intended is composed of sheep hunters and would-be sheep hunters. For the task of writing it I believe I have some unique qualifications. First, I am reasonably literate. Second, I am myself a sheep hunter of more than average experience. I began hunting sheep long before sheep hunting became fashionable and I got to prowl around in the Sonora Desert when sheep were little hunted, were more plentiful than they are now, and had in many areas no competition with domestic stock. I was also fortunate enough to be one of the first hunters in the great Stone-sheep country around the heads of the Prophet and the Muskwa right after World War II. I hunted bighorns in Alberta when the country was unspoiled and almost untouched, and Dalls in areas in the Yukon where a shot had not been fired for many years.

Another qualification I possess is the fact that I came along in time to know some of the famous pioneering sheep hunters and guides. I never met William T. Hornaday but I knew old Jeff Milton, Arizona lawman and gunslinger, who went along with Hornaday on the trip to the Pinacates that resulted in *Campfires on Desert and Lava.* In my boyhood I listened to the tales of sheep hunts spun for me by my pioneering grandfather, James Wiley Wolf, and my lawless sheep-poaching uncle, John Woolf.

I knew Bert Rigall, who was the pioneer sheep outfitter in southern Alberta and who led Martin Bovey to the bighorn which today has the largest horns of any bighorn trophy in existence. I did some desert-sheep hunting with Charlie Ren, who used to outfit in Sonora back in the 1930s, and I hunted Stones with the fine mountain man, sheep guide, and great gentleman Frank Golata. I made my first Dall-sheep hunt with an outfit furnished by the pioneering Jacquot brothers of Burwash Landing, Yukon. I knew very well Alex Davis, an Irishman who was a bellhop at New York's Plaza Hotel but wound up as a trader and outfitter in the Yukon. I have met William Morden, who wrote *Across Asia's Snows and Deserts,* and I knew James Clark, his companion on that famous trip. A great pal and a sheep-hunting companion of mine was N. Myles Brown, who was probably the first dude hunter ever to hunt that fine ram country of northern British Columbia's Prophet Bench.

Because the world is changing so rapidly this book is to some extent a record of hunts that have been taken that will never be taken again. I have been exceedingly fortunate in that I was born just about the right time. I am glad I was not born later.

—Jack O'Connor
Lewiston, Idaho
May 7, 1974

1

The Relatives of the North American Wild Sheep

In 1908 in his book *Camp-Fires on Desert and Lava,* an account of a hunt for desert sheep in the Pinacate mountains of northwest Sonora, William T. Hornaday, director of the Bronx Zoo in New York, big-game hunter, and pioneer conservationist, used the phrase "the great chain of wild sheep." By it he meant the more-or-less continuous stretch of sheep country that begins in the mountains and rocky hills in the southern Sahara of the central African Chad Republic with the sheeplike Barbary "sheep" or audad and extends through three continents. It includes the hills and ranges of the Sahara, the lofty Atlas mountains, and islands in the Mediterranean Sea. It includes vast stretches of Asia, runs into Alaska, and stretches down the mountains of the North American West to the tip of Baja California and into the rocky little hills and ranges of the Sonora Desert. The late James Clark, taxidermist and naturalist of the American Museum of Natural History, lifted the phrase from Hornaday's book and paraphrased it as the title of a book he wrote on the wild sheep of the world, *The Great Arc of Wild Sheep.*

It is believed that the genus *Ovis,* the true sheep, originated during the Pliocene or possibly the late Miocene epoch in the mountains of central Asia and then spread into suitable country. Both the sheep and the goats are presumed to be descended from mountain-dwelling antelope of more remote times. In his book *Mountain Sheep: A Study in Behavior and Evolution,* the Canadian biologist Valerius Geist says the immediate ancestors of all sheep were probably the goat-antelopes of which the North American white goat and the Asiatic serow are examples.

As is the case with all mammals, nature did some experimenting along the way. One very large extinct sheep (*megalovis* or "huge sheep") was as large as an ox. Large sheep were plentiful in Asia during the early and middle Pleistocene, but they were replaced by smaller sheep toward the end of the epoch.

There are approximately forty races of wild sheep in the world. These vary enormously in size, color, and horn shape, and to some extent in habits. The heaviest of the wild sheep, the Siberian argali, may weigh 450 pounds on the hoof or possibly even somewhat more. On the other hand, the little Cyprian "mouflon" will weigh around 80 pounds. Sheep as a group have never really been systematically studied over much of their range. Few biologists have had the opportunity to study and observe more than a few races. In the single country of Iran, for example, although considerable work has been done on sheep, much more should be done. I have never read about it in books and nor have I hunted it, but I have seen pictures of what may well be the world's smallest wild sheep. It is found in southern Iran.

Sheep are very adaptable animals. They are at home in the frigid arctic and subarctic mountains of the Yukon, Alaska, and eastern Siberia, and they are also at home in the broiling deserts of Sonora, southern Arizona, and California's Death Valley. I have hunted sheep in mountains so rough that a man climbing around in them constantly risked his life—and I have hunted sheep in country so round and smooth that a horse could be galloped over it.

The various races of sheep are all interfertile, and anyone who has moved extensively through various sheep areas learns that if given the chance the sheep will mate with other varieties. Over a generation ago I knew an old Mexican who scratched out a living of a sort in a little oasis in southern Arizona near the Mexican border. He had a horse, five or six head of cattle, a few goats, and some sheep. There were desert bighorn in all the rocky hills around, and wild bighorn rams were always coming in and impregnating his ewes. Some of his sheep wound up being about three-fourths desert bighorn, and except that they were hairier they looked about like bighorns.

Free movement between the closely related snow-white Dall sheep and the very dark Stone sheep is impeded by a chain of lakes that runs roughly along the British Columbia–Yukon border and by the wide Yukon River, but nevertheless wandering Dalls manage to get into Stone country and wandering Stone rams impregnate Dall ewes.

Actually the western end of this great arc of wild sheep is occupied by the audad or "Barbary" sheep, an animal that has both goatlike and sheeplike characteristics but which is probably more goat than sheep. It does not belong to the genus *Ovis* but to *Ammotragus.* It occupies a genus all by itself. The audad can interbreed with goats but not with sheep. At one time there were true sheep in northern Africa, but they have long been extinct. Most books refer to the audad as being found in *northern* Africa. Actually he is not only found in the high Atlas mountains of northern Africa but throughout the Sahara. His sign can be found in just about every rocky jebl and mountain range in that vast desert. In 1958 I shot an audad ram in the southern Sahara of Chad Republic, just about as close to the geographical center of Africa as one can get.

The audad *(Ammotragus lervia)* is called *mouflon 'a manchettes* by the French because of its large beard or neck ruff and the tufts around its knees. I first picked up the only audad ram I have ever shot because I noticed through binoculars the waving of his neck ruff as he fed. The audad is a rather large, heavy animal as sheep go. In his book *Man and Beast in Africa,* the Frenchman François Sommer says that rams will weigh from 175 to 260 pounds. The only one I ever saw weighed went 175 field-dressed. That would give a live weight of about 225 pounds.

The audads have been transplanted to Texas and to New Mexico and have done very well. There are restricted open seasons on them in both states. The first audad I ever saw unconfined was on Mark Moss's pioneering game ranch near Llano, Texas. The species is now found on many Texas ranches.

All true sheep, members of the genus *Ovis,* are animals of small to medium size, and of from light to chunky build, varying with the species. They have narrow, pointed muzzles, carry their heads high, and are covered with fairly fine hair except for a naked area above and between the nostrils. They have glands between the hooves of the feet and frequently below the eyes. Ears run from small to moderate size;

some are rounded, some pointed. Males have no beard but some species have a long neck ruff. They are without the strong odor of goats. Both sexes have horns, but the horns of the males are much heavier and more massive than those of the females. Their flesh is considered a delicacy, among the most palatable of all game.

It is believed that sheep are the members of the family Bovidae that evolved last, later than the antelopes and even the oxen. Besides the audad the sheep have other goatlike relatives. The bharal or "blue sheep" found in the Himalayas is akin to both sheep and goat, but lacks the face glands of the sheep and the rancid odor of the goats. The Caucasian tur resembles the bharal, but is more goatlike than sheeplike. Incidentally, the only non-Russians I know who have ever shot bharals are Prince Abdorreza Pahlavi of Iran and Jay Mellon, the American big-game hunter.

True sheep are found on some of the islands in the Mediterranean Sea—Corsica, Sardinia, and Cyprus. These are popularly called mouflon. They are small, sturdy sheep. Those of Sardinia and Corsica are called *Ovis musimon.* Clark says these sheep weigh about 150 pounds, a weight which seems high to me. The European mouflon are reddish-brown and have a white belt around the middle. They have been successfully transplanted to the mountains of Germany, Austria, Czechoslovakia, and Yugoslavia. Some pureblooded mouflon are likewise found on ranches in Texas where they can be shot for a fee, but more commonly these Texas-ranch "mouflon" have been crossed with a domestic breed known as the "Barbados sheep." The cross is supposed to have made them hardier and more disease-free. The best European mouflon head I have ever seen pictured was one Prince Abdorreza shot in Yugoslavia some years ago. Clark says the European mouflon stands from 26 to 33 inches high at the shoulder. In shape the close-curl horns of the European mouflon that I have seen look much like those of miniature Rocky Mountain bighorns.

The Cyprian mouflon *(Ovis ophion ophion)* is another species. It is certainly one of the smallest of the wild sheep as the shoulder height is 24 to 26 inches. The horns of the Cyprian sheep curve outward like those of the smaller varieties of urial found in Turkey and Iran. Like these urial it has a small neck ruff. All of these island sheep are found in steep mountains covered with brush, one of the few wild sheep with a brushy habitat. At one time wild sheep were found on other Grecian islands and on the Balearic islands. Presumably they migrated to their island homes during one of the glacial epochs of the Pleistocene when much of the world's water was locked up in the polar icecaps and the Mediterranean was an area of inland lakes and marshes with much larger areas of dry land around mainland and islands.

One of the things that the observant sheep hunter learns as he moves from sheep range to sheep range is that the various subspecies and species of sheep merge and that lines of demarcation are difficult to establish. I have seen this with the Dall and the Stone. I shall go into this in more detail later but it is impossible to say exactly where the Stone ends and the Dall begins, and vice-versa. No one will ever be able to say where the various subspecies of the brown bighorn began and ended. Sheep are mutually fertile and are great wanderers. Friends who have hunted and observed sheep all over Iran tell me that the various subspecies of the Iranian sheep merge one into the other. The Kopet Dagh urial of northeastern Iran merges at one end of his range with the red sheep and at the other in Russian Turkestan with the smaller examples of the argali.

From the Turkish mainland north of the island of Cyprus east and south to northern Iran, Pakistan, and northern India runs a belt of small-to-medium-size sheep collectively called "urial" but varying a great deal in size, coloration, build, and configuration of horns. These include the Antolian urial *(Ovis ophion antolica)*, and the Armenian urial *(Ovis ophion armeniana)* from the area where northern Turkey, Russia, and Iran come together. According to Clark this sheep has a yellowish-brown body, a saddle patch, and a dark-brown throat ruff. The Laristan urial is a very small sheep, possibly the smallest of all wild sheep. It is found in south-central Iran and sometimes it can be seen from salt water in the rugged hills along the Persian Gulf. David Laylin, an American who is a professional hunter and outfitter in Iran, sent me a picture of a full-grown ram from this area. It did not look to me as if it weighed 50 pounds.

In the fall of 1970 my wife and I hunted sheep in the Mohammed Reza Shah game reserve north and east of the Caspian Sea in Iran, and later we went sightseeing to the cities of Shiraz and Isfahan. Some Iranian friends took us out to a country estate about 15 miles from Isfahan. The owner of the estate had in a pen several wild sheep captured in the rugged nearby mountains. These were undoubtedly Isfahan urials *(Ovis gmelini isphannica)*. The rams were chunky, solid, short-legged sheep that were built much like the North American sheep. To me they seemed a good deal heavier and stockier than the closely related "Persian red sheep" I shot in the Zagros mountains south of Tehran in 1955. I would estimate that the largest ram would weigh about 130 to 140 pounds live, whereas the red sheep farther north seemed to me lighter in build and longer-legged. A sheep similar to those of Isfahan is found in large numbers on an island in Lake Urmia in western Iran. These were at one time planted on the island to afford hunting for an Iranian nobleman. They are so plentiful now that the Iranian game department has introduced leopards to help hold their numbers down.

The relationships of the various Middle Eastern sheep need more study before hard-and-fast classifications are made. Prince Abdorreza Pahlavi and Iskander Firouz, head of the Iranian game department, both say that Clark's book is no more than a good start and that it contains many inaccuracies. This is no wonder. "Jimmy" Clark himself, as far as I know, had never been in Turkey or Iran or Russian Turkestan.

Probably the correct scientific name of the "Persian red sheep" is *orientalis*. They are found in the Zagros mountains south of Tehran and also in the Elburz range, which rises above Tehran and cuts it off from the Caspian Sea. In 1955 I shot a red sheep in the Zagros and one in a little range adjacent to the main Zagros. Iranian friends tell me that in the northern part of the Zagros the "red sheep" merge with the larger white-necked Kopet Dagh urial—and scientific investigation bears this out.

The red sheep I saw were slender, light-boned, lively little sheep. I believe they are the spookiest sheep I have ever hunted. At the time I was hunting the rams were in bunches and the moment I'd stick my head over a ridge one of the rams would spy me. Away they would all go! The sheep have been hunted by human beings for 25,000 years, by everyone from Neanderthal men to modern men with scope-sighted rifles. They have had to be smart to survive.

The "red" sheep come honestly by their name. They are a reddish tan. Their horns are light and curve to the side and backward so that often the points almost touch on the backs of their necks. The two rams I shot looked to me as if they would weigh field-dressed a good deal less than 100 pounds. Prince Abdorreza told me he had seen them somewhat heavier.

In the northern Zagros the range of the red sheep overlaps that of the real urial. These handsome sheep are found in northeastern Iran, in Afghanistan, in Pakistan, and in the mountains of India, but they reach their largest size and grow the finest horns in the Mohammed Reza Shah Wildlife Park in northeastern Iran and other ranges in northeastern Iran and Russian Turkestan. In the reserve, according to a study made for the Iran Game and Fish Department by Eugene Decker of Colorado State University and his assistant Gerald Kowalski, these sheep are best classified as *Ovis ammon vignei,* but they have also been listed as *arkal* and *dolgopolovi.* They have red-brown bodies, handsome white neck ruffs, and horns that either curve back and up like those of most American sheep or pinch in close to the face and then flare out—the type common with the various forms of argali.

These white-necked urial are the largest of the Iranian sheep. Decker and Kowalski give the mean live weight of eight rams as 148.9 pounds. The heaviest weighed 182 pounds. From what I have seen I would guess that rams weighing over 200 pounds on the hoof are not uncommon. In comparison, transitional rams that were hybrids between *vignei* and *orientalis* (red sheep) weighed on the average 124.7 pounds with the heaviest 135. The red sheep rams *(orientalis)* weighed from 77 to 140 pounds, which would agree pretty well with my guess of the field-dressed weight of the two red rams I shot as less than 100 pounds.

Hunters generally call these big urial from northeastern Iran the Kopet Dagh urial. Kopet Dagh ("Apple Mountain") is partly in Russia and partly in Iran. Many fine rams have come from its slopes. Although the horns of these big urial are much more slender than those of North American sheep they compare favorably with them in length. Prince Abdorreza has collected several well over 40 inches. Some have been taken over 45.

As a layman it has occurred to me that one way to classify wild sheep for practical purposes is to divide them into climbing sheep and running sheep. The climbing sheep escape their enemies by heading for rough country, rocks, cliffs, and shale slides where they can get around faster than any soft-footed predator. The running sheep run like antelope. The red sheep and the Isfahan sheep are climbing sheep, rough-country sheep. So are the sheep of eastern Siberia and those of North America. The climbing sheep tend to be stocky and have short powerful legs and wide rumps. The running sheep, on the other hand, have longer legs and more slender builds. The urial of the Mohammed Reza Shah reserve were the first running sheep I had ever seen. When a bunch is frightened, the animals take off over the rolling juniper-dotted hills like so many North American pronghorn antelope, leaving a cloud of dust behind. The argalis, the big sheep of central Asia, are all running sheep and are found in rolling country. They are not very good climbers.

Most of the sheep popularly called urial are low-altitude sheep. The sheep hills in the reserve are around 7,000 to 8,000 feet in elevation. The country looks like the rolling foothill country of approximately the same elevation in the Western states—gray, rolling hills, with sparse grass, forbs, dark junipers. I have often wondered if these urial would not do very well in the Western United States. They have lived for generations in overgrazed country in competition with domestic sheep and goats. They are immune to domestic sheep diseases that sometimes wipe out our native bighorns. Furthermore they are very prolific, twins being as common as single births, and triplets sometimes occurring.

Clark divides the wild sheep into the Moufloniformes, of which the urials are a part; the argalis, the eastern Asiatic bighorns; and the wild sheep of North America, the Dalls and Stones (thinhorns) and the various bighorns. The range of the argalis is next to that of the urials, and argalis and urials have much in common. In fact, the smaller argalis resemble urials, just as the large urials like those of northeast Iran resemble argalis.

The argalis, the order of sheep which produces the longest horns, the heaviest horns, and the greatest body weight, and which is the least accessible of all the divisions of wild sheep, occupy the central part of the great crescent of wild sheep. Until recently few of these big sheep had been taken by trophy hunters. Back in the 1920s, William J. Morden and Jimmy Clark, the author of *The Great Arc of Wild Sheep,* made a long, difficult, and exhausting expedition for argali from northern India into Siberia. Morden wrote a book called *Across Asia's Snows and Deserts.* The book, published by Putnam in 1927, has long been out of print, but it is one of the world's classic books of big-game hunting and an important source book on the argali. Now and then a secondhand copy can be picked up. I knew Jimmy Clark and his charming wife Sally in the last years of his life, and I met Bill Morden and his wife in London in 1953. The Mordens were on their way to a safari in Africa and so was I.

Theodore and Kermit Roosevelt made a similar trip to that taken by

Morden and Clark about the same time. Their book about the expedition is called *East of the Sun and West of the Moon.* The late Roy Chapman Andrews of the American Museum of Natural History hunted and collected argali in Mongolia and western China. Prince Abdorreza Pahlavi of Iran, a dedicated sheep hunter, was as far as I know the first trophy hunter since the Roosevelts to get into the country of the *Ovis poli,* the variety of argali that grows the longest horns and occupies the highest country. This was in the summer of 1957. The prince hunted in Afghanistan and also in a Russian spur of the Pamirs. In the fall of 1959, Herb Klein of Texas and Elgin Gates of California hunted *Ovis poli* in Hunza. Gates also slipped across the border into Chinese territory. Since that time several other American hunters have made it into the Pamirs for *poli.* Prince Abdorreza was likewise the first trophy hunter to get into the Altai mountains for Mongolian argali since the late 1880s, when St. George Littledale, an Englishman, and E. Demidoff, an Anglicized Russian, hunted there. Demidoff wrote a book called *After Wild Sheep in the Altai and Mongolia.* This book was published by Rowland Ward of London in 1900. The original edition is rare and costly but it has been reprinted by offset lithography by Abercrombie & Fitch of New York and it is available at a moderate price. Demidoff is also the author of *A Shooting Trip to Kamchatka,* just about the only primary source of information on *Ovis nivicola,* the wild sheep of the Siberian Kamchatka Peninsula and close relative of the North American Dall sheep. This book was likewise published in London by Rowland Ward, in 1904. It is rare and expensive.

Since Klein and Gates hunted *poli* in Hunza a few other Americans have managed to get into the Pamirs, as the *poli* is certainly one of the world's most prestigious trophies. Among them were my friends Jay Mellon and John Batten. The country is very high, very cold, and the trip is exhausting. John Batten almost died there of high-altitude sickness, and one of Jay Mellon's companions actually did die. An *Ovis poli* hunt is only for the healthy, tough, and determined.

All of the sheep classified as argali are not large. In fact the two westernmost examples, *Ovis amon severtozi* and *O. a. nigrimontana,* are about the size of the Kopet Dagh urial of the Iran–Russian Turkestan border and greatly resemble them. In fact, I have seen mounted heads of the Bokharan argali (apparently the same thing as *nigrimontana*), and to my ignorant sheep-hunting layman's eyes it is the spit and image of my old pal the Kopet Dagh urial from the Mohammed Reza Shah reserve. Clark says the heavier corrugations on the horns and the smaller ears put them into the argali rather than the urial group.

Clark puts the members of *Ovis amon* (the argalis) into three groups: the small northwestern argalis I have just mentioned; the lighter flaring-horned argalis of which the *Ovis poli* is the most famous but which includes three other subspecies; and the massive, heavy-horned argali of which the type species and the best known is the Altai or Siberian argali, *Ovis amon amon.*

All of the argalis are what I call running sheep, and the country they inhabit, although sometimes very high, is generally not rough. In the Pamirs at 16,000 to 18,000 feet above sea level, *poli* hunters are able to ride yaks when they hunt. As one of the underprivileged I have never ridden a yak, but from what I hear it can be classed as an Experience. I understand that horses can be ridden over most of the sheep country in the Altai. Jack Atcheson, the Butte, Montana, taxidermist, who has hunted sheep in Mongolia, tells me that much of the sheep country can be navigated by a jeep.

There have always been some pretty phony characters among big-game hunters. Those who are trophy-happy have stretched hides, built up horns with fiberglass and plastic wood, lied about the weight and the size of trophies and the localities where they have been shot. But one of the boldest attempts to con the public took place about the time of World War I. A man on the West Coast (in Portland, Oregon, I believe) got hold of the horns of some species of argali, had them mounted with a Rocky Mountain bighorn scalp, and claimed the world record bighorn.

Back a half-century ago there were fewer sophisticated sheep hunters than there are today, but even then the trick was soon discovered. I saw the picture in an old hunting-and-fishing magazine and instantly detected the fraud. The horns were pure argali and anyone knowing much about sheep would not have been fooled. Argali horns have much more prominent corrugations compared to the smoother horns of the Asiatic and North American bighorns. In some species they are also much longer, and in others they are larger at the base. The longest Rocky Mountain bighorn head I can find listed in *Records of North American Big Game* is 45½ inches, but there are several around 45. The longest desert sheep horn I can find is 43⁶⁄₈, the longest Stone 51⅝, the longest Dall 48⅝. On the other hand, in an old copy of Rowland Ward's *Records,* I see a *poli* head with a length of 70¾ inches and another (owner's measurements) that is 75. A Siberian argali is listed in the same old Rowland Ward with a horn 62¼ inches around the curl and with a base of 19¾. Since some big sheep heads will shrink an inch in circumference at the base when thoroughly dry, this ram when first shot probably had horns with a circumference of well over 20 inches. But a North American sheep with a dry base of 16 inches is good, and the largest bases listed in the records are about 17¼ to 17½ inches.

During the Middle Ages the Venetian trader Marco Polo traveled with a caravan across the Pamirs, the lofty "Roof of the World." In his famous book he described the cold and the bitter winds, the thin air, the bare forbidding landscape. He also described a large sheep with enormously long horns. For generations those who read the book thought old Marco was telling a tall tale. They were used to the little domestic sheep which were descended from the small urials of the Middle East, and they *knew* a sheep that big with horns that long was an impossibility. If Marco had told them he had run across a covey of dragons he would have been believed, as the Middle Ages were high on dragons and everyone who knew anything knew that dragons were not uncommon in faraway Cathay and adjoining regions. But sheep as large as donkeys? Ridiculous! Then, finally, adventurous Englishmen penetrated to the Pamirs and found the sheep. They were named *Ovis amon poli* in old Marco's honor.

The *poli* are large sheep but not as large as some writers would have us believe. In *Across Asia's Snows and Deserts,* William Morden wrote: "The Pamir sheep are surprisingly lightly built and their bones are very delicate for animals living in rugged country where traveling through deep snow is necessary during much of the year. . . . Neither are these sheep exceptionally muscular, no more so in fact than the Virginia deer (whitetail) of North America. The necks of the rams seem lightly built for carrying such heavy heads. A carefully weighed ram totalled 239 pounds, though in the fall he would probably have weighed from 25 to 50 pounds more."

The book contains a diagram giving the body measurements of a *poli* ram. It does not say if the measurements are for the body alone and do not include the hair. Since the ram was shot in the spring the measurements from brisket to rump and from top of shoulder to bottom of chest might be greater in the remains of the spring coat than they would be in the shorter summer coat. The diagram gives a measurement of 18 inches on a straight line from shoulder to bottom of chest and 40 inches from chest to rump. Measurement from top of shoulder to hoof is 44 inches. These give the picture of a rangy, rather lightly built sheep—and not an exceptionally large one. A very large Dall ram I shot in August 1950 in his summer coat gave a shoulder-to-bottom-of-chest measurement of 22 inches, and a brisket-to-rump measurement of 40 inches. One September-killed ram in his fall coat measures slightly more, but the extra was mostly hair. Like the Kopet Dagh urial and the other running sheep, the *poli* is not found as a rule in very rough country. In *The Great Arc of Wild Sheep,* Clark comments on a photograph of the *poli* habitat group in the Chicago Natural History Museum: "This group shows an unusual amount of rocky outcrops and stony ground cover where sheep would not ordinarily be found because of lack of grass. They might, however, be en route over a high pass from one valley to another."

Morden describes the *poli* as creamy white with brownish saddles. The horns, though long, are triangular in cross-section and relatively light. Clark says the skull and horns of a *poli* specimen weighed 25 pounds when dry. A large American bighorn skull and horns may weigh 40 pounds, and Clark says a Siberian argali *(Ovis amon amon)* skull and horns weighed 49 pounds.

Some of the argalis have white neck ruffs like the larger urial. Among these is the Tibetan argali *(hodgsoni),* which British officers stationed in India used to make long pack trips out of Srinigar and Leh in the Kashmir to shoot. An old edition of Rowland Ward gives the weight of one *hodgsoni* ram as 212 pounds. This was surely a dressed weight. Another ram of the same species stood 43 inches high at the shoulder, was ten years old, and weighed 205—probably another dressed weight.

In his book Clark lists three types of argali. The first is the small, western sheep that are much like urials. There are two species of these—*severtzovi* and *nigrimontana.* The second group contains the *Ovis amon poli* and the other argali with relatively thin widely flaring horns—*hunei, karelini,* and *littledalei.* The third group consists of the argali with the heavy horns—*sairensis, collium, amon, dalai-lamae, hodgsoni,* and *darwini.*

All these argali have horns with deep corrugations that are quite unlike the much smoother horns of North American sheep. Those with the flaring horns are tremendously impressive, but if I had my pick of trophies I think I'd take one with the greater mass and closer curl—the big *amon* from the Altai.

The classification of the argali has undergone considerable change in the past twenty years. It will undoubtedly undergo more as more is learned of these fine sheep. With better relations with Russia and China more systematic work can be done.

The least known of all the Asiatic sheep and the closest relatives of our North American sheep are the Asiatic bighorns, of which there are supposed to be five subspecies—*Ovis nivicola nivicola, O. n. borealis, O. n. potanini, O. n. alleni,* and *O. n. lydekkeri.* One wonders if these classifications would stand up under further study. These are found in eastern Siberia, with some ranging on mountains close to the Bering Sea. These sheep appear to be about the size of the Dall sheep across the straits in Alaska. Like the North American sheep, they are stocky "climbing" sheep. A picture in Clark's book shows a Clifton's bighorn *(lydekkeri)* with a dark band across his nose below his eyes. The color of *nivicola* is a grayish brown. They have short ears as do the Stone and the Dall. Their horns are relatively smooth like those of the *dalli* group in North America. Demidoff gives the measurements of his best *nivicola* ram—39 × 14½ and 38½ × 14½. This would be a better than average Dall trophy.

These Asiatic bighorns range over a wider area than do even the argalis. From the descriptions and pictures in Demidoff's book *A Shooting Trip to Kamchatka,* the country looks about like the country in Alaska and the Yukon. How these sheep are faring I have no idea. Siberia is being developed, and as it is developed the sheep will come under increasing pressure just as have their relatives across the water.

2 The North American Sheep

Europeans who first encountered North American wild sheep were astounded at the size of their horns. Accustomed as they were to the domestic sheep descended from the small urials of the Middle East, they thought the wild American sheep were enormous. Coronado, who explored the Southwest, wrote that the sheep were "as big as horses, had very large horns, and little tails."

Another Spaniard told of an animal they called "sheep, because it somewhat resembles ours." He went on to say that this animal was as large as a big calf one or two years old, had a head like a deer, and very large horns. He added that the flesh of this animal was delicious.

Yet another explorer said that the horns of this wild sheep were as large around as a man's thigh and 6 feet long. That would have been one for the record books!

The American mountain men and explorers who encountered wild sheep in the Rocky Mountains were also impressed by their horns. They called the animals "bighorns." They felt that these great horns should have some useful purpose besides fighting, so they invented the tale sometimes heard even today—that the rams could leap from cliffs, land on their horns, turn a flip, and be safe and sound.

The term "bighorn" has a romantic sound, and of all the names of the North American trophy animals, "bighorn ram" is probably the most evocative. The term "grizzly" is right behind and some might even put it first. There is no doubt that the mounted head of a large mature ram of any species is an impressive trophy, one of the most impressive in the entire world. The head of an old bighorn ram, either Rocky Mountain or desert variety, massive, battered, close-curled, is a trophy that ranks right up with a 10-foot tiger, a heavily maned lion, an Alaskan brown bear, a 100-pound elephant, or one of the big Asiatic wild sheep called argalis.

The term "bighorn" is both descriptive and romantic. For a long time it was applied to all North American sheep. In a pre-World War I copy of Rowland Ward's *Records of Big Game,* an English publication, the Stone sheep are called "Black bighorns," the Dalls are called "White bighorns," and the intergrades between Stones and Dalls, for a time thought to be a separate subspecies, are called "Grey bighorns." Later the Stones and the Dalls, because their horns run generally less massive than those of the bighorns, were referred to as "thinhorns." However, the term has never been popular.

The massive curling horns of bighorn rams impressed even those who shot sheep for meat. My maternal grandfather hunted sheep for excitement and sport as much as for meat in the Rocky Mountains of Colorado and New Mexico and also in the desert ranges of Arizona. He was no trophy collector and like most men of his era he generally threw the heads away, but once he could not resist bringing back the skull and horns of an exceptionally large desert ram he shot on Camelback Mountain near Phoenix, Arizona. For many years it was in the basement of his home in Tempe. I remember the head well. It was massive, battered, broomed back several inches at the tips, and made more than a complete curl. If it were in existence today it would be high in the records.

Trophy hunting is basically what might be called an aristocratic sport, the sport of a leisured class. The European noble hunted stags and displayed the skulls and horns on the walls of his castle to show that it was not necessary to scrounge around for meat as the peasant did. Instead he hunted for something more in keeping with his aristocratic status—excitement and trophies. The peasant hated the aristocrat, who protected the stags and wild boar that foraged in his fields and ate his crops. He thought the noble insane for being interested in antlers and tusks rather than meat. The saying "Antlers make poor soup" is primarily a bit of peasant wisdom.

The aristocrat, on the other hand, looked on the peasant as a rude and gluttonous clod who could never get his thoughts above his belly. Killing a royal stag, bringing in the meat, and leaving the antlers back in the woods was as immoral to the aristocrat as taking the antlers and abandoning the meat was to the peasant. That conflict is still in existence today. Peasant sportsmen prod peasant legislators into passing laws prohibiting the trophy hunter's leaving meat in the hills. It might be argued that the trophy hunter has reduced the animal to his possession, that it is his, and it is no more immoral for him to leave the meat up on the mountain than it is for the meat hunter to leave the horns or antlers.

During the last half of the nineteenth century and well into the twentieth, the British were the trophy hunters of the world. The British Empire was worldwide. The pound was the currency by which all other currency was judged. Transportation, although slow by modern standards, was available and reliable. If a wog got funny with a Britisher, Queen Victoria would send out a gunboat to teach the lesser breeds a lesson. Furthermore, England was full of nice, new money, the product of British manufacture and trade. When Papa had a bundle, Junior could afford to pack up his guns and kit and go adventuring in far places—to Tibet and the Northern Frontier of India for sheep and ibex, to South Africa for elephant and lion, to Central Asia for *Ovis poli* and other species of the great argali, to India for tiger, and to the wild Rocky Mountains of the North American West for bighorn and grizzly.

Actually the English were responsible for the first American outfitters for big-game hunts. English trophy hunters in the late '70s, the '80s, and the '90s used to go by railroad to some small town in the mountains of the West, hire local guides, wranglers, and cooks, and rent horses, pack saddles, and other equipment. They made up their grub lists and bought the food. From them American ranchers and frontiersmen got the idea of going into the outfitting business themselves. Outfitting as it is known on this continent originated in the Wyoming Rockies to supply the needs of sheep and elk hunters, largely British. Its terms and vocabulary are cowboy western-Texas–Mexican.

Outfitting for mountain game moved into Montana and Idaho and then into Canada, primarily into Alberta. Today it is most flourishing in northern British Columbia, the Yukon, and Alaska. It is primarily the wild sheep that has made outfitting go. Today outfitting has seen better days in most American states and in southern Canada. It has been killed off by local hunters, by lumber and cattle interests, by mines and oil exploration.

After World War I, Americans started replacing the British as the international big-game hunters, but the British in the interval between the two big wars still came to Alberta for bighorn, to the Yukon for Dall sheep, to Atlin and Telegraph Creek in northern British Columbia for Stones. After World War II, high inheritance taxes, currency restrictions, and the collapse of the British Empire kept the English home. The Americans took their place as the international big-game hunters. Air transport became fast, reliable, and cheap. The United States was full of new money and of people who could arrange for leisure. Americans became the most numerous trophy hunters. They swarmed into the sheep country of the Canadian Rockies and Cassiars, to the ranges of Alaska and the Yukon. They made safaris to Kenya and other African countries, and shot tigers in India. As Europe settled down, men of other nationalities followed in their footsteps. Among foreigners I know who have hunted sheep in the United States and Canada are Frenchmen, Mexicans, Iranians, Spaniards, Germans, Italians, Swedes, and Danes. Big-game hunting has become international. The Weatherby trophy, an award given by the rifle manufacturer to outstanding big-game hunters, has been awarded to an Iranian, two Mexicans, and a Frenchman. Big-game hunters all over the world have been caught up by the romance of North American sheep with their great curling horns. No trophy in the world has more prestige.

Like most species of North American big game, the wild sheep are of Asiatic origin. A land bridge connecting Alaska and Siberia existed off and on during the Pleistocene era and sank out of sight in the rising sea water for the last time only about 10,000 years ago. Today sheep are found within sight of salt water on both sides of the Bering Straight. If the bridge still existed it would be no surprising feat for adventurous bands of sheep to cross the land bridge to North America. Wild sheep are great wanderers, and it is the feeling of old sheep hunters that the animals will travel as long as they can see mountains in the distance. After they had established themselves in Alaska the sheep moved gradually south, as there is a chain of mountains running clear from Alaska to the length of Lower California and midway down the state of Sonora in northwest Mexico. Sheep also spread west from the main mountain chain wherever there was suitable refuge country—canyons, isolated ranges, badlands, and even rough little buttes out in the plains.

It is just as logical to presume that sheep from Alaska wandered back across the land bridge into Asia as it is to presume that Asiatic sheep crossed into North America. Throughout the long Pleistocene age the seas rose and sank as ice alternately melted or piled up at the poles. During the periods when the two continents were connected, sheep undoubtedly traded back and forth and exchanged genes.

There are various theories as to the causes for the evolution of North American sheep into the two species—thinhorn *(dalli)* and bighorn *(canadensis)*. One is that the sheep that were the first migrants from Asia were driven south into what is now the western United States by the great ice sheets that formed during certain periods of the Pleistocene age. The extensive ice sheets would have made the mountains in Cassiars and Rockies between 45 and 62 degrees north latitude unsuitable for sheep. Helmut K. Buechner, in his monograph *The Bighorn Sheep of the United States, Its Past, Present, and Future* (1960), says that the sheep that moved south would have been sealed off from those in Alaska for at least 45,000 years.

The sheep that moved south into the mountains of the United States developed into the various races of the brown bighorn. Then as the ice receded these sheep worked north again into suitable country until they were stopped by the wide belt of low, heavily forested country and the humid, heavily forested Coast ranges. The sheep below the ice also moved gradually south into suitable country until they were eventually found in mountains opposite Tiburon Island in the northwestern Mexican state of Sonora, throughout the length of Baja California, and in most of the desert ranges and canyons in Arizona, Utah, Nevada, and southern California. The brown bighorns were also found as far south as the Big Bend country of Texas and in some desert ranges in Chihuahua, and as far east as the Missouri River breaks in Montana and the Badlands of South Dakota.

A theory held by Russian zoologists is that the thinhorn sheep (Dall and Stone) are descended from a later migration across the Bering land bridge, and it is true that these sheep are much more like the sheep of eastern Siberia than are the bighorns. The most popular theory today is that the ice sheet divided the North American sheep population into two segments, those north of the great glaciers and those to the south. Those to the north survived the worst rigors of the Pleistocene in the arctic between the Brooks and Alaska ranges, where the snowfall is not heavy enough to form large masses of ice. Then as the ice receded, exposing more suitable sheep country, these northern sheep worked south, gradually evolving into Dall and Stone, both subspecies of *Ovis dalli.* They were stopped in their migration to the south by the wide Peace River and by the low, wet, heavy forests of the Skeena Valley.

It is certainly true that the thinhorn sheep more nearly resemble the sheep of eastern Siberia than do the bighorns and that horn types found in Asia are more common among the thinhorns than they are among the bighorns. However, it is also true that in the southern portion of the range of Stone sheep, horns more nearly approaching the bighorn type are often found. It is presumed that the thinhorns and the bighorns have been separated for many thousands of years, but just as one sees thinhorn sheep with horns of bighorn type so one also sees bighorns with horns that look as if they should be on a Stone or Dall.

I am not a biologist but I would guess that sheep were an earlier arrival in the New World than the wapiti (elk), the moose (called elk in Europe), and the caribou. At least they are more different from their Old World relatives. The Dall and Stone sheep are similar to the various races of *nivicola* (snow sheep) found in eastern Siberia, but they are by no means identical. Valerius Geist in his book *Mountain Sheep* does not consider *nivicola* and *dalli* very closely related. On the other hand, the average experienced big-game hunter would be hard put to tell a Wyoming elk from a Tian Shan wapiti from central Asia, a caribou from the wild reindeer of northern Siberia, or an American moose from the "elk" of Siberia and northern Europe.

Another fairly early arrival from Siberia must have been the white Rocky Mountain goat, as he has evolved into quite a different animal from any of his Old World relatives. Americans are great subdividers and classifiers. The British are not. In *Wild Oxen, Sheep, and Goats of All Kinds,* a rare and valuable book that came out in 1898, R. Lydekker, a famous British zoologist, lumps all North American sheep and those of eastern Siberia into one species, *canadensis,* because *canadensis* was the first described. By this classification the Stone sheep would be *Ovis canadensis stonei,* the Dall *Ovis canadensis dalli.* The sheep of the Kamchatka Peninsula become *Ovis canadensis nivicola.* However, today most biologists recognize two species of sheep in North America—*canadensis* and *dalli. Canadensis* was first encountered in the form of desert bighorns by Spanish friars and explorers in Lower California and in Arizona in the sixteenth century.

In his book on mountain sheep, Valerius Geist says that the sheep moved into grassy areas that followed the melting of mountain and continental glaciers. Then as the trees followed behind the grass the sheep were cut off by forested areas. Sheep do not like forests and feel uneasy in them. Increase in forests limits sheep habitat, and in effect habitat suitable for sheep has in the north been decreasing as the centuries since the Ice Age have passed. A thought that occurs to me is that if the sheep arrived in North America fairly early in the Pleistocene their range would have expanded and contracted several times as the ice melted and then built back up.

The brown bighorn was officially described and classified until the early part of the nineteenth century. At various times several subspecies of *canadensis* have been described, but in 1940 Prof. Ian McTaggart Cowan of the University of British Columbia, after an extensive examination and comparison of sheep specimens in various museums, reduced the subspecies of *canadensis* to seven.

Sheep hunters do not pay much attention to these fine-spun subspecies. They lump all North American sheep into four classifications—bighorn, desert, Dall, and Stone. There might be some argument for putting the California bighorn in a separate category, but on the whole I am inclined to agree with my fellow sheep hunters. There is a great deal of variation among sheep (even those found on the same mountain) in size, horn type, and color. I have shot several examples of *mexicanus* in Sonora. I have also observed desert bighorn in Arizona and Nevada. To my layman's eye they look pretty much alike. Actually the brown bighorn has been exterminated over so much of its range that the relationship of the surviving groups is difficult if not impossible to establish.

Many questions occur to me. We can assume that sheep would have found it difficult to cross the Colorado River and that therefore it would be logical to assume that the sheep east of the Colorado would be different from those west of it. But why should the sheep of the northern part of Baja California differ greatly from those of the southern part? At one time there were sheep all over the Indian country of northern Arizona—on buttes, mesas, canyons. Were these a form of desert sheep or of *canadensis*? What sort of sheep were found in northeastern Nevada? Just where do the desert and Rocky Mountain (*canadensis*) bighorns come together? Just what is the relationship between the California bighorn and the various desert bighorns? These are just a few of the unanswered questions about the origin and wanderings of the various subspecies of the widely distributed brown bighorn.

Much contradictory evidence as to the weight of sheep exists. One reason is that estimates are generally no more accurate as to the weight of sheep than they are in the case of deer, bear, and tigers. Another is that the weight of sheep varies with season, age, feed, and species. The bighorn is supposed to be the heaviest species, and the big brown rams grow largest in the limestone mountains of the Alberta and British Columbia Rockies. The California bighorn is supposed to be lighter, and the Nelson sheep of the California and the Nevada deserts the smallest and lightest of the bighorns. The Stones are supposed to average heavier than the Dalls.

In general these statements are true, but in favored localities both Stones and Dalls can grow very large. I have seen one Stone and three Dalls I thought would weigh somewhere between 225 and 250 pounds field-dressed. All were old rams in fine condition. All were about twelve or thirteen years old. A ram continues to increase in weight (just as most human beings do) as long as his teeth remain good and until his final decline sets in.

In general I believe it is safe to say that the larger varieties of North American mountain sheep and mule deer weigh about the same but that with his massive horns the mountain ram will probably average heavier. A mature ram is deeper through the chest than a mule deer. The average large mature buck mule deer having antlers with four points to the side will measure about 18 inches from the top of his shoulder to the bottom of his chest in a straight line. With lungs, liver, and entrails removed he will weigh 180 to 195 pounds. I have weighed many such deer. Now and then an exceptionally large buck will measure 20 to 22 inches from shoulder to brisket. Such bucks, if fat, may dress out as much as 300 pounds, although I have never seen a buck that heavy. As I write this I have recently received a letter from a correspondent in my home state of Arizona stating that in the famous

Kaibab forest north of the Grand Canyon in 1971 about thirty buck mule deer weighing 225 pounds or over field-dressed were taken, and one weighed on the hoof around 340. It may well be that rams that heavy have been taken. Col. Richard Dodge, who hunted and explored in the West before cattle and domestic sheep took over the best range, considered the bighorn to be larger than deer. In *The Plains of the Great West,* he writes that the bighorn "among the horned beasts of the Great West ranks next to the elk in size."

On the whole, bighorn rams taken today are not as heavy as they were when the white men first invaded the West. Ranchers have taken over the best sheep winter range for domestic sheep and cattle. Lambs born of half-starved mothers, even if they survive their first few months, never grow as large as lambs born of well-fed mothers who have access to good feed when they are nursing their young. I am convinced that the low survival rate of bighorn lambs comes from most of them entering the world as weaklings because of ill-fed mothers and getting a poor start in life for the same reason.

Sheep vary greatly in size with the fertility of the territory in which they live. Stone rams taken in the limestone ranges of the Rockies around the heads of the Muskwa and Prophet rivers are heavy-bodied animals with heavy horns. On the other hand, the Stones taken in some of the ranges around Atlin Lake in northwestern British Columbia are the smallest North American sheep I have ever encountered. In the '30s and early '40s the Sonora sheep ran heavier than they did in Arizona after the season was opened there. The reason, I am sure, is that the Sonora sheep had less competition with cattle.

The terms "thinhorn" for Dall and Stone sheep and "bighorn" for the brown sheep are not particularly happy. Some of the thinhorns actually have quite massive horns and some of the bighorns do not. In *Records of North American Big Game,* only four bighorn ram heads of the first ten have bases measuring over 16 inches. A good many "bighorn" heads in the record book have bases less than 15 inches. Of the desert sheep only five have bases over 16 inches in the first ten. In the first ten Stones, on the other hand, four heads have bases of over 15 and one of these is over 16! Of the first ten Dall sheep not one head has a base of 15 inches. The largest in the group is 14⅞. It is certainly true that the horns of *canadensis* average larger than do those of *dalli,* but in reality the difference is not very great.

Of these principal horn types found in North America, the thinhorns produce more wide-spread horns and horns of the "argali" type that pinch in close to the face and then flare out, and the bighorns produce more horns of the close-curl type. However, I have seen argali-type horns even among desert sheep and fairly close curls even among Dalls. Generally the horns of the Stones and Dalls are more triangular in cross-section and more commonly have a "ledge" on the outside of the horn. In cross-section the horns of the Rocky Mountain and desert rams are more nearly round and seldom have the ledge. The horns of the brown sheep are generally a good deal darker in color. However, I have seen bighorn rams with triangular horns with the ledge and Stones with round, close-curl, heavily broomed horns that look as if they had come from *canadensis*. We'll go more thoroughly into the horn business in a chapter devoted to the subject.

The so-called "thinhorn" sheep were classified much later than the bighorns. The white sheep were first described in 1884 as *Ovis montana dalli*, but the name was changed to *Ovis dalli dalli* when the thinhorns were recognized as a separate species. *Ovis dalli dalli* is a pure-white sheep with amber eyes and yellow horns. One white subspecies of the Dall is recognized. This is *Ovis dalli kenaiensis*, the white sheep of Alaska's Kenai Peninsula. This was declared a separate subspecies because of minor skull differences.

Superficially the other main subspecies of *dalli* is as different from it as sheep could be. This is *Ovis dalli stonei* or Stone's sheep. The type locality is near the head of the great, brawling, muddy Stikine River in northern British Columbia. The Stone is one of the most interesting of all wild sheep and he shows the greatest variation in coat. The typical Stone has a brown-black saddle, a white rump, a black tail, forward part of legs brown-black, inside white, gray neck and face, horns varying with color of hair on neck from pale yellow to medium brown.

At one time it was thought that the intermediate sheep between Dall and Stone belonged to a separate race. W. T. Hornaday so described them. He called them *Ovis dalli fannini* and said they were "white with a gray blanket on the body, gray facings to the legs, and dark gray tail." The type locality was near Dawson City, Yukon Territory. Actually this is a pretty good description of a light-colored Stone. Sheep this light are not uncommon in northern British Columbia.

An observant person does not have to be around the various species of North American wild sheep very long before he realizes that they are all closely related and that their differences are rather minor. All are *climbing* sheep, stocky animals with wide bottoms, stout muscles, and legs that are short compared to the long legs of the argalis and some of the urials. The larger American sheep do not stand as high as the larger Asiatic sheep, but they are actually among the largest of the world's wild sheep. A large, fat eleven- or twelve-year-old bighorn from southeast British Columbia or southwest Alberta, where the North American sheep reach their optimum size, is not a great deal smaller than the great Siberian argali and may well be as heavy as many *Ovis poli.*

Americans are lucky. On their continent they have large, handsome sheep with spectacular horns that range from the arctic to the subtropics, from the Boreal zone to the lower Sonoran. These sheep are among the most sought-after of the world's big game.

3 Sheep Country

The first mountain sheep I ever saw was a big desert ram. I encountered him in a place where I thought he had no right to be, and he caught me by surprise. Instead of being high on a mountain where I thought all decent mountain sheep belonged, he was crossing an ancient and little-used wagon road that had been made to take supplies to a mine long since abandoned. He had been feeding in the cool of a May morning down on the lowland desert. He had filled up, and when I saw him he was headed back to find himself a comfortable bed up on the mountain so he could rest through the day with safety.

As I tell in my chapter on the Grand Slam, the first Stone sheep I ever saw was lying with some companions, all old rams, on a ledge of a canyon wall overlooking Nevis Creek in northern British Columbia. Later on that day I saw a herd of ewes and lambs on the walls of a side canyon made by a noisy little brook that emptied into Nevis Creek. Also on that trip but much later we saw about fifty Stone sheep in a rocky but relatively shallow canyon way out in the muskeg and scattered subarctic forest.

In primitive times the North American sheep were almost as much "canyon sheep" as they were mountain sheep. Early explorers found them plentiful in the breaks of the Missouri far out on the plains. The first white men found hundreds of sheep in the canyon of the little Colorado and in the side canyons of the Grand Canyon itself. The sheep were very plentiful throughout the Grand Canyon, and it was said that Bright Angel trail, the first trail from the South Rim down into the depths of the canyon, was "built on sheep meat." All over the West, sheep were found inhabiting canyons. I live in Lewiston, Idaho, in a house which overlooks the Snake River. Above Lewiston the Snake River Canyon was at one time great sheep country. Indians hunted sheep there, and on the rocks of the canyon are many petroglyphs of mountain sheep. Actually there are drawings of sheep on rocks all over the West and in many places where sheep have long since been extinct. Some of these petroglyphs are not too accurately drawn, with rams having horns more like some of the Asiatic goats than like sheep. I believe this is responsible for the ancient myth that there had at one time been ibex in the West. One windbag I knew claimed he had actually shot ibex in southern Arizona and told me that they had migrated up from South America. Even if there had been ibex in South America the migration would have been quite a feat.

In many areas sheep feed on the top of plateaus, then bed down on the rocky sides. Along the Bill Williams River and other tributaries to the Colorado in Arizona, the sheep do a good deal of their feeding on top of the plateaus and then go down to bed. Around Ptarmigan Lake in near the Yukon border in eastern Alaska, Dall sheep can be hunted from horseback. The hunters ride along the edge of the plateaus and get off to glass or shoot the rams below them.

In many such areas the sheep were quickly shot out because access to them was so easy. Old-time Arizonans have told me of hunting sheep from horseback along the edge of the canyon of the Little Colorado and pronounced it like shooting fish in a barrel.

The mountain sheep requires a dry climate, sufficient feed, and rough country to which he can flee and high places from which he can observe his enemies. If these requirements are met he can put up with many inconveniences. He has adapted to the 80° below zero cold of the Alaska, Yukon, and British Columbia mountains, to the 125° heat of the barren desert mountains of Death Valley in California, Nevada, Arizona, Sonora, and Baja California. If there are water-bearing cacti he can get along almost indefinitely without water. He is primarily a grazer and in many areas he lives almost exclusively on grass, but when he has to he can shift to browse.

The North American mountain sheep does not do well in areas of heavy rainfall, deep snow, and heavy timber. In this respect he is very different from his remote cousin the Rocky Mountain white goat, which is found in the coastal mountains of British Columbia and Alaska. When I have hunted black bear on the coast of the Alaska mainland south of Juneau I have many times seen goats from a boat perhaps 500 feet above the sea. I have likewise seen the remains of winter-killed goats right on the narrow little mainland beaches. The Dall and Stone sheep, however, are never found in these wet coastal ranges. They are animals of the dry interior.

Sheep avoid heavy timber, and their instinct seems to be to travel and to bed where they can see the approach of their enemies from a distance. I have seen sheep hesitate to enter timber when a short run through timber would be the quickest and easiest way to rocks, cliffs, and safety. However, in some areas I have seen sheep bed down by choice in open timber. In the Middle Fork area of the Salmon River in Idaho the days of the September open sheep season can be very hot, and it is common for the rams to bed down in timber on the north slopes. Whether they do this for concealment or not I cannot say, but in the bighorn country of the Smoky River region of Alberta and in the Stone-sheep country of northern British Columbia I have seen rams bed down during the middle of the day in patches of arctic willow and in "shintangle," the dense tangled patches of alpine fir that grow right at timberline.

If the country that sheep inhabit contains caves, the sheep make use of them to get out of heat, or rain or away from excessive cold. In the mountains of Sonora I have seen caves where sheep dung was six inches deep. The first Dall sheep I ever got a good look at was a trim little ewe standing just inside the entrance to a cave in the lava of one of the mountains in the Solomon range above the Klutlan glacier in the western Yukon. I once knew a Mexican who was an inveterate sheep poacher. He managed a cattle outfit near a big Sonora mountain called Sierra del Viejo ("Mountains of the Old Man"). It was named after an old Mexican who used to make moonshine there. He was a *sotolero* and he distilled his fiery booze from the fermented roots of the century plant. Anyway, Venturo's employer was a very rich but notoriously stingy old man who lived in the village of Pitinqito. He paid Venturo just about enough to keep him in tortillas, frijoles, pinoche (crude sugar), and coffee, and maybe a new shirt and a pair of pants every year or so.

A rusty old .30/30 went along with the job, and once a year the *patron* gave Venturo a box of .30/30 cartridges. With them he was supposed to keep himself in meat. There were a good many big desert mule deer around the Sierra del Viejo, some whitetails and javelinas, but Venturo preferred the flesh of the desert bighorn, the animal he, like most rural Sonora Mexicans, called the *cimarron*. Anyway, when Venturo rode the range he usually carried the .30/30 with him in a homemade rawhide scabbard. Often he saw sheep low on a hillside in a position where they could be stalked. Sometimes he even caught them out on the flat. Sooner or later he shot quite a few sheep, and now and then when he was riding an agile horse he actually ran one down on the flat and roped it.

Poor Venturo once had an unfortunate experience. He felt he simply had to have some mountain mutton, and he climbed high in the sierra. It was May, a month with cool mornings but hot middays. Along after noon, Venturo still had not got a feasible shot. He decided to head back home. About halfway down the mountain he jumped down from a ledge above a cave and three startled rams ran over him. Poor Venturo was knocked over a little cliff, and emerged with a sprained back and a couple of broken ribs. But what was more serious, he broke the buttstock of his .30/30 and knocked the front sight cockeyed. His Winchester was out of service for months!

North American mountain sheep are found in so many different types of country that defining typical sheep country is difficult indeed. Artists are fond of painting pictures of wild sheep surrounded by rocks so devoid of plant life that a chipmunk would starve to death. Such pictures are as unrealistic as Russell's paintings of packtrains traveling through country without the vestige of a trail and composed of nothing but rocks and cliffs. Such stuff is good theater but it is enough to make anyone who has had to do much traveling by packtrain retch. Artists as well as writers like to ham it up.

Yet the experienced sheep hunter can look at an area and tell quite well what is sheep country and what is not. Some years before I wrote this, a hunting friend of mine, who was looking for a tax dodge that he could have some fun out of, financed a windy Canadian to an outfit of horses, riding and pack saddles, tents, and gear of all sort. He invited my wife and me to go along with him and his wife on a sheep hunt that was to be a trial run for the new operation.

The outfitter whom my friend had financed met us at the Canadian town where we got off our flight from Vancouver. We spent the night there and arranged to fly into a lake by charter plane the next morning. The outfitter was a real personality boy who talked a very fine sheep hunt. Within fifteen minutes I was suspicious of him.

When we landed at the lake where camp was set up and I saw the tents he had picked I was even more suspicious. When I watched him packing the horses the next morning I was convinced he was a phony. He led our outfit for a couple of days' rough traveling to what he had described as one of the finest pieces of ram range in North America. When I pressed him he admitted he had never hunted there himself, but he said that his pal Old Joe Blow had trailed some horses through there a couple of years before and said he saw "worlds of sheep" and some of the "biggest rams he had ever laid eyes on." We traveled through country where rocky granite hills rose sharp above creek bottoms tangled with brush and across little flats where stunted jackpines grew thick. We turned away from a main stream up a tributary creek toward some high, rugged mountains 12 or 15 miles ahead. There was a great deal of muskeg, and we traveled along muddy moose trails through the willows and now and then up on rocky benches. About an hour before sundown we came to the first spot I had seen that looked feasible for a camp. It was a level, grassy flat above the stream. On the hillside above there were several dead trees. The place had grass, water, and wood and good ground for pitching tents.

I suggested we camp there in this good spot while we could still see. The outfitter insisted that we push on to this wonderful ram country he had told us about. We wound up making camp in the darkness on a ridge about 150 feet above the stream. Every drop of water used had to be lugged up a steep trail. The ground on which we pitched our tents was bare, slanting, and gravelly. My wife had a little cot with an eiderdown quilt below the canvas. She slept warm, but even in a down robe and on my air mattress laid on that bare ground I almost froze that first night. Incidentally, in the far north the best place to lay a bed is on the thick sphagnum moss that grows almost everywhere. It is springy and soft, and it retains heat like a good mattress. I padded the ground under my bed the next day.

In the morning I looked the country over and told the outfitter that it was goat and moose country, not sheep country. If we saw anything besides moose and goats it might be a wandering caribou. The mountains were steep, rocky granite with bare granite outcrops and cliffs. The river valley below was thick with brush and willows, and a lovely clear stream ran through it. There were none of the upland pastures and grassy basins that sheep love.

The outfitter swore this was where his pal had seen those noble rams, and for want of something to do, I took a rifle and binoculars and explored. My wife said it was not sheep country and she'd be darned if she was going to wear herself out proving the obvious. She got out her trout rod and her little box of flies, and found a gunny sack she could use as a creel. Every day she fished the icy stream. Noon and evening she'd trudge up the path staggering under a load of 20-to-28-inch grayling. If it hadn't been for her we would have been very short of protein on that trip. We had started out on August 1. Sheep and caribou were open but not moose. In the course of her fishing my wife saw several bull moose, but they, of course, were forbidden. Then one day she saw some caribou tracks. The next morning in addition to her fishing tackle she took along a battered old scope-sighted 7 x 57 Mauser sporter she has used all over the world. She leaned it up against some brush and began fishing. Presently she heard the rattle of hoofs on gravel and looked up to see a big bull caribou, horns in velvet, trotting toward her. She dropped her rod, picked up her rifle, and the camp was in red meat.

Many believe that limestone mountains make the best sheep country. It is certainly true that the limestone mountains of the Montana and Canadian Rockies have produced the largest sheep and the heaviest heads in North America. However, sheep are found in many different kinds of country. The famous sheep country around the head of the White River in the Yukon is mostly igneous, with large areas of volcanic ash and chunks of white pumice that float in the icy little streams. The mountains around Rapid Roy Creek in the Atlin Lake district of northern British Columbia are schist overlaid with a thin layer of soil built up by decaying mosses and lichens. The Grand Canyon of the Colorado, once a famous sheep country, is fashioned out of sedimentary rocks, mostly sandstone. In Sonora the Sierra del Viejo is solid limestone. So is the great sheep country in the Mohammed Reza Shah reserve in northeast Iran. The Pinacate mountains of northwest

Sonora, where W. T. Hornaday hunted and gathered material for his classic sheep-hunting book *Camp-Fires on Desert and Lava,* is all igneous—cinder cones and lava beds. The lofty Cobabai mountains just below the Arizona line in Sonora are granite as are many other Sonora sheep ranges. The Sierra Los Mochos in Sonora is composed of some red rock which I take to be igneous in origin.

Goats are always rough-country animals, but sheep primarily are not. Over most of their range the sheep use rough country only as refuge areas. When threatened they head for the rocks. When they lie down to rest they usually bed near slides or cliffs to which they can escape if bothered. Sometimes the old rams will bed down on rocky points overlooking great expanses of country.

Sheep know they can get around over rock sides and in steep cliffs better than soft-footed predators, and the predators likewise know it. The refuge areas need not be particularly large or extensive just so they are rough. Once I saw a grizzly approach three old rams that were crossing an open basin. The rams saw the grizzly first, stopped, then backtracked toward some slide rock about 75 yards away. The grizzly lumbered closer along a trail. When he was about 40 yards from the rams he made a rush. The rams ran, climbed up on the slide rock and stopped. The grizzly likewise stopped. He looked at them and they looked at him. They knew he couldn't catch them and so did he. Presently he lumbered off and never looked back, as if saying he had not really expected to catch them and he didn't like mountain mutton anyway. On another occasion I saw a couple of wolves rush two Stone ewes and a lamb that were cautiously working their way down to a salt lick. The sheep went bounding up the cliff and the moment they hit the rocks the wolves stopped.

It is the presence of rough refuge areas that is essential to inhabited sheep country. Sheep worked their way from refuge area to refuge area. In primitive times they were found in many places where no one would expect to see sheep today—in the breaks of the Missouri River in Montana, in rough little buttes and hills in Wyoming and Montana, in the badlands of South Dakota, in the lava beds of northern California. I have shot sheep from above timberline at 11,000 feet in Wyoming to hills that dipped their feet in the surf of the gulf of California in Sonora. I have hunted sheep in freezing winds and pelting snow in the subarctic and in the 120° heat in Sonora desert hills.

Although sheep must have rocks and cliffs for refuge if they are to long survive, they prefer to feed in softer, more gentle country. In the north the best sheep country is composed of open, grassy hillsides adjacent to cliffs and rocks, big open basins, smooth grassy ridges. A theory of mine is that sheep and wolves go in cycles in the far north. When the wolves are not plentiful the sheep increase and population pressure pushes them into areas of smooth, open mountains where there are few refuge areas and it is not difficult for wolves to take them. I have seen sheep plentiful in low, rounded hills that can be galloped over on horseback and look more like caribou country than sheep country. Then as the resident wolf population increases or wolves move in following herds of caribou, the low-country sheep are killed off or are driven back into the higher, rougher hills.

In the deserts of the American Southwest and northern Sonora, sheep often do the bulk of their feeding down in the valleys between low mountains. Where there are no predators and they are not much bothered by hunters, sheep will feed in the valleys until the sun begins to get hot. Then they will move up the mountain until they find a comfortable spot with a good view, and then they lie down and rest through the day. Back in the 1930s I used to hunt sheep in Sonora by getting up at first light and walking quietly along the bases of the mountains hoping to surprise rams moving up to bed. Rams have been known to bed down during the day in dry, shady sand washes, or arroyos as they are called in the Southwest. Back in the 1930s one of old Charlie Ren's clients was hunting desert mule deer in an area of scrubby desert trees, large *chollals* (cholla patches), low hills, and wide, dry washes. There were big mule deer out in the flats and whitetails in the hills. While Charlie was making camp, the dude heard some quail calling and went out to see if he could collect some with a 12-gauge Remington shotgun. He scared a big ram out of his bed at about 30 feet and killed him with a charge of 1⅛ ounces of No. 7½ shot. The ram was about 40 feet away when shot.

Writing about bighorn sheep and sheep country in *The Plains of the Great West,* a book published not long after the Civil War, Col. Richard Irving Dodge writes:

"This splendid animal, which among the horned beasts of the Great West ranks in size next to the elk, can scarcely be called a native of the plains. His home is among the crags and broken rocks, generally at an elevation above tidewater of not less than 5,000 feet.

"It must be remembered, however, that the plains proper rise to an altitude of 8,000 or 9,000 feet . . . and their surface is cut with many huge canyons and deep barancas and torn and broken into confused and tumbling crags, forming congenial homes for many animals usually inhabitants of only mountain regions."

Most mountain sheep herds are migratory. In some areas, such as the Grand Canyon of the Colorado, the sheep movement between summer and winter range may be almost entirely vertical, the sheep going up in the summer when it is hot in the depths of the canyon and down in the winter when it is cold and snowy near the top. In other areas sheep travel long distances between summer and winter ranges. Generally the rams summer higher than do the ewes and lambs. Bunches of old rams like to find grassy basins above timberline where there is water, good feed, and slides and steep hillsides available nearby for safety. They will spend the entire summer in from two to three basins, and it is in such country that they are usually hunted in the early fall.

Rams go back to the same summer range year after year. One of the theories as to why overshooting rams may be dangerous is that old rams lead younger rams who have joined their club to the favored summer spots. If the old rams are killed off the young ones may never find these places.

Where sheep are plentiful, sign will be found in most likely places. Where sheep are scarce, all the rams over a wide area may summer in one locality. Such a place is or used to be a long plateau in the Wyoming Rockies near the very crest of the Continental Divide. It was called Pendergrast Mountain and I was told it was named after a former head of the Wyoming game department. The plateau was flat on top and on it were two or three depressions where rainwater and melting snow collected to form little ponds. The edges of these were all tracked up by rams. The top of the plateau was just above timberline. The soil was thin and looked sterile. Some grass grew but there was nothing like the rich vegetation found farther north in the summer ram range of the Canadian Rockies. Little canyons headed near the edges of the plateau and dropped sharply off to great purple valleys threaded by little silver creeks a couple thousand feet below. There must have been five or six bunches of rams that had taken up their summer abode in these various canyons. In all I estimated that about forty-five rams were summering there. The late Ernest Miller, my outfitter, told me that the rams on that plateau were the only ones over a considerable area and that the ewes, lambs, and young rams summered about 20 miles away.

In 1967 my wife, my son Bradford, and I hunted Stone sheep in the Cassiar section of British Columbia in an area where the rams spent the summer under almost identical conditions. The section of the Cassiars where we hunted had once been a lake bottom and had been cut into mountains by erosion. The tops of many of the mountains were as flat as billiard tables. The summering rams fed and bedded down under the rims on grassy hillsides and in velvety basins. We saw one bunch of about fifty rams, another bunch of about fifteen, and another of nine. Oddly enough we saw not one ewe on the fifteen-day trip!

A folder put out by the Fish and Wildlife Branch of the Department of Recreation and Conservation of British Columbia sums up the matter of mountain sheep very neatly:

> Mountain sheep prefer grasslands, which generally occur in the rain shadows of mountain ranges. In addition in winter sheep require areas of light snow where they may obtain food easily. Such ranges may be found on low-elevation, windswept, south-facing slopes or on high, rounded alpine ridges where inversions cause warm temperatures and frequent strong winds keep the range relatively free from snow. Most sheep ranges are within easy reach of rugged cliffs interspersed with avalanche chutes and talus slopes, which the sheep use for escape from predators. This rugged terrain adjacent to the winter ranges often doubles as the lambing ground. The ewes and rams may occupy the same winter range but tend to remain somewhat separated.
>
> Where possible most herds occupy distinct summer and winter ranges which may be up to 20 miles apart. Summer ranges are typically alpine cirques, basins, and mountain ridges, and generally rams will occupy different ranges than ewes, lambs, and young rams. The areas utilized by young rams may be less rugged than ewe ranges, but they are often close to heavy timber which is used for escape from danger.

I was interested in the statement that rams go into timber to escape. It can generally be said that wild sheep lack the instinct to conceal themselves that deer are born with. Generally a wild sheep wants to be where he can see and he does not mind if he is seen. However, it well may be that sheep are learning something about how to handle men with binoculars and scope-sighted rifles. Back in the 1930s and 1940s it was very rare that sheep bedded down in brush or timber. Today many hunters report their doing so. During the open season in Idaho, rams are more often found in timber than not. In the Alberta Rockies it is now common for them to bed during the middle of the day in patches of the dwarf alpine fir which the natives call shintangle. When I was hunting Stone sheep in the northern Cassiars around Colt Lake in 1971 my guide, Frank Cooke, Jr., told me that in areas where there had been forest fires and dead timber was left standing, rich grass had grown and the sheep had moved in and often had to be still-hunted like moose.

In *Mountain Sheep: A Study in Behavior and Evolution,* Prof. Valerius Geist writes that the migratory cycle of rams runs about like this: In late September the rams appear on their pre-rut home ranges. They gather in large bands, stay from two to five weeks, then scatter to different rutting grounds, where they remain until late December. Some old rams winter with the ewes. Some return to the pre-rut home range. Some have a different midwinter range. Some rams, Geist says, hang around salt licks for a time before heading for the summer range.

Geist says that rams are led to their home ranges by older rams that they follow in their youth and that once they acquire a migratory pattern they stick to it. The ewes acquire their migratory habits from the ewe band with which they have associated.

Within the past hundred years the sheep ranges have shrunk greatly and are still in the process of shrinking. Sheep pastures have been taken over by cattle and domestic sheep. Highways, railroads, dams, and ditches have interfered with migration routes. In addition, Geist is of the opinion that habitat is slowly changing through natural forces. Forests and brush growing up reduce the grasslands which is the wild sheep's natural habitat. Geist considers the Cassiar section where he studied Stone qheep to be an area of shrinking range, too cold and too snowy to be good sheep country. He says the Stone sheep there may become extinct.

Professor Geist has made a far more systematic study of sheep and sheep habitat than I have but from what I have seen of sheep I know that there are always exceptions to rules of conduct.

Sheep do some unpredictable things. I have mentioned the ram herd that was spending the summer at low altitude in Nevis Creek in northern British Columbia whereas most of the rams of their age group summered several thousand feet higher right among the glaciers near the crest of the Canadian Rockies. Old rams are supposed to seek out the other rams of their age group and spend the summer in a bachelor's club. The first Dall I ever shot, a 39-incher, was all alone but in the same Yukon basin with a herd of ewes and lambs. It is the unpredictability of sheep that makes them so interesting.

4
The Rocky Mountain Bighorn

The bighorn, *Ovis canadensis*, or the Canadian sheep, was first recognized as a new species, collected, and sent to the Royal Society of London in the fall of 1800 by one Duncan McGillivray, a Scot in the employ of the North-West Fur Company. Dr. George Shaw managed to get under the wire with the first published name in February 1804. The fact that Shaw's was the first name published was not established until 1914. Until then names published later were sometimes used—*Ovis cervina* (Desmarest), *Ovis montana* (Schreber). These names were also published in 1804 but later. In writing on sheep, one naive American outdoor writer thought these three names referred to three different species of sheep. This type-specimen of the bighorn was collected near the headwaters of the Bow River in Alberta near what is now called Banff.

Probably *Ovis canadensis* should have been named *Ovis americanus,* or the American sheep, as the race undoubtedly developed in what is now the United States during the Pleistocene era and only moved into the Canadian portion of its range as the glaciers retreated. All the different varieties of these brown sheep are simply subspecies of *Ovis canadensis,* but for record purposes the brown sheep are divided into two classes—the bighorns and the desert sheep. As good a guess as any is that the ancestors of both Canadian bighorns and desert sheep were pushed south by the glaciers from the Canadian Cascades and the Rocky Mountains. South of the ice, possibly in northern California, northern Nevada, and Utah and southern Idaho and Wyoming, these ancestral sheep developed into the California bighorn and the desert subspecies in the west and the Rocky Mountain bighorn in the east. In the course of time the bighorns worked south into northern New Mexico, southern Colorado, and possibly northern Arizona, and as the ice receded north into the Rocky Mountains of Alberta, British Columbia, and Montana, they moved east along canyons into the breaks of the Missouri, and out into the great plains of Montana and Wyoming and the badlands of the Dakotas. The western sheep in turn spread north and south as the *Ovis canadensis californiana* and the various races of the desert sheep. Just as *canadensis* drifted east as far as the badlands of the Dakotas, the somewhat smaller "California bighorns" that evolved into the desert sheep moved south to the tip of Baja California and to the mountains opposite Tiburon Island in Sonora and east as far as Chihuahua and the Big Bend of Texas. All of these sheep have longer ears than *canadensis* and are somewhat smaller, and probably average a bit lighter in color.

The Rocky Mountain bighorn, old *Ovis canadensis* himself, is a solid-looking, blocky animal. In the fall coat at the time he is hunted he is thick-necked, heavy, burly. Although some *canadensis* horns are of the argali type and some are of the medium-curl type, a high percentage of the bighorns have massive, close-curled horns that interfere with the ram's side vision and consequently are rubbed off ("broomed") at the tips. It is not uncommon to see tips of these close-curl horns rubbed off until they are 2 and 3 inches wide. Because the horns are so often rubbed, a bighorn with horns that go more than 40 inches around the curl is comparatively rare. In the early years of this century, sheep heads were judged to a great extent by American hunters according to the size of the bases. Hunters spoke of shooting 16-, 17-, 18-, and even 19-inch heads; but it is doubtful if a bighorn has ever been shot that had a base of 18 inches when thoroughly dry. Horns of the Rocky Mountain bighorn usually carry their massiveness out farther along the curve than do other species of sheep. Sometimes, in the case of very old rams, the horn at the first quarter is actually a bit larger than the base. I presume that the reason for this is that when the animal grows old the base of the bony core of the horn around which the sheath grows shrinks. Another reason the bighorn heads appear so massive is that with the heavily broomed heads the first two or three years' growth of slender horn has been rubbed or broomed away. A characteristic of the horns of the sheep of the "thinhorn" (Stone or Dall) variety is that they generally have a heavy, overlapping outer ridge. This ridge is occasionally seen on the horns of the desert sheep of Sonora and Arizona, and I have heard it was fairly common with the Nelson sheep of Nevada and southern California. It is very rare among Rocky Mountain bighorn rams if it occurs at all. Horns of the bighorn are more like a rounded oval in cross-section, whereas the horns of the thinhorn variety of North American sheep tend to be more triangular. Horns of all varieties of bighorn are a dark umber brown. Eyes are a golden yellow.

The sheep are darkest about the time the hunting season rolls around about September 1. By that time the winter coat is growing rapidly. I have never shot a bighorn in August but I have shot Stones, Dalls, and desert rams then. The coats are then quite short. Any northern sheep shot around September 1 is getting pretty well into its winter coat and by October 1 it is thick and warm. As the winter wears on the coats begin to fade and some of the hairs break off to reveal the lighter bases. The hairs of the face are severely rubbed in feeding, and this causes the face to appear gray. By late spring some of the bighorns appear very light. Sheep in the Sun River herd in Montana seen in the spring of 1974 were so faded they appeared to be almost as light as Dalls.

The muzzle of the bighorn is white, and so are the belly, scrotum, and rump patch. The tail is brown-black and short.

The Rocky Mountain bighorn is one of the largest of the world's sheep. In *Lives of the Game Animals* Ernest Thompson Seton says the "average weight" of a big six-year-old ram is 300 pounds. In W. T. Hornaday's *Campfires in the Canadian Rockies* the weight of a bighorn shot by John M. Phillip is given as 316 pounds. Audubon, the famous naturalist, gives a weight of 344 pounds for a badlands bighorn he shot. The late Bert Rigall, dean of the Alberta sheep guides and the man who led several hunters to trophies right at the top of the world records, told me in 1949 that just before the rut one November he shot a bighorn near his ranch, packed it in, and weighed it. The scales said it went 365 pounds. The bighorns reach their greatest size in limestone slopes of the Rocky Mountains of southeast British Columbia, southwest Alberta, and northwest Montana. Not only have most of the largest heads come from this general area but the heaviest sheep. Much of this area is now in Canada's Waterton Park and in Glacier Park in Montana.

Most of the subspecies of *canadensis* are some variety of desert sheep. The subspecies most nearly like *Ovis canadensis canadensis* was the badlands bighorn, *Ovis canadensis auduboni*. This is the species that Theodore Roosevelt used to hunt in the badlands of South Dakota. It is now extinct. I have driven through the badlands and it would seem to me that sheep there would be very vulnerable. The cliffs and steep slopes that protected them from wolves and Indian arrows were not enough to protect them from white men with rifles.

The California bighorn *(Ovis canadensis californiana)* is the sheep of the western mountains—of the Cascades of British Columbia, Washington, Oregon, of the lava beds of northern California, of Mt. Whitney and the California Sierra. For the records there is no separate classification for the California bighorn, something that is unfortunate as he is a different and interesting animal. He is somewhat smaller than the Rocky Mountain bighorn and has longer ears. His horns on average are less massive and do not run to as high a percentage of extremely close curls. The coat of the rams probably average a bit lighter. The California bighorn was very plentiful in parts of its range—in the Ashnola area of southern British Columbia, for example. The race was also plentiful in the Lillooet section of the Cascades. Col. Townsend Whelen, the famous gun writer, did some sheep hunting in this area of his youth. He also hunted Rocky Mountain bighorns in Alberta west of the Big Smoky in the early 1920s. He and his outfitter, Stanley Clark, named some of the creeks there. It was in this area that I shot my first bighorn in 1943.

The California bighorn has had tough sledding in much of its range. In the Ashnola country cattle took over much of its range, and most of the country was not rough enough to give the sheep much protection from overshooting. Overgrazing and overshooting killed off the sheep over most of Washington, Oregon, and California. The California bighorn is the subspecies that has been used to reestablish the bighorn in Washington, Oregon, and in a couple of localities in Idaho. Stock from British Columbia was used. Some of the transplants have succeeded reasonably well, and some rams have been taken from Washington herds under special permit. There is a small transplanted herd of California bighorns in the Owyhee Mountains, a "desert" range in southwestern Idaho. A few rams have been taken from it. The only "native" California bighorns in the United States are the scattered and declining herds of the Sierra Nevada in California. Human encroachment on the sheep range is blamed. Oregon has restored the California bighorn with stock imported from Canada. Like Washington, Oregon has taken a few rams on special hunts. The latest estimate from British Columbia is that the province has about 2,000 California bighorns, more actually than the number of Rocky Mountain bighorns, where a combination of poor range caused by overgrazing by cattle and a bad winter killed 90 percent of the province's bighorn herd in 1965–67. In 1969 the estimate for British Columbia's Rocky Mountain bighorns was a sad 1,200.

What happened to the bighorns?

When white men first invaded the West there were bighorns over an enormous stretch of territory. They were found from the badlands of extreme northwestern Nebraska to the eastern slope of the Cascade mountains in Washington and British Columbia, from the mountains in the Big Bend of Texas, northern Chihuahua, and extreme southern Baja California to the Wapiti River in British Columbia. They were found along river breaks and in little buttes and mountains out on the plains where people thinking of the bighorns as timberline animals would never dream of seeing them. Early explorers and trappers speak of seeing "thousands" of sheep. They wrote that sheep were "very plentiful," were "common," were "everywhere." There are all sorts of "Sheep Creeks," "Sheep Mountains," "Sheep Buttes" where no sheep have been seen for many years. In the mountains of Idaho around the Middle Fork of the Salmon River there was a tribe of Indians called the Sheep Eaters. Sheep were so plentiful that the Indians lived on them, just as the Plains Indians lived on buffalo. Seton estimates in *Lives of the Game Animals* that there were somewhere between 1,000,000 and 1,500,000 bighorns from Baja California and Sonora to the end of their range in British Columbia and from the eastern Cascades to the badlands.

The decline of the sheep came rapidly.

Sheep are in some ways very smart and in some ways they are very dumb. I know of nothing in the hills smarter than an old bighorn ram that has been shot at and missed a few times. On the other hand, sheep can seem exceptionally stupid—or trusting of man, which is the same thing. Deer are born spooky. They have an ingrained fear of man. They have to learn to trust man, but they do learn and in parks and game preserves they become very tame—even bold. Sheep, on the other hand, have to learn that running up on a rock slide and standing there will thwart a wolf but is no protection against a man with a rifle.

One time in the Canadian Rockies I was traveling with a pack train when I saw an excellent billy goat all alone at a lick in a timberline basin. I told the outfitter that I would stalk the goat, and if I got it I would take off the head and cape, put the meat where it would cool, and follow the trail of the pack string to camp. I tied my horse to a handy rock and started crawling through the stunted arctic willow in a timberline basin toward the billy. The billy was still about 300 yards away, licking busily at some clay below a big black cliff to my left, when I heard rocks roll about 200 yards away and to my right. I looked up to see a band of seven bighorn rams coming over a ridge. Possibly they were headed for the lick. They saw the billy and stopped.

I was planning to take a ram on this hunt and here was a good bunch to pick from practically in my lap. I got into a good prone position, switched off the safety of the Winchester .270 I was carrying, and put a 130-grain Silvertip through the largest ram's lungs. He dropped at the shot, dead instantly. I stood up and started walking toward the dead ram. The other rams stood around looking at their fallen comrade. As I approached they moved slowly off. I skinned out the cape from behind the shoulders to well up on the neck, and then cut off the head. While the rams watched me I removed lungs, stomach, and entrails and heaved the carcass up on a boulder so it would have a chance to cool. All the time the rams stood there a little over 100 yards away wondering what had happened. If I had been a meat hunter I could have killed all six of the rams with as many shots.

On another occasion, also in Canada, a friend and I saw an enormous bunch of ewes, lambs, and young rams in a big basin. We wanted to photograph them but there was absolutely no way we could get near without being seen. We approached them slowly from an angle, getting gradually nearer. At first they watched us apprehensively, but when we made no sudden or threatening moves they paid little attention to us. The herd fed. Lambs nursed. One young ram, overcome with curiosity, approached to within 30 yards. Eventually we must have got within 50 yards of a big cluster of ewes and lambs.

This lack of natural wariness, this trustfulness, has made sheep easy prey for market hunters. If my companion and I had wanted to and had had enough ammunition we could have killed most of the eighty-seven sheep that were in that band. I could have shot the six unsophisticated rams that hung around when I knocked over the ram I have told about above. In 1971 on what I then thought was my last sheep hunt, my guide, Frank Cooke, Jr., and I stalked three Stone rams. One was quite a good one with horns having a 38-inch curl. His companions were a good deal younger—about five or six years old, I would guess. I made a good shot through the lower part of the neck into the lungs of the big ram. He dropped and never quivered. The two young rams stood there unable to comprehend what had happened. When Frankie and I approached they moved off reluctantly. We took pictures, took the head and cape, brought the horses over so we could pack all the meat to camp. While all this was going on the two rams stood and watched us a little over 100 yards away. I presume that the big ram was their leader and with him gone they did not know what to do! If we had been market hunters or meat-hunting Indians or prospectors the two young rams would have been easy pickings.

I remember another occasion of the placidity of sheep. I was hunting once with a character with whom I never hunted again. Among his other endearing qualities he was a game hog. At the time the incident I am about to relate occurred he had already shot one ram—half of his legal limit. In the Canadian province where we were then hunting, two rams a year per license were allowed. This man and his guide were walking over a high rolling sheep pasture above timberline when they came to the edge of a cliff about 40 feet high. Below them, bedded in the shale to get out of the wind, were about thirty large rams, any one of them a real trophy. This character opened up. He killed what he took to be the largest ram in its bed, another when it jumped up and stood there looking for the source of the noise. The other rams ran up on the opposite hillside and stood there looking back toward the dead rams. That bloodthirsty man shot down two more. He was aiming at a fifth ram when the guide stopped him. He wouldn't even expend enough energy to walk up and take a look at the two dead rams on the hillside. The guide carried in the two best heads on a packboard. Two of the rams lay there, heads and meat all gone to waste.

This incident happened in an area that had not been hunted for years, and I doubt if the rams had ever before been shot at. That behavior on the part of old rams is rare indeed. Once rams have been shot at a few times they become very spooky. A very large Dall ram my wife shot was with two others just about as old and with heads almost as large. When she popped over a rise and nailed the big one the other two did not tarry. Instead they headed instantly for the highest and roughest ground they could find.

At the time I was hunting sheep in Sonora the rams were chivied constantly. Most of them took off as soon as they saw a hunter. In Iran, where the Persian red sheep have been harassed by hunters ever since men came out of their caves with their spears and clubs to get some fresh meat, one glimpse of a human head will send those wise little rams scurrying.

Most sheep have a tendency to mill around when they are surprised. A meat hunter lying in wait for desert sheep at a water hole could, I am sure, make some astounding bags. I once knew an old Mexican who had been hired to shoot desert mule deer and sheep to feed miners who worked in a Sonora range called the Sierra Pinta. He told me of shooting five, six, seven, and eight out of a bunch with the .30/30 he had been given. "Mostly they were little ones," he said. By little ones he meant ewes and lambs.

An Indian I knew in the Yukon used to hunt for the Whitehorse market prior to World War II. At the time hunting for the market was entirely legal. He told me that he shot mostly rams because the rams were fatter and the meat juicier. He also told me that he got seventy-five cents a pound for sheep meat, only thirty-five cents a pound for moose and caribou. He also said that he had shot Dall rams that weighed 175 pounds in the quarters. That is as much as the heaviest mule deer I have ever shot, quartered, and weighed myself. Many times, he said, all of the rams in a bunch would stand around after he had shot one and he would kill as many as he had pack horses to bring in or toboggans to carry them.

I read somewhere that Navajo Indians once came into Utah and departed with seven pack horses loaded with the hides of mountain sheep. That would be a great many sheep!

Along about the turn of the century it became apparent in most

Western states that bighorn numbers were very low. Laws were quickly passed to prohibit the hunting of the species. The blame was laid squarely on the hunter and his rifle. In those days the only management tool that people knew was a closed season. So the seasons were closed. The closures were generally ignored. When I was a boy prior to World War I, I knew a county sheriff who was a famous hunter of desert sheep. Closed seasons were considered an unwarranted invasion of the rights of local people. Laws protecting sheep have always been difficult to enforce. Sheep are animals of empty country. If someone poaches some sheep there is usually no one around to report the deed.

In the Rocky Mountains the bighorns were numerous through the 1870s and well into the 1880s. They were even found in what was to some extent marginal range such as river breaks and the badlands. Cattle were moved into the plains and valleys of Colorado, Wyoming, Montana, and Idaho. Then little ranches came along to run cattle in the foothills and up into the mountain meadows. Around 1880 great herds of domestic sheep were pushed up into the bighorn country. Shortly afterward great die-offs of bighorns began to be noted. Generally diseases picked up from domestic sheep got the blame. One of the worst, according to most observers, was "sheep scab" or sarcoptic mange of domestic sheep. George Post of the Department of Microbiology, Fisheries and Wildlife Biology, Colorado State University, says there is some doubt about scab being responsible for the great losses. He felt it might be pasteurellosis. Whatever it was hit the sheep badly. Observers speak of so many bighorns dying that they clogged small streams, were "all over the hillsides."

Competition from domestic sheep and cattle pushed the wild bighorns back into the roughest and most inaccessible areas. Then when heavy snows drove them down into the lower hills where the snow was not so deep, they found that domestic sheep and cattle had grazed the life-giving grass to the roots. Apparently lungworm is endemic with bighorns, but when the animals are well fed they can live with the infection with few ill effects. The lungworms *(Protostrongylus)* require land snails as intermediate hosts. The worms live in the lungs of the host sheep. Eggs are laid in the lungs. They hatch into first-stage larvae. These leave the sheep by the intestinal tract and enter the snails. Sheep pick up the snails in feeding and the merry-go-round starts again.

Dr. Helmut K. Buechner, in his monograph *The Bighorn Sheep,* writes that he considers the lungworm-pneumonia complex the most important factor in limiting the numbers of bighorn sheep. He thinks the next most important factor is pneumonia in lambs.

Unhunted bighorn herds in the United States have often had a history of slow increases followed by crash declines. The well-known Tarryall herd in Colorado has had three big die-offs. The first was in 1885 and was presumably caused by psoroptic mite. A die-off in 1923–24 was thought to have been caused by hemorrhagic septicemia. The die-off in 1953 was the result of verminous pneumonia brought about by lungworm. A report by George W. Jones as reported in *Transactions North American Wild Sheep Conference, 1971,* says: "To date we have found 157 rams (including 21 yearlings), 126 ewes and 26 yearling ewes." In all 442 animals from the Tarryall herd were found dead.

Officials of the Colorado game department believed that the loss of animals could be reduced or even eliminated by preventing the overconcentration of animals through hunting. In spite of considerable opposition a hunting season was opened in 1973 for holders of special licenses and the seasons have been held ever since.

But the problem of the bighorn is primarily a problem of range—or what wildlife biologists like to call "habitat." In the Southwest, where cattle pound the forage twelve months out of the year and where wild burros overgraze the hills, defile the water holes, and drive sheep away from water, the problem is a tough one. Sentimentalists get laws passed to protect feral livestock such as broomtail mustangs and wild burros. In the north the problem is primarily one of winter range. If the sheep have enough to eat during the winter they prosper and lambs survive. Without good forage they barely hold their own or decline.

Nothing shows better that the problem of bighorn survival is a habitat problem than the recent management of the Wind River bighorn herd in Wyoming. In the middle 1950s the Wyoming game department made a study to determine the limiting factors of the bighorn herd in the Wind River mountains in west-central Wyoming. At the time there were between 300 and 400 sheep in the area. They were largely confined to one rim of Jakey's Canyon. Forage was very limited because of heavy use by domestic stock, mostly horses. Only from five to ten lambs in each hundred survived their first year. The critical winter range was between 7,500 and 10,000 feet in elevation. In mild winters the sheep had extensive range, but in winters of heavy snowfall it was very limited. The lower portion of the bighorn range was characterized by windswept ridges, low snowfall, and steep, rocky rims for escape cover. There was grass of good quality available. Some of the land was privately owned. The rest was administered by the Bureau of Land Management, the Forest Service, and the Wyoming game department.

The Wyoming game department purchased deeded land and leases, and traded lower lands of little wildlife value for winter sheep range. Over a period of fifteen years a policy of land management primarily for bighorn sheep was worked out and in 1969 a formal management plan was signed by the various agencies. It included methods of population control, studies to evaluate range conditions, fencing for range protection, temporary road closures, and plans for further land acquisition and exchange.

About 8,500 acres of winter range are primarily managed for bighorn sheep. Sheep increased from an estimated 300 animals in 1955 to nearly 1,000 in 1971. A total of 555 animals were harvested by hunters, and prior to 1971, 468 sheep were removed by trapping to transplant elsewhere. Many have been planted in other areas in Wyoming. Some have gone to South Dakota, Utah, and New Mexico. Better forage has meant a wider and more uniform distribution of the sheep herd. Game managers have found that competition from mule deer and moose in this area has not been serious but it has been necessary to step up the hunter take of elk in order to preserve the range in its best condition for sheep.

A similar land-swapping arrangement has been made in British Columbia to benefit the California bighorns that range south of Williams Lake in the south-central portion of the interior of the province. Riske Creek Ranches, a big cattle outfit, has agreed to exchange blocks of deeded land in the sheep range for land outside the area. There are about 400 sheep in this herd, and it is from these sheep that the animals have been trapped to start new herds in suitable country in the United States.

The northern sheep are largely grass eaters and mule deer are primarily browsers, but the species compete for food when their ranges overlap. This is particularly true in the desert ranges of the Southwest. Biologists found there was considerable competition between the species in the Sun River range in Montana and in the Gallatin Canyon, Montana. A report from Allen Y. Cooperrider of the Montana game department on sheep and mule deer competition in Rock Creek says: "Although sheep do not normally eat large amounts of browse, the small quantity they eat might be quite important in their nutrition. . . . Deer outnumber the sheep by a ratio of roughly 80 to 1 on the Rock Creek winter range and can put heavy browsing pressure on the few browse species that are palatable to sheep. . . . Chokeberry plants are heavily browsed by deer and many are dead or dying. Chokeberry may once have provided an important source of protein for sheep in midwinter."

Elk compete with sheep more than do mule deer, as they eat more grass. The increase of elk in the Middle Fork of the Salmon River in Idaho is thought to have limited the number of bighorns there. The great increase of elk in Yellowstone Park has killed off the whitetail deer and has severely limited the number of bighorns. The elk is a big, aggressive, and voracious animal. He is a tough competitor. Not only does he work over the winter range but he is also found in the highest upland summer pastures far above timberline. Any plan of bighorn restoration if it is to work must make provision for limiting elk numbers and possibly the numbers of mule deer.

Sportsmen and other untrained observers are fond of making large and definite pronouncements about matters of big game. Such matters as nutrition, competition with other species, disease, and so on are pretty esoteric to them. However, they can all see the predators and they are quick to blame them for any decrease in big game. The golden eagle gets a lot of blame but he is undoubtedly a very minor predator in spite of the fact that he inhabits sheep country. Probably eagles take a very young lamb now and then. One time during the lambing season in Sonora I was prowling around and observing sheep but not hunting. Twice I found blood on rocks. I assumed at the time that the blood marked the spot where an eagle had picked up a small lamb, but I may have been mistaken. I have also seen lamb bones that have fallen out of nests occupied by golden eagles for generations. However, I do not think the eagles are serious predators. Actually adult sheep pay little attention to eagles. I have been told that if an eagle does make a pass at a lamb it can quickly find refuge under the ewe.

Mountain lions, as they are called in the Southwest, or cougars, as they are known in the Northwest, take sheep, but their natural prey is the deer. It may be that the chasing of cougars by dogs has put them in rougher country than they would ordinarily inhabit and thus has made sheep more often a target of opportunity. I have seen a few sheep kills made by cougars but not a fraction of the deer kills I have seen. The fact that cougars kill many deer and reduce range competition may make their effect on sheep more beneficial than otherwise. At least most biologists do not consider the cougar a very serious predator of sheep.

Dwight Smith, who made a study of the bighorn in Idaho and wrote a monograph on the subject, did not consider the coyote had much effect on sheep numbers. He did not find a single evidence of coyotes having taken lambs. A pair of coyotes catching a sheep out on a flat could certainly do one in, but once the sheep hits rocks and cliffs the coyote is quickly left behind. Sheep have been seen to bunch up and defy coyotes.

John Russo, biologist who made the definitive sheep study in Arizona and who is responsible for the monograph *The Desert Bighorn Sheep in Arizona,* believes that as sheep numbers declined because of competition with cattle and poaching the numbers of predators remained about the same and the drain on sheep numbers was proportionately increased. Thinning out coyotes can well be recommended when sheep numbers are low.

About the time World War II ended, numbers of Dall sheep in Alaska and the Yukon were down and the wolves got the blame. When I was doing a good deal of hunting in the Yukon, every time my Indian guides saw a weathered old sheep head that had been washed down some mountain creek they would nod wisely and say "wolf kill." They had no proof except that a sheep had died. The tendency of those who live in sheep country is always to blame predators. Many times I have heard outfitters say, "If we could only control the wolves, what a sheep country this would be!"

My own knowledge of the northern sheep country is superficial, since the only time I have observed it has been during the hunting season of the late summer and early fall. I have seen very few wolf kills of sheep. Of these, most were kills of old rams. There is more than one reason for this. One is that the "kills" may be sheep that have died of old age, or of malnutrition because of poor teeth, or have been killed in snow slides. Another may be that the ram skull and horns are conspicuous and hard to destroy. On a trip into northern British Columbia one time I saw wolves all over the place. Once I may have saved a ram's life by taking a shot at a wolf that was chasing him toward a rock slide and was not far behind. I missed the wolf, but I frightened him away. Near one of our camps was a lick which sheep used. A couple of times I saw a couple of wolves by the lick gazing hungrily at two ewes and two lambs up on a cliff above. The sheep had apparently been at the lick when the wolves made their unsuccessful rush. The moment the wolves saw or heard us they always took off. One day we saw where the wolves had caught and killed one of the half-grown lambs. There was little left—some hair, a few teeth, a couple of hooves, and a skull plate with a nubbin of horn. Those wolves must have been hungry.

In 1971 and 1973 I hunted Stone sheep with one of Frank Cooke's outfits out of Colt Lake. That is one of the best sheep areas in North America—and it also has plenty of wolves. In 1971 my companion, Jim Rikhoff, knocked two wolves off. In 1943 I had the opportunity to take a wolf but passed it up as my guide, a companion, and I were closing in on a bunch of rams.

I have always had a theory that in times of low wolf numbers the northern sheep move out into many areas that are at best marginal sheep range—low, rounded hills with a minimum of slides, cliffs, and other pieces of rough country for refuge. Probably the numbers of easily killed arctic hares have a good deal to do with wolf numbers. When the hares are plentiful the wolves can feed and raise large litters and increase. When they are scarce the wolves have a hard time. When a die-off of the hares comes along (tradition has it every seven years) the hungry wolves go after sheep in lower and easier country if plentiful moose and caribou are not available.

Predators have always been around and they are part of the balance of nature. Plentiful game means plentiful predators. The presence of wolves means the presence of game. In Africa good lion country is always good game country. However, wolves prefer to go after moose and caribou instead of sheep—and for the same reason that the meat-hunting Indians do. They are generally easier to get and there is more meat on them. The principal enemy of the sheep is not the cougar, not the coyote, not the wolf, but the domestic sheep, the domestic cow, the hundreds of roads and dams, the promotion of summer homes and ski resorts, and the lawless human being with a rifle!

For many years the only states in which bighorns could be hunted were Wyoming and Idaho. I do not believe that Wyoming ever had a completely closed season on sheep, but Idaho did off and on. Wyoming always issued a certain number of sheep licenses. These were obtained by drawings, and 25 percent of the licenses were allotted to nonresidents. I drew a Wyoming sheep permit the only time I applied for one. I was lucky enough to shoot a ram in 1944 above timberline on what my outfitter called Pendergrast Mountain. My outfitter was the late Ernie Miller, who lived in Montana but who did some sheep hunting in Wyoming with Wyoming guides. We packed in from the Turpin Meadows guest ranch near Moran, Wyoming. We had a complete outfit with cook, horse wrangler, fine tents, cook tent—the works. But the outfitter, the guide, and I spent almost all of our time around timberline with our saddle horses and a couple of pack horses. Most famous of the Wyoming sheep outfitters was Ned Frost, but he has gone on to the Happy Hunting Ground. Many good rams were taken by clients of Les Bowman, who has now retired. John Keller is a young guide with a good reputation.

In Idaho one of the favorite ways to take bighorns was to go down the Middle Fork of the Salmon River and into the main Salmon and then the Snake by flatboat. Some parties floated clear to Lewiston, Idaho, where the Snake River joins the Clearwater. At night the boat would be pulled up to a sand bar and camp made there. Every day guides and hunters would have to climb for sheep. Now and then rams would be found low, but for the most part they were found from 2,000 to 3,000 feet above the river. I have never shot a sheep in my home state of Idaho, but I once went along to kibitz with a couple of friends who had sheep licenses, and I have spent considerable time on the Salmon. It is one of the roughest spots on earth. The mountains are so straight up-and-down that it is possible to start out on a trail with a pack string with the Salmon River in view and then take a half-day to get to the water. Elmer Keith, the gun writer, was for a few years a Salmon River sheep and elk guide.

But in the years from 1900 to 1945, the golden years of bighorn hunting, the Shangri-La of the sheep hunter was Alberta. The heaviest bighorns came from the Alberta Rockies between the American border and the southern border of Jasper Park. Many of these monster bighorns weighed well over 300 pounds on the hoof, some over 350. Most of the largest bighorn heads came from Alberta, too. Of the first ten bighorn heads in the 1971 edition of *Records of North American Big Game,* seven are from Alberta, three are from the mountains just across the divide in British Columbia, and one, which was taken back in 1883, is from the Wind River Range in Wyoming. Of the first ten only three, two of them pick-ups, are listed as having been taken after 1924. The reason for the existence of those big heads and heavy rams is that the southern Canadian Rockies are largely made of limestone.

The dean of the old-time Alberta sheep outfitters and guides was the late Bert Rigall, whom I knew in his last years. Bert was a well-educated Englishman who homesteaded in Alberta well before World War I. He led hunters to some noble rams and shot a few good ones himself. The size of some of the rams shown in his photographs is unbelievable. Rigall did his hunting mostly in the area that is now Watertown Park just north of the Montana border. He guided Martin Bovey to the great ram that is listed as No. 2 in the record book. It is, I believe, the largest bighorn head in existence. The head listed as No. 1 and shot by Fred Weiler in 1911 was burned up in a fire. The Bovey head was No. 1 in the 1964 edition of the record book. It was shot on Oyster Creek.

Another famous Alberta sheep guide and outfitter was Ray Mustard. Others were Roy and Jack Hargreaves, and the Brewster brothers. I made my first bighorn hunt with Roy Hargreaves in 1943. More of that hunt later.

In the years between the two world wars a bighorn hunt in the Wyoming or Alberta Rockies was a sort of a status symbol for those with time and money. The man from New York, let us say, would take a train to Seattle by way of Chicago, then go to Vancouver and take the Canadian Pacific to one of the stations in the southern Canadian Rockies, where he would meet his outfitter. If he hunted in the neighborhood of Jasper Park he would go by the Canadian National. On my first Rocky Mountain bighorn hunt I left Vancouver, which I had reached by plane from Tucson, Arizona, by Canadian National in the evening. The next morning I awakened to find myself in mountains. I did not arrive at the Mt. Robson station, where I met my outfitter, Roy Hargreaves, until midafternoon. An hour or so later my hunting companion, Jack Holliday, arrived from Indianapolis by the way of Chicago, Winnipeg, and Edmonton. The next morning we started out by pack string to be gone for thirty days on one of the great experiences and most successful hunts of my lifetime.

On that hunt we saw not another hunter but we did encounter briefly a party of surveyors and geologists from the Canadian Geological Survey. We spent the first night at Berg Lake, where little icebergs that break off the Mt. Robson glacier float around. In the morning we took off down the Big Smoky River near its source. In the three and a half days we traveled down the Smoky we must have crossed and recrossed it twenty-five or thirty times. Hourly it grew as tributaries poured into it water milky with the rock ground to flour by the glaciers of the high Rockies. It had been warm in the high country and the ancient ice was giving up its locked-in water. The first day we traveled the horses splashed through shallow fords. Toward evening of the fourth day on the trail the water was deep and menacing. By noon on the fifth day, Hargreaves judged it too deep and dangerous to try to cross again. We turned up a very steep hill and went over a hump to a trail along the Muddy Water River. We camped on its banks that night, the fifth since we had left the railroad.

We were off for sheep the next morning—Roy, Jack Holliday, and I, all on horseback. Our horses picked their way down the sparklingly clear waters of the Muddy for a mile or so until we came to a spot where the stream bed had been blocked by a slide of huge boulders. We dismounted and led our horses up a steep hillside until we were about 1,500 feet above the stream. There we stopped to glass. Below us and about three-fourths of a mile away was Chocolate Creek, a tributary of the Muddy which gave that stream its name. Chocolate Creek runs through oil shale and, as I was to find out, the water looks exactly like the hot chocolate in a cup.

Across the canyon cut by Chocolate Creek on an open hillside more than a mile away we picked up an enormous herd of ewes, lambs, and young rams. For a long time we searched the country with glasses for big rams. Presently Roy said, "I see a couple!"

"Of what?" I asked.

"Rams," he said. "Look on the far side of Chocolate Creek. See the fifth draw from the mouth that cuts into the creek? Well, on the point above the draw you'll see a log lying crosswise. I can see one ram lying on the other side of the log and the head of another ram sticking over the log." Jack Holliday and I finally made them out.

So we led our horses down the mountain to the mouth of Chocolate Creek. Roy thought we could go upstream on the side away from the rams and be able to get a shot. We tied our horses and took off. When we got to a point opposite the rams, all I could see was the head and neck of a big old ram with heavy broomed, and close-curled horns. He was about 125 to 150 yards away. We were shielded from his gaze by willows, but I had no place for a steady rest. Even if I hit him I would destroy much of the cape. In a case like this the temptation is to take a chance and whang away, but I told Roy I didn't want to shoot and mess things up.

We went back down the Muddy to a point where we could cross out of sight of the ram, then staying under the steep wall of the canyon we edged along until we came to a draw that would give us access to the rams. I crawled up the steep, grassy slope, and peeked over. The big ram was lying with his rump toward me and the smaller one was gazing off in the direction of the ewes and lambs. I could shoot the big ram in the neck and ruin his scalp or I could lay a bullet in his rump and hope for the best.

I put a 130-grain Silvertip in his rump. He lurched to his feet and took off downhill. Another shot through the lungs as he ran rolled him. Jack Holliday took movies of the event. I still have them.

Roy had thought the head would go 40 inches. It went a bit over 39, but it was massive, heavily broomed, close-curled. I still have the head. Today, over thirty years later, it has shrunk a bit and now the longest horn measures 38⅝. I had it mounted by that master taxidermist the late Coleman Jonas.

Jack Holliday and I encountered a fantastic amount of game on that thirty-day trip beyond the Big Smoky. We saw in all about 180 bighorn ewes and lambs, at least thirty-five mature rams, thirty-three grizzlies, thousands of goats, hundreds of caribou, about a dozen bull moose, and about that many big buck mule deer, and possibly a dozen black bear.

I like to share experiences with people I am fond of and I always wanted to take my wife into the country. I didn't get around to doing so until 1961. What a disappointment! A road had been driven in to the banks of the Big Smoky. Do-it-yourself Canadian meat hunters drove as far as an Indian village called Grand Cache. There they would rent horses and pack back into what had been wilderness country. They had exterminated the caribou. We saw one bunch of five rams and one bunch of seven. Where there had been thousands of goats there were now a few dozen. We saw no bears of any kind, only one moose, no deer. The country was chopped up by winter cat trails, littered with cigarette packages and chewing gum wrappers. Planes and helicopters were constantly buzzing around overhead and twice a helicopter operated by the Alberta game department landed at our camp to see if we could be caught with any illegal meat. All in all this was the worst pack trip I was ever on. There was little game. The country was littered and there were several other parties in the area. The weather was lousy. The cook (a cute blonde of twenty-two) and the horse wrangler (a handsome lad of nineteen) were in love. They spent most of the time in the sack pitching woo instead of cooking and wrangling.

Alberta is in a frenzy of exploitation and is making all the ecological mistakes we in the United States made earlier. Roads have been driven into what were formerly wilderness areas. Virgin forests have been opened to logging. Mines have been opened. Local meat hunters drive in on mine and logging roads and shoot off the game. Winter bighorn range is leased to cattle grazing.

As a result of all this the bighorns have been in a crash decline. About half the Alberta bighorn country is closed to nonresidents and Alberta hunters want all nonresident hunting stopped. A few big trophy bighorn heads still come out of Alberta and these are usually shot around the fringes of Banff and Jasper parks. This is the story of the bighorn almost everywhere!

The old Alberta outfitters are now mostly out of business. Those who haven't died or retired have moved their outfits north—to northern British Columbia, the Yukon, or the Northwest Territories.

The horns of the largest bighorn rams are heavy and massive. They contain more horn material than do the horns of any other subspecies of North American sheep. However, the horns of the largest bighorns are not so much more massive than the best heads of other species as it is popularly believed. The largest bighorn head now in existence is the one shot by Martin Bovey in 1924 with Bert Rigall as guide. The No. 1 head in the 1971 book was destroyed in a fire. The Bovey head has a score of $207\frac{2}{8}$. The right horn is 45 inches long, the left horn $45\frac{2}{8}$. The bases are $15\frac{6}{8}$ and 16. The No. 1 desert bighorn head, although not quite as long, has large bases—$16\frac{6}{8}$ and 17 inches. I find in the record book only one "thinhorn" head that has bases larger than 16 inches. This is one taken by "Dal" Dalziel, legendary bush pilot and outfitter who now lives at Watson Lake, Yukon. Large bases are more common on bighorns and great length is more common with Stones and Dalls.

Actually a 15-inch base is a good one for any variety of North American sheep and a length of horn of 40 inches is exceptional. The largest base for a bighorn in the 1971 record book is 17 4/8 inches. It was shot in Alberta in 1968. The greatest difference between the horns of the bighorns and the "thinhorns" is that the mass is carried out farther in the case of the bighorns. The circumference of the third quarters of the Martin Bovey head are 11 6/8 and 11⅞ inches. On the other hand, the circumferences of the world-record Chadwick Stone-sheep head at the third quarters are 6 6/8 and 7. The third quarters of the world-record Dall measure 6⅝ and 6⅞ inches.

In the section on bighorn sheep in *Lives of the Game Animals,* Ernest Thompson Seton writes:

"A ram's horns should be measured as soon as secured. Horns shrink surprisingly as they dry out. In one year they will shrink as much as an inch to an inch and a half, that is 5 to 10 percent in girth; somewhat but not so much in length. . . . In perfect good faith, some sportsman announces that he secured a pair of 19-inch horns ten years ago; and when doubting critics apply the tape, and find them but 17½ inches, the sportsman is unfairly put in the wrong light."

Sheep horns do shrink. At least some of them do. Why some shrink more than others I cannot say, but this shrinkage must be related to the age and condition of the animal and possibly to the climate. I doubt if any horns shrink more than an inch in circumference. At least I have never seen any that have. In 1946 I shot on the Prophet River in northern British Columbia a Stone ram that when carefully and correctly measured the day after I shot it had bases just under 16 inches and a length of 42½. By the time it got to Coleman Jonas, the Denver taxidermist, it had shrunk to 42 inches in length and 15½ at the base. By the time it was measured for the record book some years later it had shrunk down to 14 6/8 at the bases and 41½ inches long. This amount of shrinkage is exceptional, I believe. My best bighorn head has shrunk less than an inch in length and circumference. One of the horns of a big Dall my wife shot in 1963 has shrunk about ¼ inch. The first sable antelope I ever shot had a horn length of 44¼ inches. It is still that today. However, a 54½-inch greater kudu has shrunk a couple of inches in twenty years.

Seton lists a head shot in Alberta with a girth of 19 inches and a length of 36¾. These horns must have been very badly broomed off. I doubt the 19-inch circumference very much. If there was such a thing, why don't such heads show up in the record book when measured by disinterested measurers? A bighorn head measured by Rowland Ward himself (according to Seton) had a girth of 18¼ and was 42½ inches long. I am skeptical about the 18¼ figure. I think I have an explanation. Today, the circumference of sheep heads is measured straight around the bottom of the horn. The tape does not follow the dips. I believe those big girth measurements were all taken by following the dips. Length should be taken by following the outer edge of the horn on a straight line. I have seen sheep heads measured for length by going out and back. This adds a half-inah or so.

Those who have taken trophies never sell them short. Once when I was on a hunting trip a companion shot a ram with a horn length of 43 inches. I measured it myself. Before the trip was over the horn had grown to 44½. The rule is that measurements for *Records of North American Big Game* should be taken at least three months after the animal was shot. I have heard of hunters keeping the heads frozen until measuring time came around. Another explanation for the difference in field and final measurement is that guides like to butter up to their clients and soothe egos with fancy measurements. A guide will run a tape over a head and say, "Congratulations, Mr. Jones, the head is 43½ inches long." Then the client takes his word for it, just as he takes as gospel the guide's word for the range at which he made the shot.

Here is a story about an exceptional bighorn head which I trust my readers will find interesting. This head has been seen by tens of thousands of people because it is worn by one of the bighorn rams in the habitat group of the Rocky Mountain bighorn in the American Museum of Natural History in New York. Seton lists for it the following data: It was owned by J. Simpson, and was taken on the Clearwater River. (The book says in Idaho, but this is a mistake. The Clearwater River in Alberta is apparently meant.) The longest horn is 49 inches and the girth is 16. As measured many years later by a committee from the Boone & Crockett Club, the left horn is 48²⁄₈, the right horn is 49⁴⁄₈. Girths of the bases are 15²⁄₈ and 15³⁄₈. This time the head was taken on Sheep Creek, British Columbia. I have camped on a Sheep Creek, but I doubt if this was the same Sheep Creek. In any mountains where sheep range there are generally several Sheep Creeks.

The story I have heard about this head is as follows: Jim Simpson was an old-time Alberta sheep guide and outfitter, who hunted in the country adjacent to Jasper Park. He saw this great ram in the park and told park rangers that this was the finest sheep head he had ever seen, that the ram was very old, did not have long to live, and should be shot so the head could be preserved for posterity. The park officials refused, saying that shooting this or any other ram was against park policy. So Simpson, who was afraid that the ram would go off somewhere and die and thus be lost, took a .22 rifle into the park, shot the ram, and hid the skull and horns behind the heavy foliage of a spruce tree. Park officials missed the ram, suspected Simpson. For about three years they searched his automobile every time he left the park. When they finally gave up Simpson smuggled the head out. He sold the head to Dr. Henry M. Beck, a wealthy man who did not hunt himself but who collected exceptional heads. He got $1,000 for it. Beck had the head mounted by a taxidermist. When he died he willed this and other heads to the American Museum of Natural History. At the time the head was the world record, so the museum had the horns installed on one of the bighorns in the habitat group. The present scalp is the third this old ram has had—his own, the scalp secured by Dr. Beck, and the one he is wearing at the present.

All this simply goes to show that human nature is human nature and hanky-panky has been going on for a long time.

This Dall is the best North American sheep I have ever taken. Its fine, even argali-type head is 43-5/8 inches around the curl after twenty-four years. It was shot on Pilot Mountain in the Yukon in 1950 and was No. 12 in the 1952 record book, but it is way down now.

Eleanor O'Connor and the first ram she ever shot—a magnificent 44-inch Dall that won her a Boone & Crockett medal.

The fabled Ovis poli *is considered by many to be the greatest trophy in the world. This one was shot in the Afghan Pamir by H. I. H. Prince Abdorreza Pahlavi of Iran, who is shown with the ram.*

The bharal or "blue sheep" of the Himalayas is related to both sheep and goats. This one was taken by Jay Mellon.

I took this "Persian red sheep" in the Zagros mountains of Iran in 1955. I'd guess it field-dressed at about 85 pounds.

Eleanor O'Connor shot this fair urial in northeastern Iran in 1970. With La O'Connor is Yar Mohammed Shadloo of the Iranian Game Department.

This desert ram is probably the wearer of the future world record desert sheep head. He was part of a transplant to desert country near Winkelman, Arizona. The photo is by Duard Sanford, the rancher on whose land the ram is now ranging.

This young desert ram got lonesome and came in from the hills to join a herd of cattle.

The world record desert sheep head. It was taken by an Indian in 1940 in the Sierra San Pedro of Baja California and is owned by Carl Scrivens. The score is 205-1/8 points.

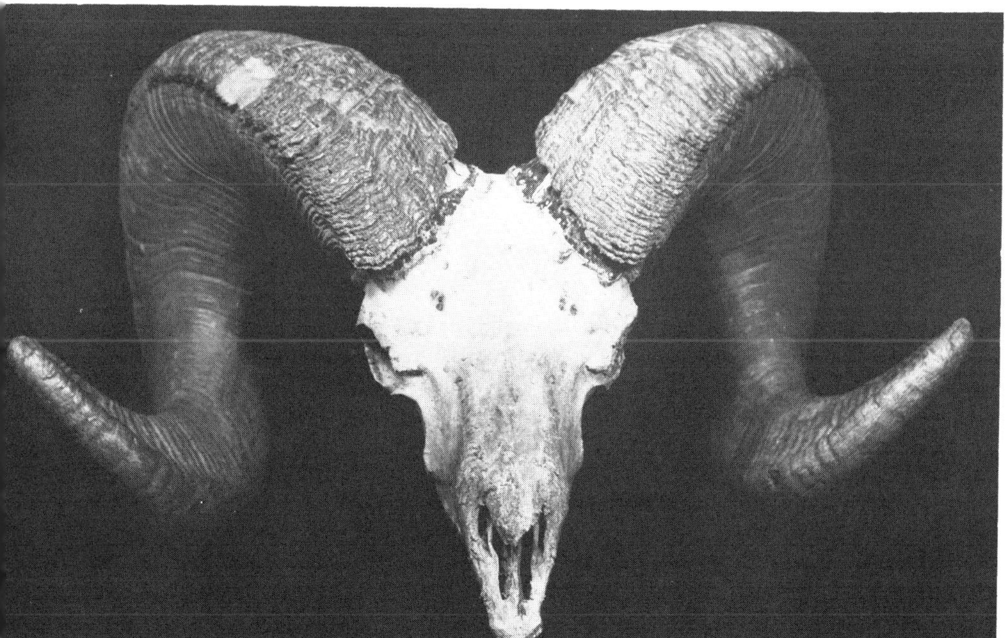

This is a very old picture. Who the guy is I cannot say. Note the Model 95 Winchester. The ram, one of those hungry desert rams who has had to compete with cattle, is only a fair trophy.

Another old picture, taken in the Pinacates of Sonora in the bad old days. When sheep are confused and mill about a whole bunch can be slaughtered. The ram in the middle has a very fine head and is the only real trophy in the lot.

Eleanor O'Connor looking at a sheep bed in the Cirio Mountains on the Sonora coast. A bunch of sheep had bedded on the ridge so they could look in every direction.

A tremendous desert bighorn on the Desert Game Range near Las Vegas, Nevada. He has a droopy-type head well up in the record class.

The late Charlie Ren (left) with me on a sheep hunt in Sonora in the 1930s. Charlie's favorite calibers for sheep were the 7 x 57 Mauser and the .300 Savage Model 99 he's holding here.

The author on a desert sheep mountain many years ago. When sheep come down to feed they prefer to do so in interior valleys and not out on open flats such as shown here—good country for javelina and desert mule deer.

Bringing a trophy desert ram off a hill in the Pinacates of Sonora. The Pinacates are volcanic and have big cinder cones where horses can be used.

The great sheep hunter José del Rosario, with a ram taken in the Sierra del Cubabai in Sonora.

Victor Bernal of Mexico City with a tremendous ram taken in Baja California. It scored 193 points and is large and heavy, unlike rams that have to compete with cattle, goats, and burros. Famous sheep hunter Oscar Brooks sent me the picture.

A desert ram and ewe off the mountain and feeding on the flat. Photo by John Russo.

This tremendous desert ram was transplanted as a youngster, lived in a release area for about ten years, and was found dead. It has not been officially scored but John Russo, who took the photograph, thinks it is an Arizona record.

5 The Desert Bighorns

Once in the late 1940s a group of sheep hunters was gathered in a New York hotel in the suite of an old hunting companion of mine, the late N. Myles Brown. In the group was another friend, Grancel Fitz, who is also now doing his sheep hunting in the Happy Hunting Ground. "This is quite a coincidence," Grancel said after the second drink, "but only six men in the world have shot all four varieties of North American sheep—and three of them are in this room!" By that the meant himself, Myles Brown, and me.

"Have you counted me? I have shot all four varieties," one of the men said.

"I didn't know that," I said. "I knew that you had taken bighorns, Dalls, and Stones. Where did you hunt desert sheep?"

"Sonora," he said.

"That's interesting," I said. "I have hunted in Sonora. What ranges did you hunt in?"

"I have forgotten," he said. "Some Mexican names."

"What kind of country was it?" I asked, growing suspicious.

"Oh, the usual sheep country," he said. "Big high grassy basins above timberline. You know—regular sheep country."

"Oh sure," I said, now more than suspicious. "Which side of the Southern Pacific of Mexico tracks did you hunt on—east or west?"

"East," he told me.

Grancel winked at Brown and Brown winked at me. We all knew the man was indulging in a flight of fancy. In the first place, the desert sheep in Sonora are found west of the railroad. No mountains in that area go anywhere near timberline, and none of them have big grassy basins.

Unlike the northern sheep, which are generally found on high, cold mountains mostly above timberline, the Sonora rams dwell on steep, rugged, but relatively low and often very hot mountains that rise from level desert that varies from sea level to 1,400 feet in elevation. A couple of the peaks rise to the neighborhood of 5,000 feet, but few of them are higher than 3,000. All of them give sheep the kind of country they like—high points from which they can sweep the lowlands with their incredibly keen eyes and rough crags and canyons among which they can elude predatory animals and man.

The variety of bighorn sheep known collectively as "desert bighorns" were the first mountain sheep to be seen and reported by European observers in North America. Coronado first saw desert sheep in 1540 and reported them as having large horns and little tails. They were seen in Baja California in 1697, and they were noticed in Sonora and southern Arizona by soldiers and missionaries. Yet in spite of the fact that the sheep were reported almost three centuries ago they are even today the least-known of the North American sheep. In reality no one knows where the desert sheep originally merged with the Rocky Mountain bighorn. No one ever will know, since desert sheep as well as the Rocky Mountain bighorns have vanished from much of their original range and are found in isolated pockets cut off from other sheep by cities, railroads, irrigation ditches, heavily traveled super highways.

In his monograph *The Native Sheep of North America,* Prof. Ian McTaggart Cowan writes:

"Along the valley of the Colorado River the open-horned, heavy-toothed, pale desert sheep of Arizona gradually gives way to the close-horned, light-toothed, dark-colored sheep inhabiting the Rocky Mountains. The trend is so gradual that it is impossible to draw an arbitrary line between the two. However, the Rocky Mountains from Colorado, Utah, and Wyoming north through southern Idaho, Montana, and into

Alberta, and British Columbia is inhabited by the most highly specialized population. In its large size, closely curled horns with very heavy basal circumference, large skull without prominent orbits, the population differs more radically from the hypothetical ancestral type than do the sheep of any other part of North America."

Dr. Cowan knows a lot more about sheep than I do, but I think I can say that I may know more about the desert bighorns of southern Arizona and Sonora than he does. His statement about the characteristics of the desert bighorns is open to modification. In the first place, the desert sheep have almost as high a percentage of close curls as the bighorns. In the second, there is a great deal of variation in the pelage of all bighorn sheep. I have seen desert sheep as dark as any bighorn I have ever encountered. In fact, the darkest bighorn I have ever run into was a melanistic desert bighorn I encountered many years ago in the San Francisco mountains of Sonora. All of the brown of this big ram was replaced with black. The hair of his neck was so black that his brown horn appeared almost yellow against it. I was within 10 or 12 feet of this ram. He was lying on a point. I climbed up hand over hand with my rifle strapped across my back. Suddenly the ram and I were face to face. He outwitted me and I never got a shot. I have a color photo of another melanistic desert bighorn that was shot some years ago in Arizona. However, black desert bighorns are freaks. So are albinos. Some years ago near Las Vegas, Nevada, a hunter shot an albino desert bighorn. The man was a meat hunter. He cut the head off right behind the ears.

In my trophy room I have the mounted heads of two desert bighorns. One shot in late November is what I would call rather light brown and in color somewhat lighter than any bighorn I have shot. The other ram was shot in February and he is in his full winter coat. I would by no means call him "light" in color but his pelage is somewhat lighter than that of an old bighorn ram I shot in Alberta. However, I doubt if a Sonora or Arizona desert bighorn is much "paler" than a Rocky Mountain bighorn of the same age and shot at the same time of year.

I believe that old rams tend to be darker than young ones, rams somewhat darker than ewes. I once looked over carefully a bunch of seven- and eight-year-old rams with binoculars in September when they were beginning to grow their winter coats. They were what might be called a rich "gunmetal brown"—or what Cowan calls "mummy brown." Along in April I looked over the same bunch of rams—or at least I thought they were the same rams. They were in the same mountains, were the same age, and the bunch contained the same number. The hair was longer and lighter. I presume it had faded in the bright desert sun. One characteristic that I have noticed in desert sheep is that one now and then sees a ram with a nose less white than is typical with the Rocky Mountain bighorns. Sometimes the nose instead of being white is a buffy white, and with scalps of this type the light-colored nose merges gradually into the brown of the face. Another thing I have noticed, which may or may not be typical, is that old Rocky Mountain bighorn rams often have considerable gray on the face. I have never noticed this in a desert bighorn. This may be a sign of age.

Back in 1906, Dr. W. T. Hornaday, who was a hunter, a naturalist, and the director of the Bronx Zoo in New York, made a sheep hunt in the Pinacate mountains of northwest Sonora. The book he wrote is a hunting classic. It is called Camp-Fires on Desert and Lava. Here are his comments on the desert sheep of the Pinacates:

"The hair of the Pinacate sheep is thin, short, stiff, and dry, and next to the skin has practically none of the fine, woolly hair that is often found on specimens farther north. It is only about one-half the length (or less) that one finds on the mountain sheep of Wyoming and British Columbia in November. . . . I expected to find the pelage of the Pinacate sheep bleached from the heat and strongly inclined to gray tones, or the salmon pink of the sheep killed by Nelson in July in the Funeral Mountains (in Death Valley, California); but we found nothing of the kind. The smoky-brown colors of our new specimens were just as deep and rich as they were on the British Columbia specimens; and from head to tail tip the color pattern was precisely the same."

The winter coats of the sheep in warm Sonora are much thinner than those of the northern bighorns, who live in country where in the winter the temperature goes far below zero. This gives an old desert bighorn a sort of a scrawny, thin-necked look, as though his big horns were just too heavy for his thin neck. All in all the desert bighorn has a more slender, more deerlike look than does the northern bighorn, which is actually a rather blocky and burly animal. In his winter coat an old Alberta bighorn looks as blocky as a polled Angus bull.

The tails of the desert sheep are longer. They run 5 inches for the desert sheep as compared to 3 inches for the northern bighorns. The longer tail combined with the short coat makes the little black tail of the frightened desert ram conspicuous. It sticks up like a twig when he runs. On the other hand, the shorter tail of the northern bighorn is not conspicuous in the longer fall coat. The Stone and Dall sheep likewise have short tails. I have had many views of the southern exposure of northbound Stone and Dall rams but I have never noticed erect tails, even in August when the sheep were still in their thin summer coats.

The ears of the desert sheep, like those of the California bighorns to which it is related, are longer and more pointed than the small, rounded ears of Rocky Mountain bighorn, Stone, or Dall. Some Sonora sheep have a fringe of lighter colored hair just above the hooves. Whether this is ever present in the Rocky Mountain bighorn or not I cannot say.

The desert bighorn is smaller than the Rocky Mountain bighorn, but under primitive conditions not as much smaller as some believe. When for the first time in a half-century it became legal to shoot desert bighorns in Arizona I was surprised at the small size of many of the rams reported. Many presumably mature rams field-dressed only 110 to 120 pounds, and for years the heaviest ram shot in Arizona weighed dressed only 160 pounds. However, about 1970 a ram that weighed 175 pounds field-dressed was shot in the Catalina Mountains overlooking Tucson, Arizona. That ram would probably have weighed between 215 and 220 on the hoof. There is less difference in size between rams and ewes in the desert sheep than there is in the Rocky Mountain variety.

Sheep of all kinds are more often than not found in rough country where it is difficult and laborious to bring out the carcass to weigh. I have weighed only two desert bighorns. Both were weighed because they were larger than average. One ram was shot by a companion as he ran down a canyon directly away from the hunter. My companion fired but the ram ran on. He was sure he had missed but I thought I had seen an almost imperceptible flinch and insisted that we go down to where we had seen the ram and look. I found a few specks of blood. Then I found a thin sliver of abdominal fat. We went on down the canyon. Now and then we would see a drop or two of blood. At the mouth of the canyon we could see the ram's tracks going out on the sandy floor of the desert. I had followed them a little way when I saw something shining on the top of a *bisnaga* (barrel cactus). It was the ram's stomach. The bullet had slit the skin of the ram's abdomen and the stomach had apparently protruded. When the ram jumped over the *bisnaga* the stomach had caught on the thorns, and as the ram continued on everything behind the diaphragm had been pulled out. My companion and I took up the track and found the ram dead in an arroyo about a quarter of a mile away. We could drive the pickup truck we had right to the dead ram. At camp, with heart and lungs out as well as stomach and guts, the carcass weight, as I remember, was exactly 175 pounds. At the time we commented that he was a good big ram, somewhat larger and heavier than average.

The largest and heaviest desert bighorn I have ever seen was one that my old pal Charlie Ren and I collaborated on in the Pinacates. He was a very old ram. We counted thirteen annual rings and we thought one had been broomed off. He was living all alone in a basin and from his tracks and droppings it appeared he had been there for a considerable time. He had been feeding largely on Indian wheat. He was the fattest ram I have ever seen to this day. He was so heavy that we resolved to weigh him. Charlie, a Papago Indian, and I managed to get him back to camp. I took no notes at the time but as I recall the ram dressed out 225 pounds. He was so fat that the Indian we had along to cut wood, look after camp, and keep the pot of frijoles simmering over an ironwood fire rendered out enough fat to fill a 5-gallon tin. I have heard of one heavier desert ram. An issue of the *Arizona Daily Star* of the 1880s tells of a ram that was shot in the Tucson Mountains and displayed at a local butcher shop. It is supposed to have weighed field-dressed 235 pounds.

On his Pinacate hunt Hornaday shot a thirteen-year-old ram which he records as weighing 192½ pounds. Presumably this is live weight. He wrote that the ram was very thin, that its teeth were badly worn, and that if fat it would have weighed at least 40 pounds more. This would have brought the weight to about 235.

The desert sheep do not stand as high as do their Rocky Mountain cousins. An adult ram will go 34 to 38 inches at the shoulder, whereas the Rocky Mountain bighorn will stand 40 to 42 inches. In spite of the smaller size of the desert sheep, their horns compare favorably with those of the *canadensis* variety. The total score of the No. 1 Rocky Mountain bighorn (length of both horns and circumference at the quarters added) is 208⅛. The ram was shot in Alberta. The world-record desert sheep, a Baja California ram poached by an Indian, scored 205⅛.

Wild sheep continue to grow in body size until they are eight or nine years old, and they get heavier every year as long as their teeth are good, just as human beings usually do. When the teeth go the sheep do not last long. Apparently the age of thirteen is in sheep the equivalent of the biblical three score and ten in human beings. I have shot several rams with thirteen annual rings but I have seen only one I thought had fourteen. As the ram gets old he begins to lose weight and condition. He gets swaybacked. His hip bones protrude. His rump is hollow. This is particularly noticeable in the case of the desert sheep with their shorter hair.

At one time during the 1930s and 1940s I did most of my big-game hunting with a custom-made .270 rifle mounted with a 2½× scope with a Lee dot reticule subtending 4 minutes of angle. This means that the dot covered 4 inches at 100 yards, 8 inches at 200, and so on. Knowing the approximate distance in a straight line from the top of an animal's shoulder to the bottom of the brisket, the amount of the animal the dot covered used to give me a pretty fair idea of the range.

I generally carried a tape measure with me and I gathered a considerable amount of data on the depth of various animals from shoulder to chest. The average large ram taken in Sonora measured about 18 inches. This is about the same measurement as that of a large four-point buck mule deer, but the body of the sheep is not as long. The very large, fat ram weighing 225 pounds that was shot in the Pinacate measured slightly over 20 inches. This is exactly the measurement of a heavy Stone sheep I shot in the northern Cassiars in 1973. It does not pay to generalize too much about sheep, as they vary a great deal in size, color, and horn type in the same area and even in the same bunch.

Just as extra-large sheep are encountered, so are stunted sheep. The dwarf ram that Charles Sheldon collected in the Sierra Rosario—and which was the type specimen of *Ovis canadensis sheldoni*—was a runt and in weight about like some of the stunted adult rams that have been taken in Arizona where they have had to fight with cattle and wild burros for every mouthful of grass and browse. It was thought for a time that the dwarf sheep represented by Sheldon's stunted ram were isolated on that one mountain and were a separate subspecies.

On a trip into the Dawson Range in the Yukon a companion of mine shot an old, fat, very heavy Dall ram. A few miles away I shot a ram with horns that I thought would go 45 inches. They went slightly over 40 inches. His horns had looked large because he was a small sheep. His skull was an inch and a half shorter than the skull of my companion's heavy ram. My ram probably weighed about 50 pounds less.

I did my desert sheep hunting in Sonora in the 1930s and 1940s. At the time there were very few cattle in any of the areas inhabited by sheep, and large areas had no cattle at all. As a consequence the sheep could feed down in the valleys where the forage was better. In Arizona, on the other hand, ranchers dug wells and built "tanks" to hold rainwater wherever there was a chance that a few cows could get enough to eat to stay alive. The sheep in Arizona had to stay higher and eat the less plentiful and less nutritious forage on the rocky hillsides. Most of the Arizona sheep country is true desert with less than 9 inches of annual rainfall and some of it with less than 3. As a consequence it is land that no one wanted very badly. Until the establishment of the Bureau of Land Management there was no pretense of control. In the early years of this century most ranchers felt that if a blade of grass was left when the rains began the range was not overgrazed. Consequently more of the fragile arid and semiarid land of the Southwest was desperately overgrazed and much was permanently ruined.

The constant overgrazing and overbrowsing by cattle and in some cases by sheep and goats not only resulted in the desert bighorns being driven out of the fertile valleys between the mountains but resulted in half-starved ewes and low lamb survival. The sheep is a natural eater of grass, but in many areas the once-abundant grasses have been killed by overgrazing. The cattle interests in the Southwest have always been exceedingly powerful. When the Kofa Game Range was established the agreement was that the wildlife would be administered by the Fish & Wildlife Service and the grazing by the Bureau of Land Management. An astounding total of 3,987 animal units (cows) a year were allowed on what was supposed to be a refuge for a vanishing and greatly endangered species. This is in an area where the average annual rainfall is only 3½ inches a year. The Bureau of Land Management deals principally with the cattle interests and is exceedingly sensitive to pressure from cattlemen. A paper written by A. F. Halloran of the Fish & Wildlife Service and presented in 1949 at the Fourteenth North American Wildlife Conference says: "In narrow mountain canyons containing water at their heads cattle compete with sheep for both feed and water. This is particularly true in dry periods when sheep are forced into the lower waters and are of necessity using feed close to the tanks. In these instances the coffeeberry bushes *(Simmondsia)* in the arroyos close to the water are overutilized. . . ." He adds: "It is the present policy of the Fish & Wildlife Service to discourage additional applications for cattle range on the Kofa, which because of its low rainfall and prolonged periods of excessive temperature can be considered marginal range for cattle."

As this is written, twenty-five years after Halloran's paper was prepared, there are still cattle on the Kofa. In the past, anyway, the practice among permitees on government land has been to run from two to five cows for every animal unit they had permits for. If officials of the Forest Service or the Bureau of Land Management got after the ranchers for running this "trespass" stock, the ranchers went howling to their senators and congressmen and the government official who had troubled the rancher was transferred to another area or demoted to an office job.

In 1946 I went on a deer hunt in the Tonto Basin with a well-heeled local rancher. As we rode along through badly wrecked and overgrazed country my host continually cursed the Forest Service because it had cut back on his allotment. How many cattle was he permitted to run? I asked innocently. He said he had permits for 400 head. We dropped the subject, but presently I asked him how many calves he had sold this last year. When he said he had sold 950 head I observed that he had a remarkably fertile bunch of cows, as all of them would have to produce twins and some would have to produce triplets. "Oh, hell," the rancher said. "I run over 1,000 head of cows. Everybody goes over his allotment!"

Some years before, an intelligent and conscientious supervisor of the Tonto National Forest had tried to cut down on trespass stock and had attempted to educate the public and the ranchers themselves as to the dangers of overgrazing with the subsequent deterioration of the range. The ranchers went after his scalp and got him demoted and transferred. His successors got the message.

This competition for water and the sparse forage with domestic livestock in what is a marginal big-game range and an even more marginal cattle range has resulted in the stunted desert sheep of Arizona and other areas where the bighorn must compete with cattle. It is also responsible for the low survival rate of bighorn lambs. Now that more cattle have been pushed into the Sonora sheep country the Mexican bighorns will be dwarfed like their Arizona relatives.

The desert bighorns of Arizona are not increasing. If anything they are slowly going down in numbers. There is too much interference from cattle, from wild burros, from land developers, from 4-wheel-drive vehicles. There were probably about 2,500 bighorns in Arizona in 1948 and there are probably somewhat fewer today in 1974.

Incidentally, the Catalina Mountains area from which the 175-pound Arizona ram came is not browsed or grazed by domestic stock. The only competition is from whitetail deer and possibly some from javelinas.

The fact that the sheep spend more time high in the hills than they did formerly may result in a serious lack of trace elements in their diet, as these leach out of the higher soil.

The desert sheep of the American Southwest have been classified into various races. Hornaday, writing in *Camp-Fires on Desert and Lava,* felt that the desert bighorns he encountered in the Pinacates were not deserving of classification as a subspecies but were instead straight *Ovis canadensis canadensis.* In *Lives of the Game Animals,* Ernest Thompson Seton lists *mexicana* from Lake Santa Maria, Chihuahua, Mexico; *nelsoni* from the Grapevine Mountains, Inyo County, California; *sierrae* from the eastern slope of Mt. Baxter, Sierra Nevada, California; *gaillardi* from the Arizona-Sonora border; *cremnobatis* from the San Pedro Martir mountains, Baja California; *texiana* from the Guadalupe Mountains, El Paso County, Texas; and *sheldoni* from the Sierra del Rosario, Sonora. All of these "subspecies" are desert bighorns. Their classification into all these various races shows a considerable lack of knowledge of desert sheep and their habits and no end of desire to get with it and name a new subspecies.

Desert sheep, unless their movements are interfered with by canals, roads, railroads, fences, and so on, are highly migratory. They have had to be in order to survive in a land of scant food and little rainfall. Early zoologists assumed that the sheep were isolated on the various mountain ranges and would not cross level open country to another range. I have seen sheep far away from mountains in flat country. Before the days of fences, highways, railroads, and urban sprawl, sheep used to travel back and forth from the Catalina Mountains north of Tucson to the Tucson Mountains 20 miles or so to the west. Old-timers have told me that there was a regular trail used by the sheep. Unless the migrations are stopped by formidable obstacles, the sheep move about and exchange their genes pretty freely. The subspecies *Ovis canadensis sheldoni* is a case in point. I have prowled around in the Sierra del Rosario, the type locality of *sheldoni.* I once saw about thirty rams in one bunch there. Sometimes the Rosarios had a good many sheep and sometimes I could find no fresh sign.

Prof. Ian McTaggart Cowan in his monograph on the North American sheep cuts down the number of races and lists four subspecies of *canadensis* that can be called desert sheep. The one with which I am familiar is *Ovis canadensis mexicanus,* which is found in Arizona, Sonora, southern New Mexico, and into Chihuahua. The desert sheep of California west of the Colorado River are listed as *nelsoni.* These are supposed to be smaller than *mexicanus,* lighter in color, and with out-flaring, more nearly triangular horns. Cowan speculates that *mexicanus* mixed with *canadensis* along the Colorado River in northern Arizona and southern Utah, and that *nelsoni* and *canadensis* did some gene exchanging in eastern Nevada. He lists two subspecies in Baja California, *cremnobatis* in the northern part of the peninsula west of the head of the Gulf of California and *weemsi,* named for that fine gentleman and sheep hunter Carrington Weems, in the southern part of the peninsula. *Ovis canadensis californiana,* the long-eared relative of the various desert sheep, has a range from southern British Columbia to southern California. The so-called Sierra bighorn, if there is such a thing, would have been an intergrade between *nelsoni* and *californiana.* It is reasonable to suppose that the sheep west of the Colorado River are somewhat different from those to the east and that the *weemsi* at the extreme southern portion of Baja are somewhat different from those to the north. However, the thing classifiers forget is that the sheep in the same area vary in horn type, in size, and in color. All the desert sheep of whatever variety have longer ears and tails than their cousins the Rocky Mountain bighorns. They are generally somewhat lighter in color. They look gaunter and more slender, partly because their hair is shorter and partly because they live in a hard land of little food and little water.

I was once on a sheep hunt in Sonora with a companion who shot his first desert ram at about 250 yards from one low rocky hill to the next. We crossed a valley to get to the hill on which the ram lay. After my companion had looked the dead ram over he turned to me and said, "For Christ's sake, Jack, this old ram is all horns, feet, and balls!" And he was right. The largest heads of the various desert species compare favorably in size with the largest *canadensis* heads. The knockers of the two species are both large, and the feet of the desert ram are little if any smaller than those of the Rocky Mountain bighorn. The heavy horns, the large testicles, and the large hooves look out of place on a skinny old desert ram.

Actually, there is not as much difference in the size of the hooves of the different species of North American sheep as one might expect. In my trophy room I have a gun rack made with the front feet of the four species of North American sheep recognized by the Boone & Crockett Club for record purposes. The Dall feet are from the Solomon Mountains of the Yukon, the Stone feet from the Besa River of northern British Columbia, the bighorn feet from the Wyoming Rockies, and the desert sheep feet from the Sierra Los Mochos in Sonora. There is surprisingly little difference in size.

The desert sheep of the Southwest are found in a variety of terrain. Today they are mostly confined to small and rugged mountain ranges that rise out of the deserts of the lower Sonoran zone. When white men first arrived in the Southwest, however, there were sheep in all suitable country. There were many sheep throughout the length of the Grand Canyon. Old-timers in Arizona said that at least some of the Grand Canyon sheep migrated to the San Francisco peaks near Flagstaff and spent their summers around timberline. Today some of the sheep of the Grand Canyon herd range up into the Upper Sonoran and Transition zones. In Nevada and Utah the sheep likewise on occasion range up into the yellow pines. They have been seen in the pines on the Catalina Mountains near Tucson.

First explorers in the country north of the Santa Fe railway in northern Arizona found sheep in the canyons and on the rocky little buttes throughout what are now the Hopi and Navajo reservations. Overgrazing by Navajo sheep and the population explosion of the hunting Navajos resulted in the extinction of the sheep in the Navajo country. An old Indian who lived in the ancient Hopi town of Orabi told me that a lone ram had been seen and killed in a little canyon not far from the Hopi town in the early 1920s. As I have mentioned in an earlier chapter, sheep dwelling in small canyons are very vulnerable as hunters can get above them and shoot down without the trouble of climbing.

Sheep were found all over the Southwest wherever they had sufficient rough country for refuge. In Yuma County, Arizona, the rainfall is only about 3½ inches a year. In the winter the temperature almost never goes below freezing. In the summer the temperature can go up to 125 degrees in the shade. In the sheep country of Death Valley it can get even hotter. Sheep are found in southern Arizona deserts only 200 feet or so above sea level, and in Sonora in the summer I have seen rams lying on rocks by the sea so the salt spray of the breakers can cool them. In the northern part of Arizona the sheep adapt themselves to canyon country at 7,000 feet and over and temperatures that sometimes go below zero. The cliff-dwelling Indians who were the ancestors of the present Hopis and other Pueblo tribes used these canyon sheep for food, along with mule deer and wild turkeys.

Actually the Indians probably arrived in the Southwest before the sheep did. Until the end of the Pleistocene era about 12,000 years ago the Southwest was a well-watered land of stream and forest, a land unsuitable for sheep. Excavations by Southwestern archaeologists in Ventana cave in southern Arizona show that the Indians had occupied the cave for centuries, eating mule deer, whitetails, and antelope before they started bringing in sheep. The inference is that the sheep did not move in until the forests had died out from lack of rainfall and the country had opened up.

There were sheep literally all over the Southwest. I have not hunted sheep in Sonora since 1947, but in the 1930s and 1940s sheep sign could be found in every desert mountain range in the northwestern part of the state and on almost every rough little hill. Some of the sign would be fresh, some old, but sign could always be found. I am sure the same was true of southern Arizona and Nevada. My grandfather Woolf, who came to Arizona in the 1880s, shot rams in the rocky hills in and around the Salt River Valley. One especially large ram he shot on Camelback Mountain near Phoenix, an area now occupied by palatial winter homes of the rich. As a boy before World War I, I found and brought home the weathered skull and horns of an old desert ram from a cave in the hills around Hole-in-the-Rock near Tempe.

In the 1930s I knew an old Mexican who in his youth had smuggled merchandise from Guaymas, Sonora, across the Sonora, Arizona, and southern California deserts to San Diego. He and his pals traveled by pack train from water hole to water hole. He told me that in those days (1870s and 1880s) sheep were more plentiful than deer and that he and his campañeros killed many for food along the way. He also told me that in his youth, before overgrazing had denuded the country, the Altar River ran the year round and that there were grizzly bears in the thickets of mesquite, willow, and cottonwood along the banks.

The extent of the denuding of the fragile land of the Southwest by overgrazing is something difficult to realize. Lieutenant Abert, for whom the Abert squirrel is named, described the country along the Little Colorado River in northern Arizona as a sort of an earthly paradise. There were *cienegas* (marshes) along the river in which he found elk, wild turkeys, and mule deer. There were antelope out on the grassy plains and mountain sheep in all the rocky buttes and mesas. Overgrazing by hordes of Texas longhorn cattle brought in after the Santa Fe railway was built in the 1870s quickly denuded and destroyed the fragile land, and it is now a barren waste that can hardly be restored in one hundred thousand years.

Desert sheep are found in mountains of many different compositions, and what mountains are made of doesn't seem to make much difference as long as they are rough enough to afford escape routes. The famous Pinacates, where Hornaday made his historic hunt in the early years of this century, are volcanic—composed of cinders and lava. Actually the Pinacates are a recent scene of volcanic activity. The Sierra del Viejo ("Mountains of the Old Man") is solid limestone. The Sierra Blanca near the Pinacates, the San Franciscos, and the Cobabais are granite. The Sierra Los Mochos is surely igneous in origin but just what its red rocks are called I cannot say. So is the Sierra Picu. The mountains north of Puerto Libertad in Sonora appear to be igneous, but the Cirios that run south of Libertad to Disemboki are decomposed granite, as is Topopa, a big triangular peak to the south where I once shot a handsome ram. From the spot where he fell I could have thrown a stone into the sea. It is firmly believed by many familiar with the Rocky Mountain bighorn that the sheep do best in limestone mountains. That does not seem to be the case with the desert sheep.

I did some of my first sheep hunting with Charlie Ren, whom I've already mentioned. He had led a remarkable life. Born in the 1870s in the Jackson Hole country of Wyoming, he had trapped and hunted all his life. He had been a market hunter in the Northwest and had shot deer and elk to furnish meat for mines. Like W. D. M. Bell, the famous elephant hunter, he had hunted moose, caribou, and sheep for the market in the Yukon during the Klondike rush. When I knew Charlie he ran a semi-legal outfitting business from an establishment just south of the American line near Sonoyta, Sonora. Northwest Mexico was pretty lawless back in the 1930s. Sonoyta was a long way from Mexico City and the sheep ranges of northwest Sonora were a long way from the state capital at Hermosillo.

As far as I know, Charlie kept his clients from getting arrested, but his methods were somewhat devious. None of Charlie's dudes ever took his desert sheep head across the line with him. Instead the trophy appeared at his hotel room after he had got back to Ajo. Although the sheep season had been closed for years the law was disregarded. Now and then one of Charlie's clients would actually have a legal museum permit. Charlie would always retain it after the dude had left. Then if by some remote chance one of his parties was actually stopped by a Mexican official, Charlie would display the permit, argue in his mixture of pidgin Spanish, profanity, and ungrammatical English, and generally slip the official some *mordida* in the shape of a 50- or 100-peso banknote.

Charlie knew a lot about desert sheep and their habits. He always maintained that desert sheep could get by with absolutely no water as they could obtain sufficient moisture from the dew on the vegetation near the Gulf of California, from the sap of various plants, from cactus fruit, and from water-bearing cactus like the *sahueso*, the saguaro (both forms of giant cactus), and the *bisnaga* (barrel cactus). He also maintained that the best sheep country had no water at all, as water enabled mountain lions to come in and prey on the sheep. Actually many of the Sonora sheep mountains have absolutely no water, particularly those made of decomposed granite. In these the rain sinks in as into a blotter. Whether Charlie was right or not I cannot say, but he held that if the country contained water-bearing cacti the sheep did not need open water at all.

I know that I have seen sheep in the searing heat of August in mountains of decomposed granite along the Sonora coast and I knew there was no open water in many miles. Whether old Charlie was right about water bringing in the lions or not I don't know. On the southern portion of the Sahara Desert in Africa there are many cheetahs and some desert lions, which are able to survive on the moisture they obtain from the blood of their prey. It may be that mountain lions can adapt themselves to do without open water. I once found a fairly fresh lion kill of a nine-year-old ram in the interior basin of Tepopa, and as far as I know the nearest water was at Pozo Coyote about 25 miles away.

Sheep are dry-country animals by nature. All desert game has been able to adapt to an existence without open water. One of the most heavily populated whitetail deer ranges I have ever been in was a little range of granite hills near the sheep range of broken red volcanic rock called Los Mochos, "The Cuts." It is so called because one time some Papago Indians waylaid a party of cattle-stealing Seris, killed all of them, cut off their heads, and brought them in gunny sacks into Mexican ranches to collect the bounty the ranchers had placed on the thieves.

However, many sheep ranges have few water-bearing cacti or none. These cannot be inhabited by sheep during the hot months of late spring and summer. A. A. Nichol, the University of Arizona ecologist and a good friend of mine, made the first desert-sheep survey that was ever made in Arizona. He felt that water was a limiting factor of the sheep population and that if the sheep were to increase more water would have to be developed. He predicted that the sheep around Lake Meade would increase because they would be protected from poaching and water would be available. This has come to pass. When the desert game ranges for the protection of the desert bighorn were established in the Kofa and the Cabeza Prieta mountains the development of water was considered an important management tool. At the time John Russo, biologist with the Arizona game department, was making his excellent sheep study that resulted in his book *The Desert Bighorn Sheep in Arizona*, one of his methods of determining sheep numbers was to count sheep coming into water holes in the hot months. Russo felt that the majority of sheep in an area would visit water within a three-day period.

During the many decades when there was no legal season on sheep in Arizona but when the sheep were not protected, thousands of sheep were killed when they came into water. Indians, and white and Mexican cowboys and prospectors built rock blinds or found natural hides within easy range of water holes used by sheep and then waited. When the sheep came in they opened up without regard to sex and age. There used to be (and probably still is) a big pile of weathered old sheep heads near water in the Pinacates. Rocky blinds were considered private property by Indians and Mexicans and were passed on from father to son. I have been told that Tucson, Arizona, got its name from the Papago name for a pile of desert sheep horns that was near what is now called "A" Mountain. Once years ago I went with John Russo to a blind that had been used for at least a half-century in some low desert mountains near Gila Bend. Within the blind were weathered cartridge cases dating from such old rifles as the Model 76 Winchester to the contemporary Model 70 Winchester and the Springfield. I saw fired cases that just about covered the history of centerfire metallic cartridges—.45/70, .40/82, .44/40, .30/30, .32 Special, .30/40, .30/06, .270. There must have been at least a hundred empty cases within the blind, and since the range was short and the riflemen could shoot from a rest each empty case probably meant a dead sheep. John and I sat at the water hole for a few minutes and quietly talked about sheep. While we were so engaged a handsome full-curl ram with heavy broomed horns came to water.

Old and ill sheep hang around water. Often they die there. Sometimes old and feeble rams have gone down to water that is difficult of access and have been unable to jump out and have died there. Predators often waylay sheep at water holes. Bob Housholder, head of the Phoenix-based Grand Slam Club and Arizona sheep outfitter, writes in a paper on the hunting of desert sheep that he has found the remains of about fifty dead sheep near water holes. Of these, he wrote, about half were large old rams.

In Sonora and southern Arizona the sheep use the saguaro, *sahueso,* and *bisnaga* cacti as a source of water and probably as a source of carbohydrates also. The largest bunch of desert rams I have ever seen was in a wide sandy valley where many *bisnagas* were growing. It had been very dry and the rams had been breaking them open. It is not uncommon to find saguaros completely girdled and *bisnagas* with their tops knocked off. Sheep also come down out of the hills and eat cholla fruit in *chollals* (cactus patches) out on the flats. In this they compete with the desert mule deer.

Near the coast of the Gulf of California in Sonora the dew is usually very heavy, and browse consumed by sheep in the early hours must furnish a good deal of moisture. I remember one time when for a couple of weeks I was camped near the sea. It was fearfully hot and very damp. I would turn out of my camp cot at dawn, boil some coffee, eat a hasty breakfast, then leave with rifle, binoculars, a 2-quart canteen of water, and usually something to eat—a can of Vienna sausages, a small tin of Dutch cheese, or maybe an orange. In the middle of the day I would try to get out of the sun—in a sheep cave, or on a shaded ledge. There I would alternately doze and use my binoculars until the sun began to slant down. Then I'd climb and look some more. All the time I was thirsty and every evening when I came back to camp my canteen would be empty.

Climbing around in all that humid heat in temperatures that went to 115° in the shade without much to eat and without quite enough water to drink was exhausting. When my companion and I got to camp we were usually so tired that we would have a stiff belt of Scotch and water or a bottle of warm but precious Mexican beer first. Then, somewhat restored, we would build a fire and cook supper. Sometimes we would open a tin of salmon or corned beef and heat up a can of green beans, but more often than not we'd simply cook up a pot of quick Quaker Oats, eat a dish full with sugar and condensed milk, and then turn in.

We had long before exhausted the good well water we started out with, and what we had with us had come from a stinking tank that contained part of a decomposed coyote. We had halazone tablets with us and suffered no ill effects, but the water smelled bad and had a disagreeable taste. However, it sustained us, and when we were on some high rocky ridge burned by the sun, often tantalized by the sight of the blue, cool-looking water of the Gulf of California below us, the damned stuff actually tasted pretty good. In spite of the heat we were always damp from our copious sweat. When we got ready to lie down on our cots we would take off damp ulderwear, pants, and cotton shirts wet with sweat and hang them on bushes. In the morning when we put our clothes back on they would still be wet.

In the north, sheep are to a great extent grazers, but in Arizona and Sonora they largely depend on browse. They feed on brittlebrush, coffeeberry (jojobe), beans of the mesquite, ironwood, and paloverde, various forbs, and annual grasses. The best time for the desert bighorn is late winter and early spring after good winter rains, and the sheep have adjusted their rutting times so that the lambs are born in February and March.

During droughts (and that means much of the time in deserts where annual rainfall averages as little as 1½ inches a year and never more than 8 or 9) the desert is a grim place—gray, dry, barren. The glaring sun bounces blindingly off of light-gray sand glittering with mica. From a distance the sheep mountains look as barren as the face of the moon. The giant cactus and the organ cactus look gaunt, and the leaves of the prickly pear shrink and shrivel and give the collapsed appearance of fat men who have lost too much weight through crash diets.

But following good rains, the desert comes to life. Wet winters are followed by springs where in places whole acres are golden with California poppies and blue with little desert flowers. Then the paloverdes are masses of golden bloom, and the ironwoods thick with blossom look like drifting blue-gray smoke. Then the desert is fragrant with the blossoms of the mesquite and the little desert bees sing and hum in the blossoms. Often the Indian wheat is high and rich, and the filaree carpets acres with green. The saguaros and prickly pears grow plump with water, and ocotillos flaunt scarlet blooms.

Summer rains can be heavy, and when they are the desert springs to life. Hornaday in *Camp-Fires on Desert and Lava* referred to much of the southern Arizona and Sonora deserts as arboreal desert. This, I believe, is generally an area of subterranean water not too far from the surface. Much of it resembles the Northern Frontier District of Kenya, with paloverdes, ironwoods, and mesquites instead of thornbush, jack rabbits instead of dik-diks, Gambel quail instead of guinea fowl, desert mule deer instead of lesser kudu, gerenuk, and beisa oryx. The Sonoran and Somali deserts are much alike. Rains can turn either into a jungle. Following good rains, grass and weeds are tall, all trees and bushes are in leaf, and vines pop up out of nowhere to clamber over the trees.

The desert rains that fall in the summer are spotty. Many times I have gone through a belt of gray, gaunt drought to a belt of lush green, of waving plants, climbing vines, and plump cactus.

Because of the spotty rains the sheep have to be migratory to survive. Once in the summer I was in the San Franciscos of Sonora. In three days I had not seen a sheep nor any fresh sign. It was late July and very hot. Every afternoon big gray clouds with black bellies rolled in from the Gulf of California. Now and then at night I would hear a rumble of thunder and see a stab of lightning. Then late one afternoon it started to rain. The storm lasted a couple of hours before the clouds passed over, leaving the desert cool and fresh-smelling. The next afternoon I saw a herd of seven ewes and four of last February's lambs. The next morning I saw a couple of rams. Apparently the sheep had seen the falling rain and had come to it.

Just how far sheep will move I cannot say. Old Charlie Ren claimed that he had recognized rams in the San Franciscos and the Sierra Pintas that he had seen previously in the Pinacates. Mexican sheep-hunting friends tell me that several rams have been shot in Sonora that have been tagged by game-department biologists in Arizona. I have mentioned that some of the sheep that wintered in the Grand Canyon in Arizona in the Sonoran zone were supposed to migrate to the San Francisco peaks and summer in the alpine-arctic zone around and above timberline.

The sheep do travel. Many sheep in Arizona have been killed by automobiles on paved highways. Often they travel on moonlit nights. In January 1937, on a bright moonlit night, I saw a big ram cross the Tucson-Phoenix highway just north of the Gila River, run up on a rocky little hill, stand there and look at me. Migrating sheep have worn trails in the hills north of Puerto Libertad, Sonora, that you could ride a bicycle on. A little desert range may be full of sheep one week and not have a sheep in it the next. Near Piti Quito, Sonora, is a little chain of low but very steep and rugged volcanic mountains called the Sierra del Chino ("Mountain of the Chinaman"). I had always thought it would be a good place to find a ram, and on five or six occasions I stopped there, made camp, and scouted the country out. I always found sheep sign there but never did I see a live sheep. However, my friend Oscar Brooks of Mexico City, one of the most skillful and enthusiastic sheep hunters I know, shot on Sierra del Chino one of the very best rams ever taken in Sonora. Another lucky Sierra del Chino hunter was my old hunting companion the late N. Myles Brown of Cleveland, Ohio, who shot a good ram there in 1947. Brown's ram made him one of the first hunters ever to take all four varieties of North American sheep. At the time neither he nor I knew whether ten hunters or ten thousand had shot the four varieties.

When the desert sheep of Sonora traveled long distances they often stopped for a rest at some intermediate point. About halfway between the Sierra Picu and the Sierra Los Mochos is a little clump of hills that by no stretch of imagination could be called sheep country. Nevertheless, I have seen sheep in those hills several times. They have always been rams. From the tracks I would guess that they travel in a day the 20 to 25 miles from one of the ranges. Then they rest in those little hills from one to three days and go on. The hills themselves harbor a good many of the small Arizona Coues whitetails, and there are desert mule deer (which can get along without water as well as sheep) out in the flats. I was once camped at a well about 5 miles from the hills to hunt deer with a very unsophisticated companion. He came into camp one night and told me that he had seen a large and very odd-looking deer but had not got a shot at it. It wasn't until he started describing the strange-looking antlers that I realized he had seen a ram. He was astonished when I told him what he had seen. He thought that all sheep were white.

Sheep traveling through level country encounter many hazards. They can get around in rough country faster than any other animal, but they are not very fast and agile on level ground. Many have been roped by Mexican and American cowboys, and quite a few have been hit and killed by automobiles while crossing roads. I once encountered a big old desert ram about to cross a wandering desert track. Just to see how fast he could run I jumped out of the car and took after him. I am by no means a speedy runner but I almost got close enough to touch him. I scared the hell out of that ram. He headed for a hill and the moment he hit the talus slope of broken rock he was in his element and I drew up. At the top of the ridge he stopped and watched me for twenty minutes or so. I am sure he was convinced I was insane.

Poaching was always a major factor in the decreasing numbers of desert sheep. The sheep were "protected" from the time well before Arizona became a state—in that there was no open season on the animals. In the days before the use of the automobile became widespread very few people ever went into desert sheep country but those who did go in could do as they pleased. I have mentioned how I saw dozens of empty cartridge cases that dated from the 1870s to the 1950s in a blind overlooking a water hole in southern Arizona. Such poaching went on constantly and the people who lived in the desert thought poaching sheep or deer was their right.

John Russo showed me the largest Arizona head I have ever seen. As I remember the bases were over 16 inches and the horns were over 40. This great ram and a companion were crossing a desert road going from one rocky little range to another. A local desert rat bumped into them. He had a .30/30 handy in his pickup, shot them both, cut off the wonderful trophy heads, and buried them near the scene of the kill.

Somehow the game department found that he had sheep meat in his house, confiscated it, found the buried heads. They thought they had an airtight case but the desert-rat justice of the peace turned the poacher loose.

Along about 1912 or 1913 my uncle John Woolf brought to my grandfather's home at Tempe, Arizona, a couple of quarters of a desert ram he had shot in the Superstition Mountains. As I remember the story he had just awakened and was lying in his bedroll. He saw the ram watching him from the hill above and about 150 yards away. His Winchester .30/30 was beside him. He jacked a cartridge into the chamber, drew a bead on the ram, and knocked it off. This ram furnished the first sheep meat I had ever eaten. I was home from school with a sore throat at the time and I enjoyed cutting off strips of the tender meat, broiling it on the top of my grandmother's wood-burning range, salting and eating it. Possibly this delicious meat combined with my grandfather Woolf's sheep-hunting stories made me a sheep hunter. Incidentally, there are now no sheep in the Superstitions. For decades a remnant band managed to hold out, but poaching by would-be prospectors and hunters of Indian artifacts and competition from cattle has finally done away with them.

From what I could learn from local residents the desert sheep in Arizona were holding their own or slowly increasing during the 1920s. Then the 1929 depression came along and all manner of romantic people with a lot of time but little money invaded the desert, ostensibly to prospect, and tried to live off the country. Almost all of them had rifles of some sort and they shot everything they saw that had meat on it. The late A. A. Nichol, who made the first field study of the Arizona sheep, told me that in the 1930s some prospectors supplemented their income by market hunting and that mountain mutton was regularly sold by a butcher in a small Arizona town. These prospectors found little pay dirt, but they really shot up the sheep. The same thing happened in the deserts of southern California, Nevada, and Utah.

In Sonora the sheep were targets of opportunity. Cowboys working cattle in sheep country seldom missed a chance to shoot sheep—usually with .22 rifles since .30/30 ammunition was pretty expensive. In many places along the Sonora coast the sheep mountains come right down to the sea. Commercial fishermen nearly always carried rifles in their boats, and if they got the chance they would shoot sheep off of rocky headlands to vary their fish diet. At a fisherman's camp at

Puerto Libertad one time I saw the skinned carcasses of two ewes and a small ram hanging up. The fishermen were going to cut them up and make jerky from the meat. I was offered the pick of the carcasses for $10 American, 50 pesos Mexican, or one box of .30/30 cartridges.

The correct Spanish name for wild sheep is *borrego salvaje,* which literally means "wild sheep," but the desert Mexicans almost always call them *cimarrones.* This is a Spanish word meaning the wild form of a domestic animal. In the Philippines, I understand that water buffalo gone wild are called *cimarrones.* The Mexican name for a ram is *macho cimarron.* I have heard a few Mexicans call sheep *chivos,* "goats," probably because of the goatlike appearance of the ewes.

The government of Mexico had enough to worry about without getting in a dither about the wild sheep in a remote part of Sonora, but after his sheep hunt in the Pinacates in 1907, W. T. Hornaday got the Mexican government to declare a closed season on desert sheep. This had no effect one way or the other. The 1910 revolution came along and other revolutions followed. Now and then an adventurous American or perhaps even a European came to Sonora to collect a sheep trophy. Usually he would have to get some Arizona desert rat to outfit him.

I once knew an old Mexican who had gone along as a guide and packer for an Englishman and his beautiful blond wife who shot sheep in the Pinacates about 1912. He was particularly impressed by the woman, who, to hear him tell it, was quite a dish. He was intrigued by the fact that she hunted sheep in a divided skirt and that come hell or high water she had to have a bath every night in a folding canvas tub. He was likewise flabbergasted by her carrying a white umbrella lined with green cloth when she rode horseback. When he got to the umbrella bit the old boy used to sigh, shake his head, and say in Spanish: "How beautiful the woman! How white her skin! What a people the English!"

I also remember being very impressed by an American who was about to go into Sonora on a sheep hunt about 1914. When he got to the border at Nogales he looked up my uncle Bill O'Connor, who was a lawyer and a big wheel locally. My uncle had him to dinner and I remember listening in awe at his tales of hunting bighorn rams in Wyoming and Alberta and Stone sheep out of Telegraph Creek. I was a rifle nut of the worst kind even in those days. I was awed by his battery—a .280 Ross rifle and a 7 x 57 Rigby Mauser.

How it came about I have no idea but for a time an American, a notorious sheep poacher whom I later knew, was employed by the Mexican government to prevent poaching of the northwest Sonora sheep. This was equivalent to hiring a weasel to protect the chickens. He regularly took hunting parties into Sonora for sheep. When the Mexicans learned what he was doing and fired him, he simply took his clients into the mountains of southwestern Arizona and *told* them they were hunting in Mexico.

But mostly the desert sheep were shot for meat. Old Charlie Ren always maintained that the poachers shot more ewes than rams. He may have been right as during the 1930s I used to see more rams than ewes.

However, there was some headhunting done. I once knew a Mexican in Sonoyta who when he was not smuggling opium, heroin, or Chinamen used to improve his shining hours by poaching large rams. He jerked the meat for his own use, carefully skinned out, salted, and dried the capes, and cleaned the heads. Once a year a Los Angeles taxidermist used to pick up the ram heads, take them back to Los Angeles, and sell them mounted to rich Californians as decorations for their rumpus rooms. This guy, Ramon by name, was strictly a no-goodnick, but I rather liked him. I was sorry when the *cordada* (mobile police) hanged him. "How come? What had the guy done?" I asked a Mexican cop six months or so later. "Nothing in particular," I was told. "Everyone knew Ramon was a coyote bastard!"

Enterprising trophy hunters from California used to drive to Arizona, camp in the desert mountains, and hunt sheep. One citizen of Los Angeles who is now well along in years once told me he had shot fine desert rams in Arizona and had never run into trouble.

At the University of Arizona some of the more sporting youths used to hunt desert sheep in the Santa Catalina Mountains north of Tucson. At one time the Catalinas were a great desert sheep range, but today it probably does not contain one sheep where it sheltered ten in the middle 1930s. The Santa Ritas south of Tucson once held sheep, but they were shot out many years ago.

Human development has interfered with the migrations of desert sheep from one range to another. Railroads, highways, irrigation canals—all restrict sheep movement. I have mentioned going with John Russo to the water hole where sheep had been shot from a blind for generations. On the way there we crossed a wide irrigation canal with smooth concrete sides—an effective barrier to sheep movements.

Development of marinas, motels, and whatnot along the shores of Lake Mead in western Arizona has been bad for the sheep. Roads have been driven back into some of the best sheep country in the area. Roads, vehicles, and human presence have always been bad for sheep. In the winter of 1971 a friend of mine who was spending a vacation in Arizona was watching three desert rams with binoculars as they fed on a low rocky hill. Suddenly he heard a shot and one of the rams fell over. The man who fired the shot was in a car with an out-of-state license. My friend turned the poacher in. Such exploits are frequent and are made easy by roads into the back country.

I am profoundly pessimistic about the survival of desert sheep over much of what is even now a very restricted range. The desert sheep face more perils than Pauline ever thought of. They are the pioneers of a race that has spread halfway around the world, from the islands of the Mediterranean Sea to the barren and rugged hills on the coast of Sonora opposite Tiburon Island and down the mountains of Baja California almost to the tip.

Mostly they live in a marginal environment, a harsh land of little rain and limited food. They are in the position of the poor man who is just barely keeping body and soul together and who yet has his mother-in-law and a drunken uncle descend upon him.

Most of the desert sheep country simply cannot support sheep plus cattle plus wild burros. As if the illegal headhunters, the meat hunters, and the cattlemen weren't enough, the latest enemy to enter the lists against the desert bighorn is the feather-brained sentimentalist of the stripe that supports Friends of the Animals.

People of this sort form a very powerful lobby, and in 1971 the United States Congress passed Public Law 92-195 protecting wild horses and burros on public land, making it a federal offense to harass, capture, kill, sell, or process into commercial products these feral animals. Unless this idiotic law is changed it will mean the end of the desert sheep in many areas. A conservationist friend of mine from Phoenix recently spent some time in the sheep country of California's Death Valley. He said that the sheep there were in a crash decline principally because rapidly multiplying burros had taken over water holes and had eaten up the vegetation near water.

I quote from an article by Dr. Loren Lutz, president of the Society for the Conservation of Bighorn Sheep. It is from *Safari*, the quarterly magazine of Safari Club International:

By being such efficient foragers and being able to survive under marginal conditions, burros offer unsurmountable obstacles to native wildlife survival. They put such tremendous pressure on the vegetation that the most desirable forage plants are eliminated, and bighorn sheep and other mammals and birds such as quail have little left for food. Very few perennial grasses are left in high-density burro population areas.

Burros also cause severe soil problems. In the Granite mountains of San Bernardino County, California, burros have just about destroyed Bighorn Basin with heavy trailing and rolling areas. Soil erosion is quite heavy, vegetation propagation is severely limited in areas of this type. The change in the character of the watershed and the amount of wildlife is directly proportionate to the amount and kind of plantlife. Burros will eat virtually anything, even eat creosote bush. Once the vegetation is gone, and consequently the life that fed on it, decades are needed for vegetative regeneration.

Burros also usurp water sources and drive away other animals. Don Swarthout (V.P., Society for Conservation of Bighorn Sheep) recounts burros driving sheep away from a spring he was watching for several days. They have also been known to kill calves, fight off horses, and harass range cattle at water holes.

Areas around watering devices generally have no vegetation because of the feeding and rolling activities of burros, thus negating their use by birds and small animals for food, breeding and protection.

People counting sheep and other forms of wildlife at desert water sources generally find that in high burro population areas few sheep, quail, and chukar are found.

Burros range from below sea level in Death Valley and Imperial Valley to above 11,000 feet in Imperial county. They come down out of the mountains at night and feed heavily on the farmers' crops.

Attempts have been made by concerned groups to have sensible management plans made for these animals. In California this legislation was killed by legislators poking fun at the Bill through cries of killing off the symbol of the Democratic party, to pointing out that this was the beast of burden of Jesus Christ, and also a part of the heritage of the old West. True enough statements, but somewhat emotional claptrap.

> Eco-freak environmentalists have persuaded State and Federal legislators to ignore the dictates of common sense in the management of wildlife resources. The abrogation of responsibility by these representatives bodes ill for the wildlife of the desert.
>
> Man has usurped the water, divided the desert ranges with highways, despoiled the slopes with mines, over-grazed the ranges with sheep and cattle, introduced diseases, noxious weeds and grasses, put houses and people where they don't belong, and now as a probable final blow, man is trying to protect coyotes, bobcats, mountain lions—and burros—and then some say "Let Nature take its course."

There are probably more desert sheep in Baja California than anywhere else. An intelligent and well-informed Mexican friend of mine tells me that he thinks there may be as many as 5,000 there. The sheep in the southern half of the peninsula *(weemsi)* are supposed to be larger on the average than the sheep on the mainland. Some very remarkable trophy heads have come out of Baja, and the Mexican government regularly allows hunting on special (and very expensive) permit there. I have heard of two tremendous heads that have come out of Baja within the past few years. One was killed by an American of Chinese descent and the other by a Mexican sportsman. I have seen a photograph of this last ram and he was large, even by comparison to northern sheep.

Baja California is a big country. It has always been a country where game laws were not enforced. Sheep have been shot for the pot by hungry *paisanos* and shot to feed mine and agricultural workers.

6 Hunting the Desert Bighorns

I made my first hunt for desert sheep—and also my first hunt for any kind of sheep—in December 1934. Two friends from Tucson and I had heard that there were desert bighorns in the Sierra del Viejo in Sonora. We also heard of an American in Nogales who had been to the Sierra del Viejo, who spoke perfect Spanish, and who had hunted sheep. We made a deal to pay him $10 a day to lead us to those mighty rams.

We camped at an abandoned gold mine called El Union. One more or less rainproof shed remained standing, and under this we made our campfire and set up our cots. We had filled our canteens and a couple of 5-gallon cans at the last ranch, which was about 10 or 12 miles from the mine.

A bunch of more innocent sheep hunters you never saw. Like most beginning sheep hunters I was convinced that sheep hunting was a long-range business and I was going to have to knock my ram off at 350 to 400 yards. My rifle was a Springfield with a custom stock and a heavy 4× German scope. The outfit weighed about 10½ pounds. In those days there wasn't much material in print on sheep hunting in general and desert-sheep hunting in particular. I digested the chapter on sheep hunting in a book on North American big game by the late

Col. Townsend Whelen, who afterward became a friend of mine. The good colonel recommended hobnails for climbing, so hobnails it was. I had a pair of Gokey boots. I took them to a shoemaker who dug up some hobnails. I had a pair of 8×30 French binoculars that cost me $35 and were not worth 35 cents. Apparently the prisms had been put in place with chewing gum by a six-year-old cretin. The damned things were always out of alignment and I could not use them more than a few minutes without getting a headache.

At the time I had done considerable deer hunting, mostly mule deer but with some Arizona whitetails thrown in. In addition I had shot a few javelinas and some black bears. But what I lacked in experience I made up in enthusiasm. There was a little brush of one kind or another in some of the draws in the Viejos. Used to hunting deer, I pictured the sheep bursting out of the draws and bounding up the hillsides like whitetails.

The Sierra del Viejo is solid limestone and most of the rocks are as rough as a very coarse file because some of the lime has been dissolved away. Those damned hobnails were always catching in the little cracks and crevices and making me strain my ankles. The longer I climbed around the heavier my rifle got.

I saw sheep that day but all the sheep I saw were on the horizon and all were looking at me. I saw a great deal of sheep sign, much of it quite fresh. The Sierra del Viejo is a large mountain. It rises from land that is perhaps 1,000 feet above sea level and I should imagine that the highest peak is not far from 4,000 feet. In those days there were a good many sheep there. Sheep still inhabit the range today. Oscar Brooks, a good friend of mine, a guy who can climb like a cat and who is a good sheep hunter, got a fine ram there in the fall of 1972. I do not know the sierra well enough to say for certain if there is permanent water there or not, but I suspect there is. The mountain got its name from an old man who used to distill sotol there, and to make the mash he had to have water. Furthermore, most ranges which like the Sierra del Viejo have permanent sheep herds also have permanent water. Years after my first sheep hunt a friend of mine who had made a bundle manufacturing lace fell in with an American prospector who assured him that all he had to do to get very rich was to put about $100,000 into the old Union mine. My friend did so. He was already rich but he wanted to be richer. He put a road into the Sierra del Viejo, brought in sophisticated machinery, built permanent buildings—and lost a million dollars. I have not been back since he tried to develop the mine. What effect it has had on the country I cannot say. Undoubtedly it was not for the best.

That first day on Sierra del Viejo was the day I got hooked on sheep hunting. Along in midafternoon I stood on one of the highest peaks. All around I could see the gray and tan of the lowland desert cut with the wandering white threads of arroyos. To the west I could see the dark upthrust of the Sierra Picu and beyond it the curving red hills bordering the flat blue of the Gulf of California. All over this level desert, drab in its winter coat, I could see little bumps of whitetail hills and the sharp upthrust of sheep mountains. I was all alone in a wide, beautiful, almost untouched world. A slight breeze was stirring. The sun was bright, the air fresh and cool.

Then on another ridge, perhaps a half-mile away and a bit below, I saw the diminutive outlines of a sheep. It was watching me, standing absolutely immobile. I got him in my funny little French binocular. It was a good ram. He watched me and I watched him. I hoped he was excited and stimulated by what he had seen as I was.

I was about to get to my feet, bid the watching ram goodbye, and head toward camp when I heard a faint humming. For a moment I thought it was a distant automobile. Then I saw it was an airplane headed in my direction. It was a fairly large plane for those days. Afterward I found that it was a commercial plane that carried mail and passengers from Mexico City to San Diego. It passed right overhead, probably not 500 feet above me. I waved but the plane went on, giving no sign of having seen me. Whether anyone in the plane saw the lonely sheep hunter or not I have no way of knowing. When I turned my eyes from the plane to the ridge where the ram had been I found him gone, frightened no doubt by the noise of the plane.

When I got back to camp about sundown my companions were waiting. Both were tired and disgusted. "If this is sheep hunting they can have it," one of them said. "I walked my ass off all day long and never saw a damned thing!" "Think I'll try hunting deer tomorrow," the second one said. "I may not get a buck but I won't kill myself."

As far as I know, neither of these men has ever again set foot on a sheep mountain. The next day they hunted deer and one of them got a young desert mule deer buck. I climbed the Viejo again and worked north, watching first on one side of a ridge and then on another. Along in early afternoon I poked my head over a crest to look into an interior basin. Presently I saw something move. It was the head of an animal. It could only be a sheep! At first I thought it was a ewe, but then I realized it was a young ram, three or four years old. I felt I was getting somewhere. I had seen a sheep before it saw me! I was about to move on when I made out two more sheep, likewise young rams. I later saw a small bunch of ewes and lambs that day and another old ram, but these had all seen me first.

I have often tried to articulate just why I have had an affair with sheep hunting that has lasted forty years and has carried me from Sonora to the Alaskan border of the Yukon, to the hills of Africa's central Sahara and to the mountains of the Middle East. Possibly the principal reason is the joy of being high, of being away from the ruck of humanity, of sharing the country with the sheep and the eagles and farther north with those other mountain dwellers the goat, the hoary marmot, the caribou, the great half-blind lumbering grizzly bear. Possibly those who fly airplanes have this same feeling, but I'd think they would have had more of it when they flew in open cockpits with the seats of their pants. And I have always liked the fresh, untainted air, the brisk breeze. Like all stalking, sheep hunting extends the excitement for a long time. Often I have seen rams bed down so I was willing to begin my stalk by nine-thirty or ten o'clock and have not got within shooting position until three or four. This means five or six hours of pleasant anxiety, of suppressed excitement. Then too an old ram is a smart and an impressive animal, rare enough, handsome enough, tough enough to come by to make it something to be proud of.

At the end of our second day on that first trip to the Sierra del Viejo we were just about out of water. We went to bed thirsty but saved enough for coffee. By midmorning we were back at the ranch called Pozo Acerno drinking the cool sweet water from the deep well.

I didn't get a ram on that trip, but I did learn a few things. One of them was that the reason I had been seeing all those rams on the skyline was that they had seen me first. I decided I needed a better binocular and a lighter rifle. I got a 7×57 on a Mauser action. With the Lyman 1-A cocking piece sight it weighed a bit less than 7 pounds. I acquired an 8×30 Bausch & Lomb binocular, a very fine sheep-hunting glass, and it opened up a new world for me. I shifted for desert sheep from hobnails to basketball shoes. Of this more in the chapter on equipment.

I shot my first ram through a sort of a fluke in that I did not see him before he saw me, stalk him in the classic manner, and pick him off at my leisure. Early one morning during the late-summer rutting season a Mexican companion and I found the tracks to three sheep, a large ram and two ewes. They were low and headed into an interior valley where there was considerable growth. The head of the valley was perhaps a half-mile from the mouth. The valley headed north. It was U-shaped and was enclosed by ridges on each side that rose at an angle of perhaps 25 or 30 degrees and met to enclose the valley at the head. The country was decomposed granite. The footing was neither quiet nor good.

My companion and I decided that we had the ram in a barrel. My *amigo* would go up the ridge to the east, I to the one to the west. We knew the sheep should be somewhere in the valley below. If we went slowly and quietly and kept a careful look below, one of us should get a shot.

I had climbed about three-fourths of the way to the top. Every time I paused to look into the valley or got a new prospect up the ridge I expected to see the sheep. I had paused just under a sharp little cliff to get my wind so that if I saw something when I stuck my head over I'd be ready to shoot when ahead of me I heard rocks rolling. My heart almost jumped out of my mouth. I scrambled up the little cliff and just as I got on top a ewe came tearing around a corner about 40 yards away. I lifted the 7-mm, then put it down. Then another ewe fled by. Then here came the ram. I jerked my rifle to my shoulder, but my feet slipped on the loose stones on about a 30-degree slope. He was just about to go over the ridge into the canyon when the gold bead front sight found the dingy white of his rump. The rifle went off and I saw a big red spot bloom like a flower on the white. Then all was quiet.

I stood there shaking for a moment. Then I toiled over to the edge of a little cliff where the ram had disappeared. At first I saw nothing, then I noticed about 10 feet below a big gout of blood. Farther down, possibly 50 yards or so, I could see the curve of a sheep horn in a *torrote prieto* tree (a stunted little tree found in the Sonora Desert; it has a spicy, peppery smell). Then I could make out the whole ram through the leaves and twigs. He was dead.

Hunting the desert sheep is in many ways quite different from hunting their northern cousins. In the first place, the desert bighorn is the hardest of all North American sheep to see. He is a brown animal in a largely brown environment. The hills and mountains he inhabits look as bare as the face of the moon, but most of them have a good deal of thin brush of one kind or another. I have mentioned the *torrote prieto,* which is a dwarf tree with leaves like the ornamental "pepper tree" that was planted in the Salt River Valley for shade when I was a boy. As I have said, it also has a peppery smell. Another, a very strange plant, one that breaks and bruises easily, is called by the Mexicans the *sangren grado.* It exudes a white sap that turns black in the sun. My old khaki sheep-hunting pants were all crisscrossed by black streaks. The stain does not come out in the wash. My old friend the late A. A. Nichol said the sap contains a powerful alkaloid. Indians and Mexicans have told me that if the roots of the plant are boiled and the "tea" drunk, it is a cure for both gonorrhea and syphilis. There are other odd plants, such as the *cirio* (wax candle tree), which looks like an uprooted parsnip and grows only in one range in Sonora, the Sierra Cirio south of Libertad. I mention these plants because as far as I know the *sangren grado* grows only in extreme southern Arizona and the *torrote prieto* and the *cirio* do not grow in Arizona at all. The organ cactus (which the Sonora Mexicans call *pitihaya)* is found in Arizona only in the extreme southern part—the Organ Cactus National Monument.

In most sheep areas in North America, horses can be used for a good deal of the climbing. In some it is occasionally possible to climb off a horse, jerk a rifle out of a scabbard, and shoot a ram. In most of the desert-sheep mountains with which I am familiar it is not possible to use horses. The country is so rough a horse would break his neck, for one thing. For another, many of the sheep mountains are a long way from wells and water holes. When I was hunting in Sonora a limited use of horses could be made in the Pinacates because the cinder cones were smooth enough for horses and camp can be made near natural tanks which contain water. Water for horses can be trucked in, but a horse drinks a lot of water and for the limited use to which a horse can be put it is usually not worth it. Bob Housholder, a professional sheep guide in Arizona whose clients have taken a good many desert rams, thinks horses are more trouble than they are worth on a desert-sheep hunt.

When I hunted the Sierra Los Mochos I used to camp at a little well which was dug for cattle but abandoned because it did not produce enough water for cattle. It was about 9 or 10 miles from the mountains—about a two-hour ride. However, those rides were not fruitless, as the low country contained many big desert mule deer and the rolling foothills near the sierra were full of whitetails. Leaving camp at six o'clock, I could tie up my horse and start my climb about eight. I would try to get back to the horse by four o'clock and back to camp for a sundowner and something to eat. Horses always travel faster when they are headed for home.

In the warm months the desert-sheep hunter has to carry a canteen. I used one holding 2 quarts. This is a heavy and clumsy burden but the desert is so hot between April and November that a supply of water is a must. Even with 2 quarts I used to have to ration myself during the hot months to have enough for a final drink to wet my whistle before I headed back for camp. In the cool months I learned to do without water. I would usually take a little knapsack with a couple of oranges or sometimes a small can of tomato juice.

I once had a friend who was overweight and soft. He was anxious to get a ram, so we went sheep hunting in April. We had to camp about 4 miles from the mountain where we planned to hunt, as we could get no nearer with an automobile. Every morning he and his Mexican guide would start off, each with a 2-quart canteen of water. Within 2 miles my pal would drink his 2 quarts. Then as he continued on toward the mountain he would drink the guide's 2 quarts. That done, he would look at the mountain and head back to camp.

In the winter on the Sonora Desert I did not take a jacket if I planned to do much climbing. I would wear only a wool shirt. The first hour or so after I left camp, I would be chilly, but when I was climbing I was comfortable and not burdened by a jacket.

Most sheep-hunting camps were dry camps, in that all the water consumed had to be taken along. Hunting alone or with one companion, I could make 10 gallons of water last a long time. If my wife went with me our camps were of short duration. She was revolted by my ways of saving water. One she did not object to was an alcohol rub. I used to take a bottle of rubbing alcohol with me to use in lieu of a bath.

In much sheep country the bulk of the feeding is done down in the valleys between the mountains. The sheep start feeding in the first gray of dawn. They move about, taking a bite here and a bite there. When it begins to warm up the sheep generally move up onto a mountain. Often they won't get very far, perhaps 200 or 300 feet above the valley. If the weather is pleasant they like to lie down on points or ridges from which they can have a good view of the country below. If it is raining or the weather is very hot they will often go into caves. The rams will generally go higher than the ewes and lambs. They paw out beds by scraping away large sharp rocks. It seems to me that for whatever the reason the desert sheep change their bedding grounds more often than do the northern sheep. I have seen favored bed grounds of Dall and Stone sheep where the dung was 3 or 4 inches deep. I once saw somewhere between twenty-five and thirty old desert rams in one bunch, but big bunches of rams are rarer than among the northern sheep. I do not know why, but I believe it is more common to see lone desert rams than it is to see lone northern rams. In the desert it is common to see two or three old rams together, seldom more.

In areas where there is little disturbance and little if any competition from cattle or wild burros, the sheep often bed down under a nice shady tree in some sandy wash. Back in the 1930s when I used to hunt in the San Franciscos, south of Sonoyta, Sonora, I have on several occasions seen sheep bedded during the middle of the day right out in the valleys. At the time the only cattle that ever reached the "Friscos" were occasional wanderers who showed up during the winter rains of December and January. The San Franciscos consist of a series of isolated granite mountains with valleys between. Sheep were then almost the only large animals there. For some reason deer did not seem to care for the area and were seldom seen.

The Sierra Cobabai, on the other hand, had open water developed by Mexican ranchers. There were a good many cattle there and a large number of wild or semi-wild burros. There were also a good many whitetail, desert mule deer, and some javelinas. The Cobabai is a higher range than the San Franciscos, with the highest peak going about 4,500 feet above sea level. When the sheep come down they do so warily, never bed in the valleys, and seldom bed down less than 1,000 feet up. There is permanent water in the range—in natural cisterns worn by rain in the solid granite. The Mexicans call these *tinajas* and Americans call them tanks. The water in these *tinajas* always has moss in it, sheep droppings, and the excretions of whitewing doves. But it is always cool and wet!

Old Charlie Ren told me that once he took a client into an interior valley where they were to make camp. While Charlie was putting up the tent and a Mexican camp helper was chopping wood, the client took a shotgun and went for a stroll. He thought he might pick up some quail or whitewings for the pot. Charlie heard a shot and presently the excited client came in and told him he had shot a ram. It had been bedded down under an ironwood tree. It had stood up while the client was about 30 feet away and he had shot it with a Browning automatic shotgun and 1¼ ounces of No. 7½ shot.

Another time one of Charlie's clients had taken a look at a sheep mountain and decided he'd rather settle for a mule deer. He and his Mexican guide were pussyfooting along in a *chollal* (patch of cholla cactus) when they heard a noise and a big ram that had been eating the cholla fruit jumped up on a pile of granite boulders about 10 feet high to take a look at them. The hunter knocked the ram off the rock, got a sheep without ever setting foot on a mountain.

I used to get up early so I could be out as soon as it was light enough to shoot. Then walking upwind or crosswind I would go quietly along the edge of the hills, hoping to see rams feeding or working up the hillside to bed down. Now and then I'd stop, glass what areas of the mountain I could see. Generally as rams go up they stop now and then to nip off a choice bit of browse along the way. Many times I have seen them above me with my naked eye. What usually gave them away was what old Charlie Ren used to call that "fatel white rump patch." Charlie was not the best speller in the world. The white rump is the most conspicuous part of the sheep.

By the time the sun began to get warm and if nothing had developed the thing to do was to go high, find a good place, and start glassing. Then if a shootable ram was located the route of the stalk had to be planned.

Above all the stalker must stay out of sight. Particularly should he avoid parading in the skyline. Usually the best bet is to keep high and come at the ram from above. Sometimes it is possible to go low, come up behind a point, and shoot a ram on the opposite point. The desert sheep have been hunted continuously by Indians, Spaniards, Mexicans, and Americans since the sixteenth century. They can be very smart indeed. I remember spotting a ram bedded down all alone on a point, chewing his cud and at peace with the world. I went back over the ridge, worked down the far side, came up over the top so I could see the ram below me about 400 yards away. Slowly and cautiously I moved down the ridge toward the ram. I was about 150 yards away but out of sight of the ram when a cruising crow came by, saw me, let out a startled squawk. The ram took off like a scalded cat.

I have mentioned the black ram I got within a few feet of. This happened in the San Franciscos. A series of sharp little canyons dropped off the main ridge and were separated by steep ridges. I was moving across the little canyons near the comb of the mountain, stopping to glass whenever a ridge offered me a new prospect. I came to a spot where for about 30 feet the wall of the little canyon was almost straight up and down. I decided that I'd need both hands to climb it. I put my rifle across my back with the sling across my chest and started up. The ridge was flat on top. Just as I stuck my head over I heard a movement and a big black ram and I were face to face. He had been lying there at peace with the world when I popped up. I scrambled up as fast as I could make it. I expected to see him below me or going up the side of the next canyon. He was nowhere in sight. I looked around frantically. Then I heard rocks roll and saw his white rump and his big heavy horns disappearing over the main ridge. That damned ram had dived off the ridge, had run around the point behind me, and had headed for the crest sheltered by the ridge on which I stood and out of sight until a moment before he went over the top. That ram was *black*, darker than any Stone I have ever seen. He was also pretty smart!

But I didn't lose them all. Here is the story of a successful sheep hunt:

It was springtime in the desert and the day before an *amigo* and I had crossed the border at the Mexican village of Sonoyta, Sonora, and had driven into the San Franciscos to make camp. The next morning we were up before dawn, and when we had eaten we parted—my pal to go in one direction, I in another. Not much over a half-mile from camp I came on the tracks of two rams, one young, the other an old-timer. They had been feeding along the base of a steep granite mountain, so recently that some of the twigs they had bitten off were still damp with saliva.

The wind was right as I quietly followed the tracks. Every moment I expected to see them in front of me moving through the scant desert growth, but presently I saw the tracks swing into a canyon. They were out of sight somewhere above. I turned up the mountain to my left and made my climb. About this time the sun came over the horizon and instantly I could feel its warmth displacing the delicious coolness of the dawn. I was in my middle thirties then, tough and enduring, and it didn't take me more than a half-hour to get to the crest of the ridge. Before I went over I glassed the basin below me in case there might be sheep in it, but nothing did I see.

In the saddle at the head of the canyon into which the rams had turned there was a little sand from decomposed granite and some sheep beds. The droppings around the beds looked fresh, and so did the tracks of rams. I hoped this was the spot for which the rams were headed.

I fed a cartridge into the chamber of the light .30/06 I was carrying that day, put on the safety, and sat down behind a boulder large enough to conceal all except my head. I then took out my binoculars to see what I could see. Below me lay the ocher desert threaded with the wandering white lines of dry arroyos. The ocotillos were tipped with scarlet and the paloverdes were masses of yellow bloom. Behind me a whitewing dove perched in a low bush was giving his deep-throated melodious call.

I waited. It grew warmer and on the desert plain below me the mirage began to dance and shimmer. I began to wonder if the rams had turned out of the canyon or had bedded below me.

Then about 200 yards below in the canyon, a vague movement behind a bush—a movement almost as much sensed as seen—caught my attention. My good 8×30 glass showed me it was a sheep. Then it moved again and I made out the head and horns of a ram about five or six years old. Presently he moved out into the open and gazed down into the plain below. I finally saw what he was watching—a coyote slinking home from its night's hunting. One moment there was one ram—and then there were two. The other had somehow approached from behind the brush and boulders across the narrow canyon from his partner. At first I could see only his rump, but finally he moved and I got a look at his head. He was an old-timer with heavy close-curled horns rubbed off wide and flat at the ends.

I reached down, picked up my old .30/06, and padding the fore-end with my left hand, I laid it over the boulder, snuggled down behind it. Much to my disgust I was shaking a little and my throat was dry, but I waited for the ram fever to pass. The ram fed behind more brush and boulders and I thought he would never come out. But finally he did. He stood there broadside, lithe and taut and muscular, his slender neck looking too thin and delicate to hold up those heavy horns.

I put the intersection of the crosswires low behind his shoulder. When I completed the trigger squeeze and the rifle roared in the silent desert air he disappeared as if the earth had been jerked from under him. The younger ram stood there for one horrified moment as the sound of the shot echoed through the canyon and then came bounding up hill right toward me. I remained quiet behind my rock and he passed within a dozen feet.

Here is one to mull over. I once knew an American who did a spot of sheep hunting in Sonora. Like me he used to like to get up early and skirt around the edges of the hills and pussyfoot through the valleys. But unlike me he had a trained sheep hound, a Weimaraner. This intelligent dog would take up the track of a feeding sheep and sneak along until he saw it. He would then go on point. This dog led this friend of mine, who this time had a client with a museum permit, to within 40 yards of one of the largest rams ever shot in Sonora. This old boy had horns that went almost 40 inches around the curl and is one of the largest desert rams ever shot, not only in Sonora but anywhere!

Sheep hunters reading these lines will no doubt notice that nowhere have I mentioned using a spotting scope for desert-sheep hunting. I did not have one of those wonderful instruments until 1946. Now on a sheep hunt I would not be without one!

In the December 1967 issue of *Arizona Wildlife Sportsman* there is an interesting article about Jack Walters, an Arizona sheep hunter and guide who lived at Ramsay, Arizona. I have seen a fair number of Arizona sheep but I have never shot one. However, the Arizona and Sonora sheep are the same subspecies and they live in more or less the same country. What Walters has to say about hunting desert sheep makes a lot of sense to me.

He advises against charging around on rough desert mountains, as the only time to make the climb, he says, is after you have a shootable ram located. He advises thorough glassing, particularly on the lower third of the hills. He says that many times he has gone over a stretch of country three or four times only to find sheep that he had missed lying in plain sight. As I have said before, desert sheep are very hard to see, particularly when their outlines are broken up by thin brush. Walters advises watching the ram "until you can establish whether he is more or less going in one direction or just wandering." He advises trying to intercept the ram at the first place that looks promising. This is the method I used to ambush the big ram that was feeding up the canyon in the San Franciscos to the place where he and his mate planned to bed down.

Walters had probably spent more time with desert sheep than I have but I have found it difficult to figure out what a feeding or traveling ram was going to do unless he had an obvious route (like the two rams feeding slowly up the canyon to bed down) or was traveling on a sheep trail. Too often feeding rams are so unpredictable that if the hunter has to make a long stalk he may find the ram gone when he arrives. If it is feasible I prefer to watch the ram until he beds down to spend some hours in pretty much the same spot during the middle of the day. When he lies down he may move a bit to get in the shade or to find a breezy spot where the gnats that have been bothering him will be blown away. Along around twelve-thirty or one o'clock he may get up and browse a little to put something in his stomach, but usually unless something disturbs him he'll pretty much stay put until he moves out to feed again in the cool of the afternoon.

It is unwise to generalize too freely about sheep of any sort. Walters says that rams are usually found on the lower one-third of a mountain. I have seen them low and I have seen them high. I am a lazy character and I prefer to hunt low if doing so is productive, and I spend a lot of time looking the country over, but in some places the rams I have seen have always been high. The big black ram that outwitted me was lying on a point just under the highest peak in the San Franciscos, for example. Sometimes old rams of any species will be found surprisingly low. As I have mentioned earlier, the first desert bighorn I ever saw was crossing an abandoned mine road. The first Stone ram I ever saw was lying on a ledge on a canyon wall above a creek in northern British Columbia a long way from a mountain.

Sheep do some strange things, particularly desert sheep. A big ram was once killed on the outskirts of Sonoyta, Sonora. If I remember the story correctly the ram was lying under an orange tree. Once I took my wife and son into Sonora to do a little deer and quail hunting and to see some sheep. We camped in a wash at the northern edge of the Cirios in the exact spot shown in the habitat group for desert sheep in the museum of the Philadelphia Academy of Sciences. I had picked the spot because it was an easy walk up the arroyo and over a low saddle where one could look over a wide canyon and a lot of sheep country. We saw no sheep but when we got back we found that a large bunch of ewes, lambs, and small rams had investigated our camp and left their tracks and droppings all over it. The whole bunch was on the hillside above us watching us.

Sheep are curious creatures, and apparently they feel (until they have been shot at a few times) that enemies they can see can't hurt them. Once in Sonora I was heading back toward camp high on a ridge along a pretty fair sheep trail. A ram about four years old followed me for a mile or so. He stayed about 150 yards behind me. Now and then he would stamp his feet and lower his horns threateningly when I stopped to look at him. When I got back to my camp and was enjoying a sundowner he stood on a point about 200 yards away and watched me.

If a ram has seen the hunter it is sometimes possible for one hunter to make the stalk while another hunter or two keeps the ram interested by walking up and down in plain sight. Another time I had watched a bunch of sheep for a half-hour until they crossed over a ridge. I waited for five minutes or so to see if a ram would come back for a look. None appeared so a Mexican *vaquero*, a companion, and I started to cross an open place to get into a canyon out of sight and make the stalk. No sooner had we started out than a ram popped up on the ridge and spotted us. I put a couple of handkerchiefs on the ends of ocotillo stalks so they fluttered in the wind. Then I had the *vaquero* walk up the valley away from the other hunter and me. As the ram watched the *vaquero*, the other hunter and I sneaked away and made it to the canyon without his being the wiser. The fluttering handkerchiefs and the walking *vaquero* had him completely distracted. I tell in the chapter on sheep hunting methods how in the Yukon, an Indian guide and I led three horses back and forth on a hillside and kept three old rams, who had seen us, interested so that my wife and her guide could make a stalk. My wife bowled over a 44-inch ram at about 40 yards.

I have been writing of days that are gone and will never come again—days when sheep were more plentiful and less harassed than they are now and when there were fewer people in the deserts. There were a few good sheep hunters in those days. Most who were good have passed to their rewards, whatever they are. Mostly the hunters who shot the sheep off were poor hunters. They were out after meat, shot sheep only when it was easy, when they caught sheep crossing from mountain to mountain, when they could knock them off coming in to water, or when they simply blundered into them. Most of these "sheep hunters" either had no binoculars or very poor ones and did not know how to use them. I have hunted sheep with local *vaqueros* who were presumed to be good sheep hunters, but most of them had little idea how to go about it. There have been some excellent sheep hunters in the Southwest, and no doubt the open sheep seasons of today have developed good ones in the United States. Most of the Sonora sheep hunters I knew were poor judges of heads, were ignorant about binoculars, were indifferent stalkers, and couldn't compare as sheep hunters to such famous Wyoming guides as Ned Frost; Alberta guides like Roy Hargreaves, Ray Mustard, and Tom McCready; British Columbia guides like Frank Golata, Westley Brown, George Ball, Bruce Creake-Dennis, and Frank Cooke, Sr. and Jr.; Yukon guides like Field Johnson, Alex Van Bibber, and Johnny Johns. Unfortunately I have never hunted sheep in Alaska, but I am sure there are many excellent guides there.

George Parker of Amado, Arizona, is more or less a contemporary of mine. We were both prowling around in Sonora back in the 1930s. After the war Parker outfitted for a time in Sonora. He is now a prosperous rancher and resort owner in Arizona. He is not only an excellent desert-sheep hunter and guide but he has successfully hunted all varieties of North American sheep.

In the 1960s and early 1970s some legal licenses for desert sheep were available in Sonora and in Baja California. They are exceedingly expensive but people scramble for them. A few are available to nonresidents in Arizona and Nevada. New Mexico and Utah have taken a few desert bighorns but licenses are not available to nonresidents.

Most of the residents of the desert-bighorn states who are lucky enough to draw licenses manage their own shows, and the success ratio is really rather high. Nonresidents who secure desert-sheep licenses almost always engage guides and outfitters. From what I have heard most of these are competent.

From what I hear there are also some good outfitters in Mexico. They furnish good tents, vehicles, enough food, competent guides. But some Americans have had some hairy experiences. Right after World War II when I was still living in Tucson, two acquaintances of mine asked me to arrange a desert-sheep hunt for them. I said I'd do my best. I knew a Mexican rancher who lived in sheep country. He spoke English, had horses, trucks, tents, and *vaqueros* who could guide. I suggested a price which gave him an excellent profit. I made out a grocery list for him. A relative of his who lived in Tucson bought the food and took it down to him. At my insistence his relative also took down to the ranch a professional cook.

My Eastern friends chartered a plane in Nogales and flew down to the Mexican ranch. The rancher asked them what they wanted to eat. They said, "Oh, anything! We're not hard to please!" That was the mistake of the century. The rancher took them at their word. He kept the good American food for his own use and sent them out with frijoles, lard, and ground corn meal for tortillas, bitter coffee, and an unrefined sugar called *pinoche.* For twenty-one days the boys had beans, tortillas, and coffee for breakfast and dinner. For lunch their guides took along some cold tortillas, heated them at noon by tossing them on the embers of a fire. This with coffee made in a tin can was their lunch! After a week or so one of the men shot a ram. It was hanging in camp when the rancher drove up to see how they were doing. He took all the meat home with him. Both hunters got rams but each lost about twenty pounds. To this day they can't look a bean or a tortilla in the face.

Some acquaintances of mine had secured licenses to hunt in Baja in the 1960s. They came back and reported very primitive outfitting at a very high price. In 1972 some friends procured Baja sheep permits and engaged an outfitter. I warned them that they had better go in with their own beds and with iron rations.

The first day, not long out of camp, one of them, an experienced sheep hunter, spotted a good ram with binoculars. He spoke a little Spanish and showed it to his Mexican guide. They began the stalk. They finally came to the ridge which should put them about 200 yards from the ram. About 40 yards from the top the Mexican guide rushed ahead, popped over the ridge, and yelled in Spanish, "There he is, the big ram! Shoot him!"

The ram, of course, took off. My friend ran to the top of the ridge, sat down, and opened up with a .270. The ram went down at the second shot. The guide, a young and lively character, rushed across the basin to the ram. When my friend arrived the Mexican already had the ram cut up and half skinned. My pal couldn't even get a satisfactory picture of his trophy.

So hunter and guide carried the head, scalp, and meat back to camp. Presently the other hunter came in empty-handed.

The next day both the Americans joined forces and went out. Like the other Americans they had been living on beans and tortillas. They saw no rams that day but the successful hunter told the unsuccessful one to cheer up, that when they got back to camp he would panbroil some sheep backstraps and they would feast. But alas when they got back to camp the "cook" had cut all the delicious mountain mutton into thin strips, had salted it, and had hung it up in the sun to dry as "jerky"!

Like the Rocky Mountain bighorn the horns of the desert sheep run to the close-curl type. However, like all American sheep the desert variety produces rams having horns of medium curls, and occasionally of the argali type, which pinch in and then flare out. In his booklet called *Hunting the Arizona Bighorn* Bob Housholder pictures the bighorn with the largest head ever shot in Arizona. It was taken by Louis Dees of Buckeye, Arizona. The ram dressed out at 160 pounds and the horns scored 187 points. Both horns were over 40 inches in length. The head is of the argali type in that the points curve out instead of coming up close to the eyes and blocking the side vision. The points, from the picture, appear to be slightly rubbed but they do not block the side vision, and I am sure any rubbing came from accidental contact with vegetation or rocks. I note also that these horns, unlike most bighorn horns, have a distinct ledge on the front surface and are somewhat triangular in cross section. Except for color they could very well have come from a Stone or a Dall. I have never seen a head like this on a desert ram in the field, but my old pal Les Bowman, who for years outfitted and hunted sheep in Wyoming, shot a ram in Baja California with a head that except for the color looks for all the world like the common "argali type" head from a Stone or a Dall.

The type of bighorn heads that I have always preferred in either the desert or the Rocky Mountain species is the close-curl. Heads of this type are always broomed or rubbed. They grow close to the face and as they come up they block the side vision and the ram rubs them against rocks. Sometimes they are rubbed off as smooth as if it had been done with a file. Often they are rubbed clear back to the core. Sometimes such horns have plainly been broken—perhaps by a fall, perhaps in fighting. The horns of desert sheep are dry and brittle. They knock chunks off when they fight. I have the head of an old desert ram with one horn sheath so broken that the core is exposed about 15 inches from the base or about halfway to the tip.

Incidentally, rams lower their heads and do not butt each other with the bases. Hunks of horn are broken off and can be found at the scenes of fights. Sometimes the broken and loosened pieces do not fall off until later. I have found pieces of horns around sheep beds. They have fallen off when the rams were lying down. Rams also break horns when they fall and when they bump them into rocks.

Another type of sheep horn is what I call the droopy type. It comes back and around and far below the joint of the jaw in a wide shallow curve. Often such horns have considerable length and yet do not come up to the bridge of the nose. Horns of this type usually have perfect points as they do not block the side vision and are never rubbed. When a ram with horns of this type lives long enough for the points to come up to the bridge of the nose they are very long indeed.

Anyone lucky enough to be able to arrange a legal desert-sheep hunt these days should settle for nothing less than a good trophy head. This does not mean a head worthy of the record book. Any old desert bighorn with a broomed, weathered, and battered head is a fine trophy whether he "makes the book" or not! Since the desert sheep is a smaller animal than the bighorn the hunter who is used to bighorns will often see rugged-looking heads with horns that come down below the point of the jaw and come up even with the nose or above it, horns that have very tight curls and come up close to the face. Heads that if they were on a bighorn would go close to 40 inches around the curl will go about 35 or 36 on the smaller desert rams.

Some desert rams, mostly young oncs seven or eight years old, will have heads with heavy bases that taper rather quickly. A head I took many years ago and which is listed in the 1939 edition of the *Records of North American Big Game* had bases of 16 and 16½ when thoroughly dry, but the longest horn was only 36½. The horns were of the droopy type. I no longer have this particular head. Inexperienced sheep hunters set great store by "perfect points." These are to be sought in sheep with widespread and argali-type horns such as are common to Stones and Dalls. With the bighorns, however, the best and most typical heads do not have perfect points. The best ones are rubbed and broomed, broken and battered. They show a life of many fights and many loves and they are something to be proud of.

The hunter of desert sheep has to do a great deal of walking and sometimes a great deal of climbing. Now and then the climbing gets dangerous. A couple of times I have been in situations where I could very well have fallen to my death. Because it is always possible for the desert sheep hunter to fall and break a leg or otherwise disable himself, those who hunt should go in pairs. I didn't always follow my own advice and I have had the unpleasant experience of wondering what would happen to me if I injured myself so I couldn't make it back to camp under my own steam. Desert-sheep hunting isn't always strolling through the lowland valleys at dawn. In some ranges the sheep are almost always high and reaching them requires some real climbing.

As I mentioned earlier, my first sheep-hunting shoes were equipped with hobnails. These were almost worthless. I next tried basketball shoes. With these you can cling to dry rock like a fly on a windowpane, but unless the hunter has very strong and tough feet they can produce stone bruises and walking on broken rock is unpleasant. Light boots of the "bird hunter" type are as uncomfortable to wear in broken rock as basketball shoes, and they seldom last more than a day or two on a desert-sheep mountain. They simply aren't built for it.

The most successful footwear I have ever had for desert sheep is a good stout leather shoe with a composition sole. Some like 8-inch tops, saying the higher top keeps gravel, twigs, and whatnot out of the shoe. I prefer the 6-inch top as it is cooler and easier on the Achilles tendon. Hobnails and soles with lugs (like Vibram) are not needed in the desert mountains. The walking and climbing the desert-sheep hunter will do will be on broken talus and on solid rock, not on steep grassy slopes the hunter of northern sheep will encounter.

I have used an 8×30 Bausch & Lomb and a 9×35 of the same make on desert sheep. Both are excellent but have been discontinued. There are good German and Japanese binoculars with similar specifications. During the middle of the day there is a great deal of mirage in desert-sheep country and higher powers are not practical.

I am sure that the professional sheep guides in Arizona and Nevada carry spotting scopes for sizing up heads after locating rams with binoculars. Hunters going into Mexico should take with them a spotting scope of 20× to 25× with tripod in some sort of a case so the guide can carry it. But for the lone hunter, a spotting scope in addition to rifle, camera, binoculars, lunch, and probably canteen would be just too much.

The desert sheep's rut is in August and September. Rams get thin and do not regain their condition until after the winter rains in December and January. The ideal time to hunt them would be in March and April. They are then fat and in good condition. They have left the ewes and hunting them does not disturb the ewes and the young rams. Furthermore, in the spring the deserts are seen at their best!

7 The Dall Sheep

I saw my first Dall sheep on Edith Creek in the Yukon in 1945. The day before, my companion N. Myles Brown and I had left the Alaskan Highway with outfitter Gene Jacquot, a French cook, two guides, and two horse wranglers. Gene, who was a thrifty Frenchman, couldn't see much point in our eating store-bought Spam, expensive bacon, ham, and whatnot when there was good wild meat roaming the hills. That first day on the highway it took a long time to get the packs made up and distributed on the various horses and we got a late start. In camp at last, with the tents pitched, our beds blown up, good smells coming out of the cook tent, and glasses of Scotch and creek water in our hands, Gene gave us the plans for the morning. "We stay here," he said. "In the morning you fellows must hunt for meat. We can't have a good camp without meat!"

The country where we were to hunt was at the time pretty much the private reserve of Gene and Louie Jacquot. They had come to the Yukon in the gold rush of 1898. Both had been trained in France as cooks. They were cooking in the Fred Harvey railroad restaurant in Needles, California, one of the hottest places in North America, when they heard of the Klondike gold strike. They set out for one of the coldest spots on the continent. They backpacked over the White Pass, built a boat of whipsawed boards on Lake Bennett, floated down the Yukon. When they ran out of money for grubstakes they would go into Dawson City and cook in restaurants. Gene told me that in the palmy days in Dawson it was possible to buy as good a meal as could be obtained in Paris—escargots, truffles, pâtés, filet of moose or mountain sheep, soufflé Grand Marnier, the works. But such food was pretty expensive, Gene said. A miner in the chips (or should I say nuggets) could spend $100 for dinner without batting an eye.

Eventually their prospecting led Gene and Louie to beautiful Kluane Lake. They found a gold mine there, although not an overpoweringly profitable one. To save some money they started importing their own supplies from Seattle and Vancouver. They built a wagon road to Whitehorse so they could bring their supplies back to their mine and cabins at Burwarsh Landing. They found that the Indians in the surrounding country wanted to trade them furs for canned food, cartridges, and various supplies, so they established a trading post and bought more supplies. They presently found that well-to-do Americans and Europeans wanted to come to the Yukon to hunt sheep and grizzlies, so they went into the outfitting business with an American named Morley Bones, who had a fox farm. When Bones grew old and tired of the Yukon and went back "Outside," the Jacquots carried on with the outfitting business. Among the famous who hunted with them are General R. E. Woods, Nelson Rockefeller, Richard K. Mellon, and "Wild Bill" Donovan.

In 1919, Bones and the Jacquots outfitted a party of four for a long hunt that began at McCarthy, Alaska, and was to have ended when the hunters, Bones, and their trophies floated in a scow built of whipsawed lumber down the White River to the Yukon River, where they were to hail a Whitehorse-bound steamer. The raft capsized and most of the trophies were lost. Bones managed to find another pack outfit. The hunters were picked up, taken to the Jacquot place at Burwarsh Landing and from there by wagon to Whitehorse. They almost froze and starved. One of the men, G. O. Young, wrote a book about the hunt, *Alaska-Yukon Trophies Won and Lost.* It was published in 1947 by Standard Publications of Huntington, West Virginia. It is a classic hunting tale. On that first trip of mine to the Yukon I hunted over much of the country described in the book. The Alaska Highway had been built, but two or three miles away from it the country was just as untouched as it had been when Gene had gone along with Morley

Bones to cook for the G. O. Young party. Later, Myles Brown and I hunted out of our main camp where Harris Creek flows into the Generk River, one of the spots where the Young party had camped years before.

The first morning of my own Yukon hunt on Edith Creek I rode out in one direction, Myles in another. My guide was an Indian called Field Johnson, a fine hunter and a fine person, honest, hard-working, and intelligent. Myles's guide was Johnny Johnson, who, I believe, was Field's cousin. Myles and both the Johnsons are now dead, alas, and so are both the pioneering Jacquot brothers. Field and I saw moose and grizzly sign that first morning, and along in late afternoon we saw a lone, young caribou bull. I shot it, and since Field had been foresighted enough to bring along a pack horse we were able to bring in all the meat. While Field was loading the pack horse I was using my binoculars. Four or five miles away I had noticed about a dozen white specks on a green alpine pasture at the foot of a dark cliff. It was around the middle of August and already there had been a little snow. Most of it had melted off, but patches remained here and there. Since the dozen white specks did not move I had concluded that they were patches of snow. Then I turned the glass on the specks once more. This time I realized that some had changed position and some were moving.

I handed Field my binocular.

"Look, Field," I said. "Those white dots must be Dall sheep. Some are moving now. I had seen them before but I had thought they were patches of snow."

Field nodded solemnly.

"Little ones," he said. "Ewes and lambs. It is late now. They get up to feed. Snow only white. Sheep white and kind of blue."

What Field was trying to tell me was that Dall sheep were whiter than white.

"Ewes and lambs," Field went on. "Some dots big, some dots little. Ewes and lambs."

The next day we packed over a high pass and from it we could see the wide gray sandbars of the Generk River, the Klutlan glacier from which it sprang, dark spruce forests, green upland pastures, snowy peaks. We dropped down, forded the Generk, and in late afternoon we were in camp on Harris Creek.

When we crossed the Generk I had my first lesson in "reading" glacial streams. Field took the lead. He would go perhaps 30 feet in one direction, then he would switch 30 degrees. Those who followed directly in Field's path had no trouble. Horses who wandered a few feet away from it had to struggle out of quicksand. There were several branches of the Generk and each had to be crossed carefully. On the sandbars between I could see tracks of grizzly bears, the large deerlike tracks of moose, and caribou tracks like two halfmoons.

The Jacquot brothers had named many of the streams in the area. Edith Creek was named for some client's wife. Count Creek, where I later hunted, was so named because a German count had shot a memorable ram there. Later I named a creek for my wife, Eleanor, but whether the name ever became official or not I cannot say.

The following night Myles and I with our two guides and the little Frenchman who was brought along to do the cooking after Gene left were in a jack camp of Moose Horn Creek. We were far above timberline and at the foot of the Solomon Mountains, a range that rose above the great Klutlan glacier. We had two small tents, one for Myles and me and one for the help. Cooking was done on a campfire with dry willow branches. When we awakened the next morning the ground was white with frost and our water bucket had an inch or more of ice.

Field had never been in the country but Gene had told him in general terms where to hunt. "You'll find some nice sheep basins above the glacier on the far side," he said. "It's a long way from where you'll camp but you can make it." That was that!

The next morning Field and I rode our horses over a series of caribou barrens where flock after flock of ptarmigan rose out of the stunted arctic birch and flew squawking and protesting away. They were mottled brown and white, already turning into their white winter dress. We stopped on the edge of a deep canyon. On the other side were more rolling uplands rising gradually toward the jagged end of the range that overlooked the great white glacier. We took turns using the binocular but nothing did we see.

"Let's go other side," said Field.

We led our horses down a moose trail into the canyon and up the other side. Then we rode across the rolling barrens toward a cold, dank basin at the foot of the range. More protesting ptarmigan flew up in front of us. A couple of caribou cows and their calves trotted across our path, bouncing as if on springs, their little white tails up. Then we saw our first sheep, a couple of white dots 2 miles or more away. Leading our horses again, we scrambled down a trail into the basin and crossed to the foot of the steep slope leading to the high rough ridges beyond. There we tied our horses to boulders and commenced our climb.

We soon hit a nice sheep trail along the hillside. It had been worn into the hillside by thousands of sheep over hundreds of years. It was steeply pitched but a bicycle could have been ridden on it. We saw fresh tracks, fresh droppings.

Field was so certain that we would see sheep the moment we poked our heads over the first ridge that he insisted we lie just under it for a couple of minutes while I got my wind after the hard and speedy climb. When I was breathing normally again I took off my 10-gallon hat, put a stone on it so the frigid breeze would not blow it away, laid my .270 beside me, and stuck my head over.

Nothing! What we saw was the head of a canyon, deep, rocky, and steep with a big shale slide crisscrossed by sheep trails. When we had glassed all the country within range we crossed the slide to the next ridge. We saw fresh beds there on the ridge but the sheep that had made them were gone. Surely, though, the beautiful white sheep of the arctic could not be far away. The sign was plentiful and fresh.

"Field," I whispered, "where in the hell are the sheep?"

"Next canyon sure," he said.

We edged along steep lichen-covered slopes, over rocks, and across a shale slide so steep that the only way we could negotiate it was to do so on a dead run so our impetus would carry us along and we wouldn't fall into the glacier below.

At last we once more lay just under the crest of a ridge. I waited until I got my wind, then peeked over. Below me was as beautiful and as sheepy-looking a basin as I had ever seen. It was the head of a steep, narrow canyon that dropped sharply into the Klutlan glacier below. Patches of snow spotted the lush green of the moss, grass, and tender little flowering plants, and all around great peaks sheathed in ice gleamed white and cold. Surrounding the basin were outcroppings of black lava, and knobs of the same material jutted from the basin itself. The floor of the basin sloped sharply, and through it ran a noisy turbulent little brook fed by the everlasting ice above. The stream plunged roaring into a steep, narrow canyon that fell away into the great white glacier that twisted and turned through its brown moraine below.

On the far side of the basin, dazzlingly white against the black lava rock, lay two ewes. A little below a lamb was feeding. As I watched, another ewe popped out of a lava cave where she had been resting—the same habit possessed by the cave-loving desert sheep of Sonora thousands of miles to the south. Two others walked sedately over the ridge on the opposite side of the basin and stood there looking around and silhouetted against the crisp blue sky.

What lovely animals they were! The larger bighorn ewes farther south in Alberta and British Columbia often have a heavy, potbellied look, but these dainty white ewes of the arctic were built as cleanly and as gracefully as their remote subtropical cousins down in Sonora.

I lay there feasting my eyes on my first Dall sheep, but Field was growing impatient.

"Let's go," he said. "We gettum ram today, that fella, but I don't see no ram here!"

"The ewes haven't seen us, so let's drop back over the ridge and work up to where we can glass the whole basin," I suggested.

"Don't need to," Field said. "We go right down into basin. If ram go out we see-um that ram, then shoot-um."

Abandoning any pretense of concealment, we got up and headed down into the basin. The ewes watched us with curiosity but with no apparent fear. I doubt if any of them had ever seen a man. We walked straight toward them but they made no effort to run. Our objective was the ridge where they stood, as from it we could glass the head of the next canyon.

Now comes the strange part of this tale. We were walking along and about to pass behind one of the volcanic outcroppings that dotted the basin floor when suddenly I smelled a ram. The breeze was blowing gently from the head of the basin down toward the glacier, and I was certain that there was a ram close by. A ram has a characteristic odor that once encountered is never forgotten. I have a better smeller than most and I had caught the scent. I have smelled deer, elk, tigers, and African lions before I have seen them.

"Field," I whispered, "I smell a ram!"

"If you do you got nose like wolf," he said.

Then above us and about 175 yards away we heard rocks roll and looked up to see a big ram going off to our right from one of the volcanic outcroppings that dotted the basin. He had apparently been lying on a point that was a little higher than the ridge over which we had come. If we had gone up instead of across the basin we would have spotted the ram instantly and I would have had an easy shot. He had apparently been watching us and when I smelled him and stopped he must have thought we had detected him. Off he went in high gear.

This is how it happened, but I doubt like hell that I smelled a ram 175 yards away. I probably smelled a nearby ram bed and the fact that the ram jumped was coincidence. Just why the ram was so wild and the ewes so tame I do not know. Maybe in his youth a wandering prospector had taken a pop at him.

"Good head," Field yelled as the ram disappeared behind the point on which he had been lying. "Shoot-um!"

I flopped into the prone position, working the bolt as I did so to put a cartridge in the chamber of my .270. The ram came into sight again going full speed uphill and quartering slightly to the left. The bullet I used that day was, I believe, the first Remington Bronze Point 130-grain .270 bullet ever used on a ram. That particular experimental lot of bullets always made a sharp crack when they struck. I think the noise was made by the wedge-shaped bronze point pushing sharply back into the jacket of the bullet. I heard a sharp crack. The ram fell to his knees, then struggled to his feet and stood there weaving. A second shot beside the first started him rolling. He tumbled a couple of hundred feet down the canyon before a rock brought him up.

At the risk of breaking my neck I charged across the basin to see my first Dall ram. He was a beautiful animal. In his snow-white short summer coat he was more slender than a bighorn. I guessed his field-dressed weight to be around 150 to 160 pounds. He was larger than a big Arizona whitetail buck, smaller than a large buck mule deer. He appeared to me to be longer-legged than the average desert ram but around the same weight. His horns made more than a complete curl. One point was perfect, the other slightly broomed. Bases were 13¾ inches and the longest was 38½. The horns were a dull yellow, like faded lemon peel. Except that his horns and eyes were yellow and his black hooves were stained green from the lush grass of the basin he was pure white all over.

The ram had twelve annual rings on his horns. He was an old-timer but his teeth were still good and he was fat and in excellent condition. The incident violated a good many rules. The ram was alone instead of being with some others of his age. He was in the same basin with ewes and lambs, something not done in the best ram circles. I didn't glass him, size up his head, stalk him, and pick him off in the classic manner. Instead I shot him on the dead run as if he had been a white-tail buck. The point of this, I suppose, is that sheep don't always run true to form.

We took photographs, skinned out the head, took hams, backstraps, and ribs, and then set off down the mountain. On the way we saw another ewe, a lamb, and about a seven-year-old ram.

When Field and I reached the camp on Moose Horn Creek we had walked and ridden for five hours since we had picked up the horses we had left tied when we started climbing. It was almost ten o'clock and the arctic night was closing down. When we crested a rise about a mile from camp we could just make out the pale gleam of the tents and the orange glitter of the campfire.

In those days in the Yukon the limit on Dall sheep was two a season. The Jacquot brothers, Buck Dickson, and Johnny Johns were the only outfitters in the vast territory. The drain on the sheep population was by no means heavy. Trappers and prospectors shot them for meat and even to feed their dogs. A few were shot for trophies, but generally the prospectors, trappers, and natives simply threw the heads and horns away. The largest head the Jacquots kept in their barn was shot by an Indian trapper. He had been at the trading post when a party of hunters from "Outside" came in with their trophies. He looked their sheep heads over and announced that he had recently thrown away a better one. Gene told him that if he went back to get it and brought it in he would give him $20 for it—if indeed it was better than the heads his clients had brought in. He did and it was. It had bases of $14\frac{1}{8}$ inches. The longest horn went $43\frac{7}{8}$ inches and the head scored $180\frac{6}{8}$. According to the record book the head is now owned by Gene's son Joe Jacquot.

On that 1945 trip in the Yukon I must have looked over at least a hundred rams. I may have seen a few slightly heavier rams than that first one I shot, and I collected another with a somewhat better head. One of the rams we took was thirteen years old, had a broomed, rather close-curled head, but was a small ram. I would guess its dressed weight to have been around 135 to 140 pounds, about the weight of one of the stunted desert bighorns in Arizona that has had to fight cattle and wild burros for every mouthful of food. I am quite sure that on that trip I did not see a single 40-inch head.

Like all one-trippers I thought I knew a lot about Dall sheep. I found out later that the sheep around the head of the White and its tributaries run small. I have hunted in various ranges of the Yukon since then. In the Ruby Range the sheep average much larger both in body and in horn growth. I believe they do in the Dawson Range, too, but a ram I shot there was stunted. His horns looked very large in proportion to his body, and I thought they would go 45 inches or so around the curl. The longest horn, however, went only a little over 40—an excellen't trophy but nothing like as large as I thought it would be. A few miles away in some foothills of the Dawson Range, Bill Rae, who was then the editor of *Outdoor Life,* shot an old lone ram that was the largest Dall I have ever seen. From the top of shoulder to bottom of brisket he measured 24 inches. That is a lot of sheep, be it white, black, or brown!

Ovis dalli dalli, the snow-white sheep of the arctic and subarctic, was classified from a specimen collected by L. M. McQueston, a Yukon-Alaska pioneer, in the winter of 1879–80. The type locality was described as "The mountains south of Fort Yukon on the west bank of the Yukon River in Alaska." The area was probably the Tanana Hills. The type specimen was an adult ram, the co-type a ewe.

The Dall sheep are found in the arctic and subarctic mountains of Alaska where the snows do not lie deep and heavy, as they need to have ridges to feed on where the winds blow the snow off. They are also found in suitable territory in the Yukon and Northwest Territories west of the Mackenzie River. The pure-white Dalls also occupy a little corner of British Columbia in the St. Elias range bordering on the Alaska panhandle. As I have said elsewhere, the Yukon River and the chain of lakes that runs roughly along the British Columbia–Yukon border is the boundary between the Dalls and their close relatives, the Stones. West of the Yukon and north of the lakes the black tails and gray saddles of the intermediate, so-called "Fannin" sheep quickly disappear and the sheep become pure white. East of the Yukon and south of the lakes the sheep quickly grow darker. Oddly enough, there are a few black tails and grayish saddles in the Tanana Hills between the Yukon and Tanana rivers in Alaska—the type locality of the Dalls. McQueston was lucky to knock off a couple that were pure white.

It has long been shown that *Ovis dalli fannini* is simply an intermediate type between the Dalls and the Stones and there is really no such thing. Nevertheless, the term "Fannin sheep" stays in circulation and is used by guides to describe the lighter Stones. The specimens responsible for the name were taken near the gold-rush town of Dawson City in the Yukon and were named in honor of the director of the British Columbia Provincial Museum by W. T. Hornaday, the director of the Bronx Zoo.

Seton in *Lives of the Game Animals* says the average weight of a Dall ram is 200 pounds, a Dall ewe 150 pounds. He also says that the sheep, except during the winter, are a "dingy" white. Sometimes the coats are stained green when the sheep lie on grass, and sometimes the coats get a bit dusty. However, most of the sheep I have examined at close range are pure, clean, snowy white, as white as a fresh-washed white kitten. The horns when clean have been called a "dull gold." I have compared them to dry and faded lemon peel. However, the horns are often stained by contact with brush. The coats of the lambs at birth are white, whereas those of the bighorns are brownish gray. According to Seton this shows a complete differentiation between the two species. These sheep are not albinos. Their eyes are gold, not pink.

The Dalls vary a good deal in size and in horn development. I have never hunted sheep in Alaska, but I have hunted Dalls over a good deal of their range in the Yukon. Some areas produce big heads and heavy sheep. Others do not. In general it can probably be said that the southern Dalls are larger than those in the northern ranges. I have never heard of any large heads or heavy sheep coming out of the Brooks Range in the Alaskan arctic, but the Chugach and the Wrangell mountains have produced many notable heads. The mountains around Fairbanks do not seem to produce big sheep or big heads. The late Jack McPhee, an old sourdough pal of mine, was a market hunter in Alaska in the 1920s and shot a great many sheep around Fairbanks. He told me that of all the rams he had shot and had seen he never saw a really record-class head. There may be large and massive heads around the head of the White River along the Alaska–Yukon border where I have hunted and have glassed hundreds of sheep, but I have never seen one I thought was exceptional. The Ruby Range in the Yukon, on the other hand, has produced many heavy rams and fine heads. A fine ram my wife shot in the Rubies in 1963 was one of the heaviest Dalls I have ever seen and had a massive 44-inch head.

Except that the horns of the Dalls are lighter in color on the average than those of the Stones, I have never been able to see much difference. When thoroughly dry the horns of both species have a maximum circumference at the base of about 15 inches, whereas the circumference of bighorn horns can be as much as 2 inches greater. However, bases that measure 15 inches are good heavy bases for any North American sheep. It is true, however, that a much larger proportion of Dall horns than bighorns are slim, and it is also my impression that really slender horns are more common among Dalls than among Stones.

All the Dall horns that I have seen have a definite overhanging ridge on the outside of the horn. This characteristic is usual on the horns of the Stone sheep but now and then the horns of Stones are without this ridge and resemble in shape the horns of bighorns. This may point to an ancient connection between the southern Stones and the bighorns. Of this Seton writes, "In northern British Columbia, we sometimes find horns that are midway in type between the heavy and slender styles as well as intermediate styles of color." A Stone I took on the Prophet River in northern British Columbia has horns which except for color are just like the horns of the brown bighorn. They are close-curled, oval in cross-section, broomed, and heavy.

In North American sheep heads, a length of 40 inches is about like the 10-second time for the 100-yard dash. If a runner can't make 100 yards in 10 seconds flat he is not a sprinter of the first chop. If he can he is in the speedy class and with training may be able to play with the big boys. With sheep horns anything that is 40 inches or over is an absolutely first-rate trophy. Horns less than 40 inches, although they might make the record book, lack the class of the 40-incher. A set of horns measuring 40 inches is by no means common. Charles Sheldon, who wrote *The Wilderness of the Upper Yukon* and *The Wilderness of the Denali,* was in the Yukon and Alaska long before headhunting became popular and the heads had been picked over. In his day he probably shot well over 100 rams, maybe 200; but if he ever got a 40-inch head he certainly does not list it in his books. The best Sheldon head I can remember goes about 39. I had been hunting sheep for ten years before I ever saw a head that I thought would go 40 inches, and in my sheep-hunting career I have only shot three rams with horns over 40, one Stone and two Dalls. On the other hand the first ram my wife ever shot went 44. So it goes!

Dall sheep heads have a high percentage of horns with perfect tips because they do not run to the close-curl type which block the side vision and are consequently broomed. I have a Dall head with a tip-to-tip measurement of 18 inches, a fairly close curl. The tips of both horns are broomed off. Many Dall heads are of the argali type. Since horns of this type do not block the side vision they are never deliberately rubbed and generally have perfect points. My wife's 44-inch Dall ram has perfect points but when he was shot he was about to lose about 4 inches of his left horn. He had taken a bad fall a few days before and had so badly damaged one horn that I wrapped a handkerchief around it so the tip would not fall off on the way to camp. The No. 1 and the No. 2 Dall-sheep heads shown in the 1971 edition of *Records of North American Big Game* are both of the argali type. Both appear to have perfect points. Now and then a Dall ram is taken with horns having a very wide spread. I have seen two or three such heads in the field.

In *The Lives of the Game Animals* Seton illustrates three Dall heads. One, a head taken by the late Col. Wilson Potter, the second man to collect all four varieties of North American sheep, is of the wide-spread type with a tip-to-tip measurement of 34½ inches. The illustration shows the points to be perfect. The girth is 14¾, the length 44¾. A famous Dall head is the one taken before World War I by Capt. R. C. Dalglish of the British navy. For a long time it was considered the Yukon record. This is an argali-type head with the longest horn going 47 inches. The base is 13¾. Seton also illustrates what he calls a head intermediate between *dalli* and *canadensis*. It is actually a fairly common Dall type. It has the overhanging ledge on the outside, what appear to be perfect points, and a tip-to-tip spread of 19 inches. A head like this is a pretty fair trophy and a sheep hunter should think twice before he turns such a head down. However it is by no means uncommon.

The famous Chadwick Stone sheep head has held on to first place for many years, but the title of World Champion Dall keeps changing. I do not have a copy of the very rare first edition of *Records*, but I have a copy of the also rare 1939 edition. This shows the No. 1 Dall as having horns of 47 and 47½ inches in length, a spread of 26 inches, and bases of 13. This head was shot by an Indian named Patsy Henderson. The record book lists it as having been shot in Alaska. The story I heard in the Yukon in 1950 was that it was shot in the southwestern Yukon and was actually the head of a rather dark Stone. In those days sheep heads were ranked the way they are in the British record books published by Rowland Ward—by the length of the longest horn.

In the 1952 record book, the No. 1 head is a Yukon Dall shot by Dr. Earl Thee of Los Angeles. By this time sheep heads were scored by the present system—by adding the length of both horns and the circumferences of both horns at the quarters. The Thee head was shot near Champagne, Y. T., had horns 44⁴⁄₈ and 46⁶⁄₈, bases of 14⅞ and 14⅝. The score is 183²⁄₈. In that edition a Dall I shot in 1950 on Pilot Mountain in the Yukon is listed as No. 12. It had a score of 177⅛. Like Dr. Thee's head it is of the argali type. In the 1958 book, the Thee head was No. 2 and the new No. 1 was a head from the Chugach Range in Alaska with a score of 185⁶⁄₈. One horn is 49⁴⁄₈ and the other 44²⁄₈. By this time my own head had dropped to No. 19. When the 1964 book came out, the Frank Cooke head that had been No. 1 in the previous book was No. 2 and a head taken in the Wrangells by an Alaskan, Harry L. Swank, Jr., with a score of 189⁶⁄₈, was No. 1. It had horns 48⅝ and 47⅞ inches long. My own best Dall head by this time was down to No. 37. Dr. Thee's head was No. 7.

In the 1971 edition of *Records* the Swank head is still No. 1 and the Frank Cooke head is still No. 2, but the Thee head has dropped to No. 9. My own head, one time No. 12, was then No. 46 and the head my wife took in 1963 is No. 41.

There are still record heads to be found among the white sheep of the Yukon and Alaska, but the sheep ranges are hunted far harder than they used to be and it is now rare that the hunter could climb aboard a horse, ride out of camp a few miles, scramble up a hill, and knock off a 40-inch head. Now to get an outstanding trophy the hunter usually has to work hard and to have luck. He also needs to hunt in areas where big heads grow and where the sheep are not shot off before they get their growth. As we have seen, sheep in some ranges are larger and have larger horns than in others!

Sad to say, I have never weighed a Dall ram. I would say, however, that the figure of 200 pounds for the live weight of the *average* ram is not far wrong. However, many adult rams are smaller and many larger. As I have mentioned, a large, old, and very fat Dall ram shot by Bill Rae in the foothills of the Dawson range in 1956 measured 24 inches from the top of his shoulder to the bottom of his brisket. This was not the measurement of the skinned carcass but the measurement including the hair. At the time, however, it was in early September and the ram was not yet in his winter coat. In another month, and measured in the thick winter coat, he would have measured about 25 inches. How much did this chunky old ram weigh? I can only guess. I am a fairly good guesser. On a red deer hunt in Scotland I was able to guess the weight of all the stags brought into the larder within 5 pounds and most within 2 pounds. So, hold your hats! I would guess Bill Rae's old ram to have weighed field-dressed at least 230 pounds and more likely 250.

The ram I shot on Pilot Mountain in 1950 measured in his short August coat 22 inches from the top of the shoulder to the bottom of the brisket and in a straight line 40 inches from the front of his chest to his rump. These are somewhat larger than the same measurements for a typical *Ovis poli* given in William Morden's *Across Asia's Snows and Deserts.*

Just as there are rams that run larger than average, there are rams that run smaller. Possibly one lamb had a healthy mother that gave plenty of rich milk, whereas another had a mother who had just barely made it through the winter. Genes are no doubt important as well.

In 1956 I had to make a quick decision on a running Dall ram. A glance showed that his horns came down below the point of the jaw and well above the bridge of the nose. It looked like a 44-to-45-inch head to me. When I measured the head one horn went 40¼ inches and the other 39¾ inches. The ram was a small one and his impressive head was in direct proportion. If he had been a large ram the head would have come up to my estimate.

Another time my old pal Field Johnson and I made a long stalk on a bunch of about nine rams. When I finally stuck my head over the last ridge and could see the rams something over 200 yards away, two of them caught my eye. One which was with the bunch had a fairly wide spread and perfect points. The head looked to me as if it might go 40 inches. Another ram was lying off to himself about 35 or 40 yards farther away than the main bunch. He had a close curl and broomed tips that went well up above his nose. My guess was that his horns would measure close to 38 inches. This was in the days when the season limit on Dall sheep in the Yukon was two rams. I decided to take the ram with the close-curled, broomed horns first and then to try for the large ram with perfect points. Holding a few inches below the backbone and behind the shoulder of the lone ram, I touched off my old .30/06 Springfield with its 2½ × Zeiss Zeilklein scope. The ram never moved. The bunch took off and headed for a deep canyon beyond. I hit the second ram just as he was about to go over and later Field and I found him dead halfway down the slope.

But this reminiscence is about the ram with the close curl and the broomed tips. He was an old ram with thirteen annual rings on his horns. But the horns only went 34½ and 35 inches. He was a dwarf—or perhaps I should say he was dwarfed. His skull was almost 2 inches shorter than that of the ram with perfect points. That second ram had a rather wide spread and each horn measured 39½ inches. He was eight years old and if he had lived out the thirteen years that seems to be about the maximum for the healthy wild sheep he would have had a 45-inch curl. He was fat and in fine condition. I guessed his field-dressed weight as about 175 to 180 pounds. The thirteen-year-old ram with the close curl, on the other hand, was a little guy. He was healthy. His teeth were in fine shape, and he was fat, but he was a miniature ram, the smallest Dall I have ever got a good look at. I doubt if his dressed weight was over about 135 pounds.

The Dall sheep are the most plentiful of the four types of wild sheep in North America. This is because there has been less interference with their habitat than there has been with the habitats of other sheep species. No domestic livestock compete with them for food. One brainless director of the Yukon game department planted elk near the Dawson Range sheep. To show how bright this guy was he also planted about one hundred ringneck pheasants in an area about as suitable for them as the Sonora Desert would be for polar bears. The Yukon really needed those elk. All it had was Dall sheep, moose, caribou, black bears, and grizzly bears. If the big, greedy, and aggressive elk prosper they could become serious competitors of the Dall sheep, just as they are with the bighorns in Montana, Wyoming, and Colorado.

The Dalls occupy a vast range, most of it wilderness. There are few roads and not many people. In the Yukon I do not suppose there are over 25,000 people as I write this in 1974. Most of them live in Whitehorse. When I first hunted in the Yukon, Whitehorse had a winter population of about 300 people and there were not 10,000 people in the entire Yukon. Roads are being driven back into the Yukon wilderness areas. Mines are being developed. Whereas there were only three outfitters in the entire Yukon when I first hunted in the territory, there are now thirty or forty. Hunting parties get into just about every Yukon sheep range.

Outfitting today is entirely different from what it was when I first started hunting in the Canadian north. Businessmen with a sharp eye for the dollar have moved in. They like to have four or five hunters in one base camp and then have them go out on jack camps with their guides. Instead of hunting from several different temporary camps for thirty or forty days and moving from one to the other by pack train, supplies and hunters are taken by float plane to a base camp on some lake. The idea is to get them in, get them trophies, and get them out so a new batch of hunters can come in.

In the old days the outfitter made a good part of his living by some other occupation. He might run a trading post like the Jacquot brothers of Kluane Lake in the Yukon. He might have a summer dude ranch and raise mink as did Roy Hargreaves of Mt. Robson, B.C. He might run a winter trap line and do a little farming as Frank Golata of Dawson Creek, B. C., used to do. In the old days these unsophisticated outfitters took out maybe two parties a year. The late Alex Davis, an Irishman who was once a bellhop at the Plaza Hotel in New York and who was later a trader in the Indian village of Champagne, Yukon, was a fairly big operator as outfitters went a couple of decades ago. Alex had an enormous territory for sheep, moose, caribou, and grizzly, a lot of equipment, and over a hundred horses, but I don't think he ever sent out more than a half-dozen parties a year. Alex van Bibber, likewise of Champagne, trapped in the winter and took out a couple of thirty-day parties annually.

Today's outfitters usually try to have four or five base camps with several clients hunting out of each with guides in jack camps. They often own their own airplanes to service the camps. In the winter they answer queries from would-be hunters, attend conventions of big-game hunters, tour the country showing movies, making friends and influencing people, and giving their pitch.

In spite of all this, the Dall sheep country is still lightly hunted. In Alaska some areas adjacent to lakes where light planes can fly in may take quite a pounding, but the areas that can be hunted around such lakes is not great because most people can travel only so far on their own legs. There are many outfitters in Alaska. Few of them have horses. In fact I have only heard of two—one in the Wood River country not far from Fairbanks and another just across the Yukon border near the head of the White River and around Ptarmigan Lake.

In Alaska from what I hear many local hunters hire bush pilots to fly them into a lake. Then they take off with a back pack, camp on some creek just under timberline, and hunt on foot. Others leave their automobiles by a road and go in from 10 to 30 miles with packs on their backs. This is for the young and tough.

A couple of my friends made a deal with an Alaskan outfitter for a twenty-one-day hunt. When they landed at a lake by light plane they found nine other hunters in camp. The outfitter had scratched out a landing strip. He had two light planes equipped with doughnut tires. Every morning he would fly his dudes out, two dudes with one guide. They would land above rams he had spotted and then the dudes would hunt down on the rams and walk downhill to camp. My two pals were pretty unhappy about the deal.

Another friend of mine, a well-upholstered character who was fond of the fork and the bottle and would field-dress about 250 pounds, contracted for an Alaskan sheep hunt. The outfitter had no horses and his base camp was not near a lake. He brought his dudes and his supplies in over the tundra by a cat that pulled some sort of a wagon with automobile tires. In the morning the dudes were supposed to stumble 2 or 3 miles over the frost hummocks called "niggerheads," then climb 1,500 to 2,000 feet up to sheep country. My chubby friend didn't get a ram. Actually I am not sure that he ever got to the mountain.

Yet another pal of mine arranged for a cheapie Alaskan sheep hunt. The outfitter agreed to take in a party of four men, furnish the grub, guide some of them, direct the hunting of the others, do most of the cooking. They were to travel about 20 miles into the mountains from the highway by a cat that pulled a couple of sleds. The cat broke down two or three times and it took them three days to make the 20 miles. When they got into the mountains, the outfitter said he had some other business to attend to but that he would be back. He told the lads that there were sheep all around.

When the outfitter left the hunters discovered that they did not have enough food. A couple of them got small rams and one of them shot a grizzly. They ran out of coffee, flour, sugar, bacon, and just about everything else except vinegar and pepper, but by eating up the two sheep and chewing on the bear they got by. The four of them paid the outfitter $1,000 each—a "cheapie" trip but an uncomfortable, unsatisfactory hunt. I have no doubt but that the jackleg outfitter found it a very profitable venture.

There are outfitters and outfitters. The wildest experience I ever had myself was a trip into the Pelly Mountains of the Yukon. We didn't have enough horses, enough saddles. We were supposed to be out for thirty days but we barely had enough food for two weeks. No one in the party had ever been in the country before. Two of our guides were pool-hall Indians from Whitehorse who couldn't tell a pack trail from a moose trail, and our cook was a business executive from the East who had deserted his wife and family and had eloped with his secretary. (She went along as second cook.)

Because the country in which they live is still largely wilderness, the Dall sheep is more plentiful than any other species of North American sheep. An estimate by the Alaska game department says there are probably around 30,000 Dall sheep in that state. There are probably about that many Dalls along with their "Fannin" relatives in the Yukon. There is a substantial population of the thinhorn sheep in the Mackenzie and South Nahanni district of the western edge of the Northwest Territories.

Around 1,000 rams are taken each year in Alaska. In the past, Indians and Eskimos have killed a great many sheep. An old Indian who was the principal hunter for his clan in the Brooks range told my sourdough friend the late Jack McPhee that he had shot "several hundred" Dall sheep with a .22 Hornet. During the gold-rush days, market hunters shot off the sheep adjacent to mining camps. However, as the mines played out and the miners left the sheep came back.

The take of Dall sheep by nonresident trophy hunters has increased from 167 rams in 1969 to 226 in 1973, according to figures furnished by the Yukon game department. The same report says residents shot 55 in 1973. Compared to the dozen or so rams taken by sportsmen the first year I hunted in the Yukon, this sounds like a lot of sheep. But the Yukon sheep are certainly not hard hunted. My son Bradford has hunted in the Yukon since I have. He told me that on his last hunt for white sheep he must have seen 1,000 or more. However, J. B. Fitzgerald, director of game, thinks the annual take of rams should not be increased if trophy hunting is to be obtained. As far as I know there is only one outfitter in the Northwest Territories. He hunts in the South Nahanni country. My old friend Col. Harry Snyder, a sheep hunter of great experience, made a trip into the South Nahanni thirty years or so ago. He told me that most of the sheep he and the members of his party shot were white with black tails and scattered black hairs along their spine and occasionally on the bridge of the nose. He said the country contained more grizzly bears than any place he had ever seen and likewise had some gigantic moose.

All over the North the Dall sheep declined during the 1930s and were apparently at a low point in their numbers around the end of World War II. Wolves got the blame. Biologists said they did not think wolves were an important limiting factor in sheep numbers. Sportsmen said they were. The flack was really flying.

Lyman Nichols, biologist with the Alaska game department, wrote me that sheep numbers in Alaska were controlled almost entirely by natural influences. He says that sheep are increasing all over Alaska and that they are increasing in the few accessible areas where the hunters take almost all the legal (three-quarters curl or better) rams each year at the same rate as completely protected herds. He believes that so far in Alaska man has little lasting influence on the Dall sheep and that in some areas the sheep are approaching the point of overpopulation.

He wrote me that it is entirely possible that the Dall sheep of Alaska will continue to have periodic die-offs. Dall sheep winter high in alpine areas where the wind blows the dry, powdery snow off the slopes and ridges. The die-offs come when heavy, wet snow that is not blown off covers their feed. Then the sheep are trapped under starvation conditions in spite of the state of the range and the balance of the herd. Nichols says that a study is underway to see if the harvesting of sheep of both sexes can keep the numbers of sheep within their food supply.

In a letter to me dated November 3, 1970, he says that some of the Alaska sheep hunting is less than ethical:

> Probably the main factors connected with harvesting of trophy rams are the tremendous competition among hunters to obtain a head that will go in the Boone & Crockett record book, combined with the use of the small plane for easy access. The "prestige factor" of getting a head "in the book" encourages many hunters and unscrupulous guides to violate any laws or hunting ethics that may get in their way. The quicker and easier the head is obtained, the better. The present-day prestige appears to be in "having" a big sheep head rather than in "earning" it. The light plane enables many guides and hunters to locate large rams and to reach them with relative ease. Herding sheep past "hunters" has also been known to occur.

> Unfortunately, it is almost impossible to enforce game laws based on hunting ethics. It's hard enough to enforce any game law here with only a handful of protection officers covering vast areas, weak laws and courts, a very mobile hunting public (the number of privately owned airplanes in Alaska is amazing, to say nothing of off-road vehicles, boats and snow machines), and a dedicated group of hard-core violators-for-money.

Mr. Nichols also says that somehow the outdoor writers have failed to get over the message of sportsmanship. In defense of myself and others in this business I'll have to say the outdoor writers did not create human nature. That many human beings are greedy and dishonest has been remarked on since the first ape-man hunter in the African Pliocene left the carcass of a baboon he had beaten to death with a kudu jaw to go knock off another and returned to find the carcass of the first baboon gone. I have made my own comments on present-day sheep-hunting ethics in the chapter of this book called "The Grand Slam Caper."

So far the activities of man have had no great and permanent influence on the Dall sheep. What the future will be I have no idea. I am keeping my fingers crossed. Some years ago I wrote that the range of the Stone sheep was so remote that I did not think it would be seriously invaded during my lifetime. As I write this a railroad is being driven through it. Automobiles can drive right to Telegraph Creek. The Stone-sheep country is being explored for oil and minerals. In 1971 Frankie Cooke, Jim Rikhoff, and I had our binoculars on a 42-to-43-inch Stone ram when a helicopter came threshing around a point, scared the ram out of the country, then landed on the ridge above us and dumped off a young geologist who was prospecting the country for copper. He was hired by a large American corporation. When we told Frank Cooke, Sr., of this later he exploded. "What in the hell is this country coming to?" he said. "Used to be a man could be alone here and get some peace. Now planes and helicopters are flying over all the time and raising hell and you can't walk up a creek without bumping into some goddam long-haired hippie with whiskers two feet long!"

The Alaska pipeline will cross the Brooks Range, which is good Dall sheep country. What the effect of the pipeline on the tundra and the game no one really knows. The accompanying road will open up a great deal of territory, and sheep may well be pushed back.

Charles Sheldon, of whom more later in this chapter, wrote that sheep persistently cling to their home range and that hard hunting can kill off all the sheep on a mountain before they will move. He said this is particularly true of isolated mountains and small ranges, not so true of large continuous ranges. Actually not too much is known about this. At the present time in Alaska, sheep are being marked with dyes so their movements can be followed and studied.

My own hunch is that Dall sheep travel more than many believe. I know that desert sheep are forced to travel from range to range in order to survive. I know, too, that I have seen sheep tracks in stream beds and sandbars far out in rolling country in the Yukon. I know, too, that if shot at much, desert sheep will go clear off one Sonora range to another. Sometimes the winter and summer ranges of sheep are only a few miles apart, but sometimes they travel a long distance. In northern British Columbia, rams that summer high on the crest of the Rockies move down the high country along the Prophet River to meet the ewes at the breeding ground in lower hills and canyons 30 miles and more from the summer range. The young rams move first, the old ones last. I was on the Prophet and Muskwa for a couple of weeks in 1946 and was up with the rams every fair day. Along this migration route in that time we must have seen 250 rams. In all that time we saw but one ewe. She was on the same mountain with almost ninety old rams. Why, I'll never know!

No chapter on the Dall sheep would be complete without mention of Charles Sheldon, one of the great sheep hunters of all time. Sheldon was a man of independent means. He was a graduate of Yale in the class of 1890 in, I believe, some branch of engineering. He was an official with several different railroads and became interested in sheep hunting when he was with the Chihuahua and Pacific Railroad in Mexico from 1898 until 1902. He was the first man to collect specimens of all four varieties of North American sheep—desert, Rocky Mountain bighorn, Stone, and Dall. He hunted desert sheep in Chihuahua and Sonora and in the Grand Canyon of Arizona. *Ovis canadensis sheldoni*, a desert bighorn, was named for him. It was classified from a specimen he shot in the Sierra del Rosario, a desert range in northern Sonora not far from the Arizona border. For a time it was thought that it was a different species but it has since been realized that it was simply an extra-small sheep. He became wealthy, if I remember correctly, through the invention of some gadget which railroads use. His principal interest was the sheep of the North—the

Stones and the Dalls, particularly in the area where the two Dall subspecies came together. He spent the summers of 1904 and 1905 studying and collecting specimens of sheep in the Yukon. He shot sheep in what was then virgin country. It was not only unknown to white men but largely unknown to Indians. He hunted in the Rose Mountains, the Pellys, the Ogilvies, Selwyns, the Glenlyons—all sheep mountains that were wild country then and are still wild country today. I have hunted sheep in some of this country and much of it is difficult to travel in. There is a great deal of muskeg. The lower slopes of many of the mountains are clad in high thick brush of one kind or another—willow, dwarf arctic birch, stunted spruce and balsam. Much of the country is very steep and very rocky.

Sheldon traveled with light outfits. He usually took some trapper or out-of-work prospector along to keep camp and help him pack, but he always hunted alone and slept under a lean-to with a fire in front of it instead of in a tent. All of his camps in the Yukon were like what the modern sheep hunter calls a "jack camp."

He writes: "In the way of field equipment, I had an open canvas shelter instead of a tent, with wide wings so constructed that when pegged to the ground they inclined outward at an angle from the perpendicular, leaving extra space for storing provisions. A detachable strip of canvas a foot wide could be tied in front and sloped outward over inclined poles. This prevented rain from blowing in. No one who loves camp life can prefer a tent to a shelter. The log fire which is always made before the shelter reflects warmth directly inside so that one can sit in ease and enjoyment in all but the coldest weather . . .

"For sleeping I had a coon-skin robe eight feet square. It weighed 14 pounds. It keeps me warm enough even in winter weather. A lynx-skin robe is better and warmer but more expensive. A caribou- or reindeer-skin robe is the best of all. Equally warm, it is much lighter than the others. The wolf-skin robe is more commonly used by trappers and prospectors but it is heavier."

Sheldon wrote that until November he always wore summer underclothing, a gray flannel shirt, and gabardine trousers. He must have been very surefooted because he climbed in heavy wool socks and moccasins in the summer months. In the early fall he preferred a "rubber shoe with leather uppers soled and hobnailed." He carried a parka made of the hides of ground squirrels, a pair of Zeiss binoculars of 8× or 10×, and a small camera on his belt, and he wore an alpine rucksack for the parka and various oddments. He always carried a pocket knife, a barometer, and a steel tape.

Sheldon was not a gun nut. He did all his hunting in the North with one rifle, a 6.5 x 54 Mannlicher which used a 160-grain bullet at a velocity of about 2,300 feet per second. The rifle was made for him by Jeffrey of London, had a Lyman 1-A peep sight on the cocking piece—the same sight I used to shoot my first desert ram in the middle 1930s. With this rifle he shot about eighty grizzly and brown bears and a vast number of sheep. He also took along a .22 rimfire rifle he used to pot grouse.

By modern standards Sheldon was a pretty bloody guy. When he got the drop on a bunch of rams he was apt to pot them all. He was a cool, crack shot and almost everything he shot at including grizzlies and Alaska brown was killed with one shot.

Sheldon hunted rams among un-picked-over herds, but apparently he never made any great effort to secure outstanding trophies. In all his hunting I do not believe that he ever got a head with a horn length of 40 inches, either in Alaska or in the Yukon.

In the summer and fall of 1906 and for an entire year in 1907–08 he hunted and studied Dall sheep in the neighborhood of Mt. McKinley, Alaska, which was then called Denali. He built a cabin and spent a winter there studying the sheep. He was later instrumental in getting the McKinley National Park established.

Sheldon wrote two books about sheep which are classics of their kind. *The Wilderness of the Upper Yukon*, which came out in 1911, is the definitive book on the color variations and distribution among the Stone and Dall sheep. It is uncannily accurate. I have a battered old copy of the book which I have carried with me on various hunts in northern British Columbia and the Yukon. If the color distribution chart in the book says a certain color pattern is present in an area it always shows up. I've used Sheldon's distribution chart here in this book because there is none better. *The Wilderness of the Denali* is the account of his hunting and exploring in the Alaska range.

I have never read any accounts of Sheldon's hunts in Sonora. I wish I could find them. It has been my good luck to hunt over much of the country that Sheldon had visited thirty years and more before. I know that he was on Tiburon Island in the Gulf of California off the Sonora coast and that he visited the Seri Indians there. I have often wondered if he hunted sheep on Tepopa, just across from Tiburon, or on the

The author (with shirttail out, alas) glassing rams in a big Yukon basin. The only way to get a sure shot at these rams would have been to drive them. We didn't.

Reproduced on the next page and overleaf is Charles Sheldon's distribution chart and map from his Wilderness of the Upper Yukon. *The book came out in 1911, but the map is still amazingly accurate.*

FIG. 1. *Ovis dalli*, Type.

FIG. 5. *Ovis fannini*, Type.

FIG. 9. *Ovis stonei*, Type.

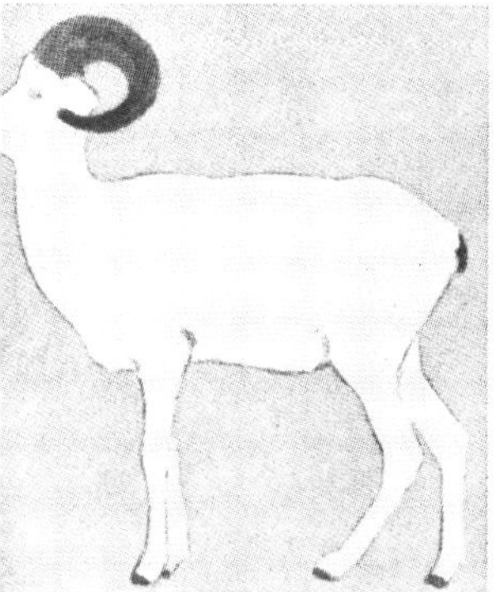

FIG. 2.

FIG. 6.

FIG. 3.

FIG. 7.

FIG. 4.

FIG. 8.

Distribution Areas.

A—Occupied by Fig. 1 (*Ovis dalli*) exclusively.

B—*Ogilvie Rockies* occupied by Figs. 2–3–4, exceptionally Fig. 5 in eastern section. Figs. 2 and 3 greatly in the majority. *Between Yukon and Tanana Rivers* occupied mostly by Fig. 2 with much less black on tail, occasionally Fig. 1. *West of Lewes River* occupied by Figs. 1 and 2 in the majority. Figs. 2–3–4–5 exceptionally.

C—Occupied by Figs. 2–3–4–5–6–7. Figs. 3–4–5–6 most common. Intermediate colors between 2 and 3 equally common.

D—Occupied by Figs. 4–5–6–7–8. Figs. 5–6–7 in the majority. Tendency toward lighter colors in the north. Fig. 4 exceptional in the north, still more so toward the south. Fig. 9 occasionally in the south.

E—Occupied by Fig. 9 (*Ovis stonei*). Rarely Figs. 6 and 7 are found in this area.

PLATE ILLUSTRATING DISTRIBUTION OF SHEEP IN AREAS INDICATED ON MAP.

res 1–5–9 were drawn from the *Types*. The other figures are from specimens illustrating the average colors, but actually every intermediate graduation of color occurs respectively between each

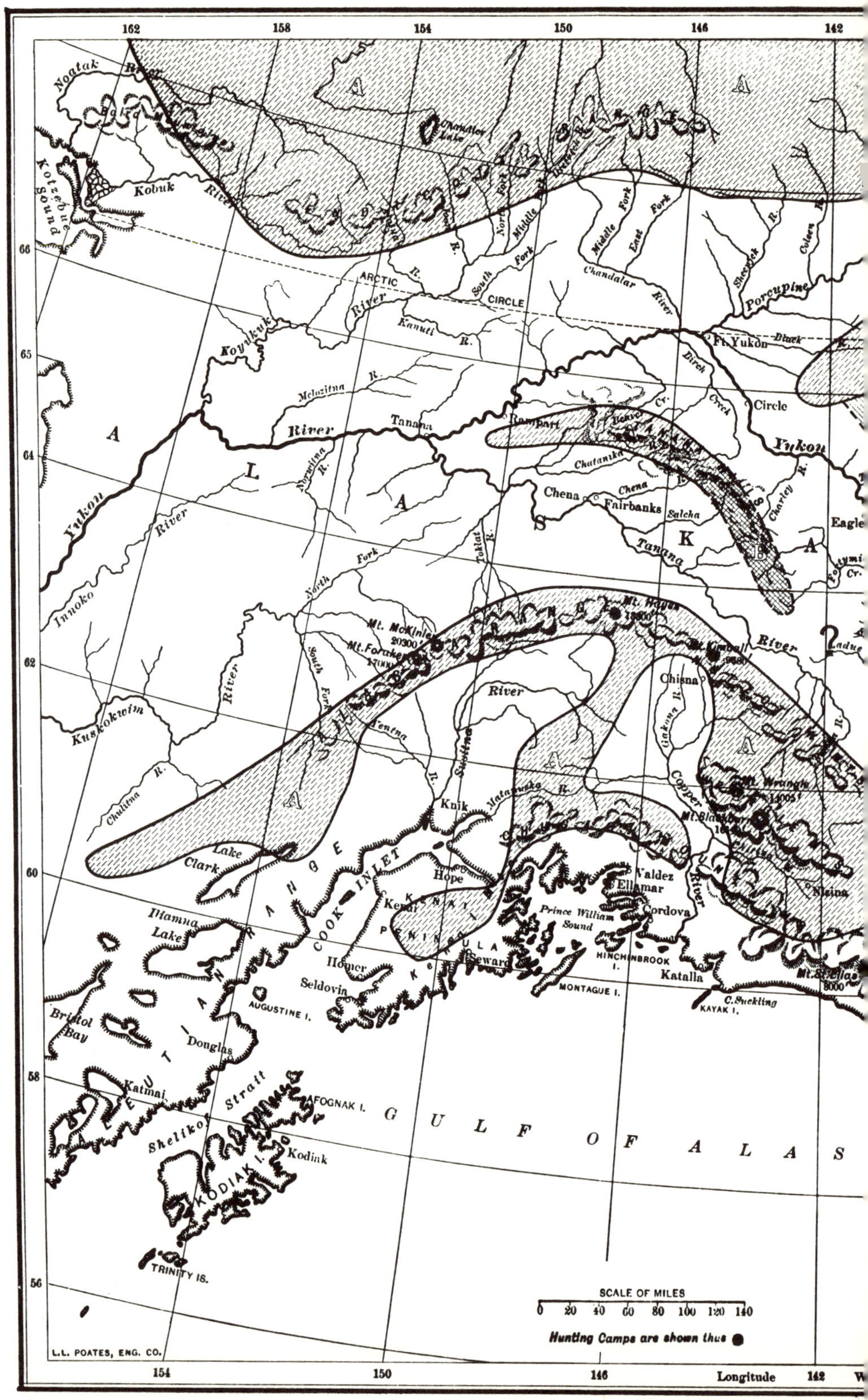

Map of Yukon Territory, adjacent port[...]
The distribution of sheep according to their colors is ill[...]

British Columbia, and North-west Territories.
d areas, the boundaries of which are, in places, only approximate.

Cirios up the coast to the north. I have also been in some of the country in the Pelly Mountains which he describes. I have never, alas, hunted sheep in Alaska.

In some ways the Dall sheep is the easiest of all North American sheep to hunt. His snow-white coat, which is undoubtedly excellent camouflage in the winter, makes him exceedingly conspicuous during the late-summer and early-fall hunting season. Charles Sheldon often speaks of the coats of the Dall sheep he hunted being stained. That has not been my experience. I have seen Rocky Mountain goats with coats so dirty that they looked brown instead of white, but I have never run into a badly stained Dall ram. As I've already said, often their yellow horns are darkened by bark and sap of the brush they go through and which darkens in the sun. Sometimes when they lie down on tender green grass they will have a green tinge on their legs and briskets, but mostly the staining does not amount to much.

The white coats of the Dall sheep make them stand out against dark rock and green grass at astonishing distances. I remember one occasion in the Yukon. With 8× binoculars I could see Dall sheep feeding and moving around against green hillside pasture clear across the Klutlan glacier and the moraine between 8 and 10 miles away. I remember another occasion. In the Pelly Mountains in 1949, Field Johnson and I were having a tough time finding sheep. I set up a 20× Argus spotting scope one day and found some white specks above timberline about 15 miles away. This was wilderness but just about gameless country. There were many old sheep trails but they had grown up in grass. Moose trails showed little use. What had happened to the game I have no idea. We didn't know where we were but we afterward found that the river across which we saw the dots was the Kitza. It took us a day and a half of travel over game trails to reach the spot where we had seen the dots. They were light-colored "Fannins," that intergrade between Stone and Dall. But all were ewes, lambs, and young rams. Some were almost pure white. One ram that grazed without concern within 100 yards while I lay on a hillside watching him was about a six-year-old with a head that would have gone 35 or 36 inches. Field and I were both hungry for meat but I held off, hoping to run into a better head. Instead I shot a grizzly. I have tasted better meat but on the other hand I have tasted worse.

I have mentioned a ram I shot on the very top of Prospector Mountain in the Dawson Range in the Yukon. This was in the fall of 1956. I had packed into that country with three other hunters—Bill Rae, editor of *Outdoor Life* at the time; "Red" Cole, who then was the sales manager of a big machine-tool company; and Fred Huntington, the president of a company that makes loading tools and dies for reloading centerfire cartridges. Of the party I was the only one that had ever shot a Dall ram. I felt somewhat responsible for the success of the others.

We saw our first sheep in the foothills of the Dawsons. While the pack string went ahead to camp, Bill Rae, one of the guides, and I cut over to some rolling country that contained some slides and cliffs where the Indian guide said he had seen sheep some years before. We located a bunch of ewes, lambs, and young rams very quickly. Then on another hill we saw a bunch of five six- and seven-year-old rams. Most had black tails and a couple had very light gray saddles. I had not expected such markings, as I had thought the sheep in the area were pure Dall. However, when I got back to camp and pulled out my old copy of Sheldon's *Wilderness of the Upper Yukon,* sure enough, his chart shows such sheep in the Dawsons.

After we had watched the sheep through a spotting scope we moved on and with binoculars found a lone ram in a basin. The spotting scope showed he had a broomed, close-curled head that was a good trophy. Bill elected to go after it.

We rode our horses as near as we could get and then went on foot. There was no cover and the ram was uphill toward the head of the basin about 400 yards away. The wind was right, so we crawled to within 200 yards. When the ram's back was turned we moved. When he was faced in our direction or even when he might see us with his keen side vision as he fed, we lay in the soft fragrant grass. Bill finally cut him down and we got the whole carcass to camp on one of the saddle horses. I wish I could have weighed the ram. He was, I believe, the heaviest Dall ram I have ever seen shot.

A few days later one of the guides and I found a bunch of about thirty sheep—ewes, lambs, young rams, old trophy rams. We got within 35 or 40 yards. I thought at least two of the heads of the rams would go 40 inches or over, and about seven were good trophies. This was an odd occasion. It was around the tenth of September and old rams are not supposed to be with the ewes at the time. I thought that if I did not disturb the bunch we could come back with Red and Fred the next day and all of us could connect.

So when tomorrow arrived we all went out. We soon found the ewes and lambs but the old rams had deserted their spouses. The guide, Sam Williams, and I located the old rams while Fred and Red were eating lunch. We got within 75 yards of the rams. They were lying on the other side of a saddle that was flat and about 35 yards wide at the top. When we went back and brought the hunters to the saddle, I told Fred and Red where the two best rams were and instructed them to crawl up the slope and along the top of the saddle until they could see the rams. Then, I said, they should take steady prone positions, signal each other with a wink or a gesture, then count three silently and shoot. Fred was to take the second ram to the left, Red the ram farthest to the right. I said I would wait until they had shot and then see if I could nail one of the other good rams on the run.

Shaking like autumn leaves, my two virgin sheep hunters started crawling over the saddle toward the rams. I waited behind with my head high enough so I could see the rams. All were lying there looking out over the basin, chewing their cuds, and reflecting on their past loves. They didn't know there was danger within miles.

But when my two sheep hunters saw the rams so close they jumped to their hind legs and opened up with a barrage that will long be celebrated by song and story in the North Country. The startled rams took off for another saddle which marked the head of a canyon about 200 yards to the right. When none of the rams went down, both hunters rushed after them.

I walked up to the top of the saddle, sat down on a rock, and began cursing in English, Spanish, Old Norse, Swahili, Hindi, and Parsi.

"Fellas get excited," Sam Williams the guide said.

"You're telling me!" I said.

Then I heard another barrage.

"See rams again," Sam said.

Then through the saddle where my pals had disappeared came three large rams. They were going full throttle. The one in the lead looked to me as if he would go 45 inches.

I switched off the safety of my Model 70 Winchester .270, swung ahead, and shot.

"Behind," Sam said.

Leading more, I shot again. I heard the bullet strike and the ram stopped. I shot again and the ram went down.

Sam and I walked over to the ram. The steel tape said 40¼ and 39¾ inches. The horns had looked larger because the ram was a small adult. My first shot had just clipped the top of the ram's back, barely breaking the skin. Since the ram was moving Sam had seen the dust behind. The next shot had broken the ram's jaw. The third when the ram had stopped had gone right behind the right shoulder. Sam said the ram was 100 yards away. Louie Johns, Fred's guide, who was watching from behind us, said the ram was 400 yards away. I think it was around 200 yards. So much for the estimates of guides. Indians do not think in terms of yards.

The tale has a happy ending. My sheep hunters got rams later, and in addition Fred knocked off a grizzly bear, a caribou, and a moose. But the rams were not as good as the ones they blew.

After Fred and Red had disappeared from sight when they had missed the first bunch of rams, they had encountered yet another bunch. These were lying down, so tame that the shooting and the sight of seven terrified rams rushing by hadn't spooked them. The ram I had shot was from the other bunch, which the boys had scared up with their zealous fusillade.

8 The Stone Sheep

Isolated as they were far from commonly traveled paths of civilized men in the great wilderness of northern British Columbia, the Stone sheep was the last of the North American sheep to be classified. It was not until 1897 that an American from Montana named Andrew Stone shot three in the Cassiar Mountains on the Stikine River and donated them to the American Museum of Natural History. What Stone, for whom the sheep were named, was doing in northern British Columbia I cannot say. A pretty good bet would be that he was prospecting, as Montana is a mining state and in the 1890s the Canadian northwest was being explored by gold-seeking prospectors, many of them Americans. The big strike in the Yukon that centered at Dawson City and the Klondike came about the time that Stone found the dark sheep named after him. Andrew Stone must have been a man of broader interests than most prospectors or he would not have bothered to bring back the specimens. Others had been combing the creeks of British Columbia and the southeastern Yukon and had undoubtedly seen, shot, and eaten Stone sheep, which were so different from the bighorn and the Dall. Like the simple men they were they just took them for granted.

The Stones were found in a vast wilderness area of mountain, muskeg, and forest. Until the building of the Alaska Highway and widespread use of light airplanes equipped with floats, getting into Stone-sheep country took a great deal of doing. They were cut off from the sea by the enormous Coast Ranges, and the only more-or-less navigable river into their range was the muddy, brawling Stikine. The sheep that Stone saw and shot on the Stikine were "typical" Stones. I, too, have hunted in the country around the Stikine, the type locality, and all the sheep I saw ran to the same typical Stone pattern. They had brown-black saddles, gray heads and necks, white bellies, black-brown legs faced with white, white rumps, and small black tails. Now and then the Stikine country produces rams with necks and faces of lighter gray. Somewhat more common are rams which have the brown-black of the body covering the necks and extending up over the jaws. Around the heads of the Muskwa and Prophet rivers farther east, sheep with light heads and necks become more common. Occasionally the area produces a ram that at a distance looks as if his head and neck are pure white. Closer examination, however, generally shows that he has black hairs scattered in the lightest areas, that his eyes are rimmed with black hairs, and that the bridge of his nose is speckled with dark hairs.

The wide Peace River is the southern boundary of the Stones, and I have been told that the sheep have been seen right on the bank. The sheep average quite dark between the Peace and the Stikine, but north of the Stikine they begin to grow lighter. In the area around Atlin Lake in extreme northwest British Columbia the sheep vary all the way from animals so light that at a distance they look like snow-white Dalls to sheep pretty much of the dark standard Stone pattern. If there is such a thing as an average sheep in this country I would say it has a dark saddle and a light-gray head and neck that often appears white from a distance.

The chain of lakes that runs roughly along the British Columbia–Yukon border—Atlin, Teslin, the Taku Arm of Lake Bennett—combined with the barriers of the Yukon River and low, wooded valleys retards the mixing of Dall with Stone. As soon as one gets north of the lakes and west of the Yukon River the sheep get immediately lighter, and there are pure-white sheep or white sheep with black tails and perhaps a scattering of black hairs on the bridge of the nose, around the eyes, and on the saddle. In 1956 I made a thirty-day hunt in the Dawson Range and in the Ruby Mountains of the Yukon. All of the sheep in the Rubys were pure-white Dalls, and so were most of those in the Dawsons. However, in the low range of hills a few miles from the main Dawson Mountains I watched a bunch of sheep through a spotting scope for an hour or more. Some were not over 300 yards from me and with the 20× scope I could see them chew their cuds and bat their eyes. Most were pure white, but a few had black tails and two had a sprinkling of gray hairs that gave a ghostly suggestion of the saddle of the typical Stone. That afternoon Bill Rae, longtime *Outdoor Life* editor and one of my companions on the trip, shot a lone ram, an ancient fellow with broomed and broken horns. I examined him closely. He had a few black hairs in his saddle, possibly a half-dozen on the bridge of his nose. However, he was pure Dall with amber eyes and golden horns. He was also the largest and probably the heaviest Dall I have ever seen. From the top of his shoulder to the bottom of his brisket in a straight line he measured 24 inches. That is as "thick" as a cow elk. He was likewise very fat. How much would he have weighed? I would guess that he would surely have gone 300 pounds on the hoof, possibly not too far from that hog-dressed.

I have hunted sheep twice in the Pelly Mountains, once around the head of the McConnell and another time in the southern part of the range about an hour's flight out of Watson Lake, Y.T. In both areas the sheep vary from fairly typical Stones to what used to be called "Fannins"—sheep with light-gray saddles and heads and necks almost pure white. On the trip in the southern Pellys in 1972 my companion Jim Rikhoff shot a handsome ram with head and neck almost as white as that of a Dall. The oddest-looking Stone I have ever taken was the one I shot near Colt Lake in northern British Columbia in 1971. He had a medium-gray saddle but his head and neck were speckled and his eyes were rimmed with dark-gray hairs that gave him the appearance of peering through goggles.

Like all species of sheep the Stones vary enormously in size. A big ram I shot on the Prophet Bench near the head of the Prophet River was a very heavy sheep, broad, chunky, fat. I am sure that hog-dressed he would not have missed weighing 250 pounds, as he was a good deal heavier than any mule deer I have ever seen. On the other hand the Stones my son Bradford and I shot in the Atlin Lake area in 1951 were the smallest mature North American rams I have ever seen. I doubt if they would have dressed out at more than 115 to 140 pounds. I believe the reason for the difference in size was the character of the soil. The big Prophet River Stones come from limestone country where the lime-impregnated feed grows big bodies and heavy horns. The little Atlin Lake sheep we took were found in a country where the mountains were shist on which the soil was just beginning to form from the decay of moss and lichens. The resulting soil was thin and sterile and simply did not grow big sheep.

It is fashionable to say that the Rocky Mountain bighorns are the largest of the North American sheep, the desert bighorns are the smallest, and that the Stones are larger than the Dalls. In general this is true—but only in general. As far as my own experience goes I believe the two heaviest rams I have ever seen taken were a Stone and a Dall, and the smallest sheep I have ever seen were the Stones which I have already mentioned and which we took around Rapid Roy Creek in hills that are an offshoot of the Cassiars in the Atlin section of northwest British Columbia. The Stones, I believe, reach their maximum size in the Rocky Mountains around the heads of the Prophet and Muskwa rivers. It is my impression that the largest Stones of this area are larger than the bighorns around the Big Smoky in Alberta and those in the Wyoming Rockies.

The horns of the Stones average longer but less massive than those of the bighorns, more massive than those of the Dalls. As is the case with all species of North American sheep the Stones produce horns in a variety of types. Generally their horns resemble those of the Dall in that they are triangular in cross-section and have a definite overhanging ridge on the exterior of the horn. Also like the Dall the Stones produce a fair number of "argali-type" horns that pinch in close to the face and then flare out. Since horns like this do not block the side vision they are never deliberately rubbed and consequently many Stones with heads of this type have perfect points. The No. 1 and the No. 2 Stones illustrated in the 1971 edition of *Records of North American Big Game* have argali-type heads. The majority of the horns worn by Stone rams are of the medium-spread type. When they are fairly close-curled and block the side vision they are generally rubbed. However, Stone heads with the extreme close-curl typical of the bighorn are very rare. Some bighorn heads will have an extreme spread considerably greater than the tip-to-tip spread. To illustrate, here are the extreme spread and tip-to-tip measurements of two Stones, a bighorn, and a desert ram in my collection.

The best Stone has an extreme spread of 23½ inches and a tip-to-tip measurement of 22 inches. These horns are quite long with the longest going 41½ inches. They curve down far below the point of the jaw and they go well above the bridge of the nose, and they do not interfere with the vision. One horn has a perfect point and the other is only slightly rubbed. The second Stone, which I thought of for a time as having a rather close curl, has a tip-to-tip spread of 18 inches and an extreme spread of 20 inches. With measurements like this he could pass for a bighorn, particularly since both horn tips are badly broomed and his horns are typically bighorn in that they are nearly round in cross-section. The only thing wrong with them is their color. They are light brown instead of deep mahogany like the horns of the bighorns.

My best bighorn has a head of the characteristic and sought-after extreme close-curl type. The extreme spread measurement is 20 inches and the tip-to-tip is 16½. The battered, heavily broomed head of an old Sonora ram I have also has an extreme spread of 20 inches but its tips are only 15½ inches apart. Bighorn heads of the close-curl type almost always have the greatest spread between the outside of the two horns at the heaviest portion, and this measurement is considerably greater than the tip-to-tip. Heads of the "argali" and wide-spread type are their widest between the tips. The great Chadwick head, of which more later, has a tip-to-tip spread of 31 inches. Another great head taken near Colt Lake in northern British Columbia has a tip-to-tip spread of 31⅜. This measurement, of course, is also the widest spread. The Stones, as we have seen, produce many heads of the argali type, as do the Dalls, and they also produce heads with fairly close curls, though by no means as close as the closest of the bighorns. For some reason I have not seen as many Stones with extremely wide spreads as I have Dalls. The current No. 1 Dall has a spread of 34⅜ inches.

The first hunting of Stone sheep by outside sportsmen took place in the Telegraph district of the Cassiar Mountains in British Columbia just off and around the Stikine River where the Stone sheep were first collected—the "type locality." Many fine heads were taken there but though long they tended to be slender. Then in 1936 L. S. Chadwick brought out from the east side of the Rockies the tremendous head which was and still is the world record. One horn is 50⅛ inches long and the other is 51⅝. The bases are $14\frac{6}{8}$ inches in circumference. Because of the great length and considerable mass this head has never been beaten and it is considered by many the greatest big-game trophy ever taken in North America.

There is an interesting story behind the Chadwick head. L. S. Chadwick was a rich man, the president of an oufit that made little kerosene stoves for emergency heating. When I was a boy in Arizona we used to warm up our bathroom with one of these stoves on cold winter days. For the hunt on which the great ram was taken, Chadwick employed what was then, as far as I am aware, the only outfit available for Stone-sheep hunting on the east side of the Rockies—Frank Golata and Curley Cochrane. Chadwick had done some sheep hunting in Alberta with Roy Hargreaves and had great respect for him as a guide. To be certain that he had a crack sheep hunter with him on his quest for Stones he took Hargreaves along.

In those days before light planes were widely used and the Alaska Highway had been built it was a long pack from the jumping-off place at Fort St. John to the head of the Prophet River. Chadwick's trip lasted sixty days. According to a ghosted story by Chadwick which appeared in *Outdoor Life,* he, Roy Hargreaves, and Golata left their camp on Lapp Creek, a tributary to the Prophet River, to shoot a ram or possibly a moose for meat. They crossed the creek on horseback and rode up through a saddle onto some rolling caribou barrens where a few sheep were feeding. They saw a mature ram at considerable distance and Chadwick took a shot at him with the rifle he used for everything—a .404 Jeffrey Magnum built by Hoffman Arms Company. I have a picture of the rifle somewhere sent me by Chadwick. He had rigged it with some sort of complicated mechanism so he could manipulate the bolt rapidly. The .404 is a cartridge more powerful than the .375 H&H Magnum. Most .404s weigh 10 pounds or so and even at that they kick like mules. I cannot imagine a much worse sheep rifle. However, I was told that Chadwick had a thing about grizzlies. He felt he needed a .404 in case he should stumble over one of the big bears and so he took his .404 everywhere.

Anyway, not realizing that the ram they had seen was outstanding, Chadwick took a pop at it with his .404. The ram took off and Chadwick said he thought he had hit it. He told Roy Hargreaves to go after it. Roy, who at that time was in his forties and so tough he could run down a ram or strangle a grizzly with his bare hands, left with his .30/06 to find the ram. Chadwick and Golata rode back to camp.

Some time later Hargreaves came into camp with the ram packed on his saddle horse. The initial wound was superficial, as Chadwick's .404 bullet had only skinned the ram across the brisket and had done little more than draw blood. If Hargreaves had not followed it up and shot it the ram would have survived to be pulled down by wolves in his old age in a year or so. The ram, Golata told me, did not have a very large body in spite of his great head.

The two guides and Chadwick measured the head and realized that it was a new world record. Ten years after this great ram was shot I camped in the same spot where Chadwick and his party had camped. The stump where the head had been placed to be photographed was still there. Roy Hargreaves had told me when I was hunting with him in 1943 about how he followed up the lightly wounded Chadwick ram. In 1946 when I was on my first Stone-sheep hunt with Golata he told me exactly the same story. I have no doubt that it is true. The only statement I doubt is the one from Chadwick's account in *Outdoor Life* that none of them had any idea that the head was out of the ordinary when Chadwick took a shot at it. Hargreaves and Golata were two of the best judges of sheep heads I have ever seen. I suspect that the tale of their not knowing the head was exceptional was a gimmick put in by the ghost writer who turned out the Chadwick piece. For a long time the Chadwick head was in a glass case at the American Museum of Natural History in New York. It is now in the National Collection of Heads and Horns at the Bronx Zoo.

The first hunters who went after Stone sheep in the Cassiars used to take a steamer to Wrangell, Alaska, then go up the turbulent Stikine by powerful little steamers and later by "gas boats" with inboard motors, a galley, and bunks for sleeping. The trip took about two and a half days of battling the swift, muddy waters of the Stikine. At night the boats tied up. The trip back down the Stikine could be made in one day. It was either go up the Stikine by boat or not go at all. The head of navigation was Telegraph Creek, where there was a Hudson Bay trading post and some Indian and halfbreed families. The local Hudson Bay factor would furnish an outfit and grub for hunting parties, secure horses, and hire Indian guides, horse wranglers, and cooks. George Ball had a "ranch" near Telegraph Creek where he kept his horses and outfitted for many years. John Creake-Dennis, a halfbreed who started out as a guide, also got together an outfit. My wife, my son Bradford, and I hunted in 1967 with a Creake-Dennis outfit, but instead of taking a gas boat up the Stikine we chartered a Grumman Goose at Wrangel, flew to a lake, and met the outfit there.

Until well after World War II the only way to get to Telegraph Creek was by boat. In 1945 when I took the Canadian Pacific steamer

Nora to Skagway, Alaska, so I could travel across the mountains on the narrow-gauge White Pass & Yukon Railroad to Whitehorse, the late Richard K. Mellon and his party left the *Nora* at Skagway to take the gas boat to Telegraph Creek. I talked guns with Dick Mellon the night before, admired his fine .30/06 and the neat fiber pack panniers in which the duffle of the party was stowed. I resolved to get a pair of those panniers and eventually I did so in New York at Abercrombie & Fitch. I also thought how nice it would be to be rich. I did not see Dick Mellon again until 1964 when I ran into him at the Boone & Crockett Club award dinner in Pittsburgh. My wife picked up a prize for a Dall sheep at that time. Today it is possible to drive an automobile to Telegraph Creek, but most hunters from "Outside" fly to some lake and meet their outfitters there.

Another way to get into Stone-sheep country was to take a steamer to Skagway, Alaska, go by the White Pass & Yukon to Carcross, take a steamer there, make a short portage, get on another lake steamer at Atlin Lake, and then go to the town of Atlin. In the early years of this century Atlin was a boom gold town second only to Dawson City in the Yukon. The late Bryan Williams, who was at one time head of the British Columbia game department, outfitted hunting parties out of Atlin for some years. He tells about it in his excellent book, *Game Trails in British Columbia.* This is out of print and expensive but if a copy can be found it is well worth adding to a big-game hunter's library.

During the depression of the 1930s and the war that followed it, hunting in the Atlin area by sportsmen from the Outside just about ceased. Since I am a romantic fellow who likes to hunt in all the classic areas, I made a trip there in 1951. It was a beautiful and interesting country. We saw a great many sheep of the light-colored Stone type, a couple of grizzlies, some moose, some tremendous caribou, a good number of goats. As far as we could find out we were the first dude outfit in the area for over twenty years. We had a Yukon outfit. None of our British Columbia guides knew all the area, and those from the Yukon knew none of it. Since the area had been heavily mined and prospected at one time, there were many roads and we were never far from a road of some sort. Most were passable to automobiles. My son Bradford shot an Osborne caribou that won the first prize for mountain caribou in the Boone & Crockett competition in the spring of 1952. The story I wrote about the trip aroused considerable interest in the Atlin area. It has been hunted a good deal since, and it has long been possible to turn off the Alaska Highway and drive to Atlin. I have often thought of going back but I have never done so. It has always struck me as a good place for an inexpensive hunt.

I believe the first dude hunters who went after Stones in the Rocky Mountains on the east side were N. Myles Brown and Tom Bright. At the time both were executives in Revere Copper & Brass at Rome, New York. To get to Dawson Creek, British Columbia, where the Alaska Highway now begins but which at that time (and also today) was the "end of steel," they had to go to Edmonton, Alberta, by train, then take a branch of the Canadian National that wandered up to Lesser Slave Lake and then turned southwest to Dawson Creek. In those days the Peace River Block had only recently been opened up to homesteading. The railroad supplied the needs of the settlers.

As I remember Myles's story, the train consisted of several freight cars, an express car, a couple of day coaches, a dining car, and another car which was a combination sleeping car and observation car. The trip was long, hot, and dusty and really penetrated the boondocks.

Myles had written around to Canadian authorities to see if he could find anyone who could outfit him for Stone sheep east of the Rockies and had found out that a trapper and trader who had a "ranch" and a trading post on the Halfway River could probably get together tents, riding and pack saddles, pack panniers, and other equipment. Since he traded with the Beaver Indians and with trappers he could undoubtedly pick up guides, a cook, and a wrangler. The trader was a squaw man, an eccentric who was the grandson of a famous figure in the American Civil War. Let's call him Finnegan, as that was not his name. His Indian wife, Susie, was a character of whom many tales were told.

Finnegan met Brown and Bright when their train pulled into Dawson Creek. He had with him a light pack outfit, an Indian horse wrangler, and the cook, an American homesteader named Johnny Cooper. Years later Johnny cooked for my own first trip into the Rockies for Stones. He was an excellent cook and a nice guy.

Even with a light outfit it was a five-day pack to the Finnegan ranch on the Halfway, where they were to pick up the rest of the outfit. When the party got to Finnegan's cabin it was occupied only by several dogs and a little girl about two years old, naked except for a wad of moss tied by strings to the strategic spot in lieu of a diaper. Presently Susie came in. Finnegan did not introduce her to his clients. Instead he said to her brusquely, "Susie, these men are hungry. Cook them some grub." A fire was burning in the stove. On it sat a blackened coffee pot, a couple of pans, and a dirty skillet. Susie said nothing. She reached out, grabbed the little girl, divested her of the wad of moss, and used it to clean out the frying pan. She then set it on the fire and started frying bacon.

Among her other endearing habits, Susie chewed tobacco. Once Finnegan took her to the rodeo that was part of the Dominion Day celebration at Fort St. John. Sitting in the grandstand to watch the bronco busting and the calf roping, Susie noticed that the other women there were not chewing tobacco and she also noticed that she had no handy place to spit. She solved the problem by disposing of her tobacco juice between her breasts.

Another Susie story, which is probably apocryphal, is that Finnegan once took Susie to Edmonton. Appalled by all the people, automobiles, streets, and buildings, Susie took a hatchet with her and blazed a trail on the walls every time she went out so she could find her way back to the hotel.

Frank Golata swore to this one. Morally Susie was pretty relaxed. Every now and then she and Finnegan would have a tiff and Susie would leave him to spend some months with her kinsmen the Beaver Indians. Sometimes when she returned she gave evidence of expecting a Little Stranger. The kindest of women, she was known to service lonely trappers and prospectors now and then. Golata related how he once dropped by the Finnegan ranch. Finnegan was gone but Susie was there with a brood of children. One little fellow was a blond. "Susie," Golata said, "You're dark and so is Finnegan. How come this little boy has light hair?" "Not Finnegan's!" Susie said. "Who is the father?" Golata asked. "Don't know," said Susie. "Long time screwum five men."

But enough of these tales of Susie. She and Finnegan have both passed into legend. I never met Susie and I am sorry I did not!

Brown and Bright were out for sixty days on that Stone sheep hunt. They spent most of their time traveling with the pack outfit. The trail they used was mostly the old Klondike trail from Edmonton. When gold was discovered on the Klondike and the word got around attempts were made to reach the diggings by various routes. One of them went north from Edmonton and crossed the Prophet and

Muskwa rivers in some of the finest Stone-sheep country in British Columbia.

I believe that Brown and Bright got no farther than the place where the Klondike trail crosses the Muskwa. Brown told me that they rode their horses up the very steep hillsides to the area of rolling grassy country between the Muskwa and the Prophet far above timberline and known as the Prophet Bench. This would not have been impossible since the footing for horses should have been good. However, it was undoubtedly very tough on the horses as the hills are steep, and both Brown and Bright were substantial men fond of their jug and their vittles. I am sure neither weighed much less than 250 pounds on the hoof. In 1946 I climbed to the Prophet Bench twice. I shudder to think how a poor horse must have labored to get up there with a heavy man, a heavy saddle, and a heavy rifle.

I'll pass on one more tale that Myles Brown told me about this hunt. He and Bright both got average rams on the bench and along the trail they shot grizzlies, moose, and caribou. In due time they got on the train at Dawson Creek and headed back to civilization. As I recall it there were two staterooms on the combination observation–sleeping car. Brown and Bright shared one. The other was occupied by an Englishman. The two Americans were talking about their hunt in the observation section the next morning after leaving Dawson Creek and the Englishman joined the conversation. Bright, who was a bit starchy, resented the intrusion, got up, and went back to his stateroom.

"Myles, you are the damnedest person I have ever seen to pick up strangers," Bright said when Brown joined him. "Who was that seedy old Limey who butted into our conversation?"

"Oh, that guy?" Myles said. "He is Viscount Lascelles, King George's cousin!"

Myles Brown, about whom you will hear more in the section on Dall sheep, was the first hunter I had ever known who had actually shot a Stone sheep. Myles and I had a great hunt for Dalls around the head of the White River in the Yukon in 1945 and I made up my mind to see the wonderful Stone-sheep country of the Rockies the following fall if it was possible. Returning from the Yukon, I flew from Whitehorse to Fort St. John and on to Vancouver. On the Whitehorse–Fort St. John portion of the flight we were going over Stone-sheep country and I practically had my head out of the window looking for sheep. In those days the Canadian Pacific Airlines plane that flew the route was a twin-motor job smaller than the American DC-3. It was not pressurized and over much of the route it flew low. Not far out of Whitehorse I saw three big bull moose with snowy-white horns newly cleaned of velvet. It was the time of the rut and all were moving through the willows of a big basin. Later I saw a collection of light-colored dots far below on a grassy ridge. I suspected they were caribou and I was seeing the white necks of bulls. I had a binocular with me. I trained it on the dots and even through the distortions of the glass window I could tell they were Stone rams. The light-colored dots were their heads and necks.

The second hunter I ever knew who had shot Stone sheep was a plump little physician from a small southern-Illinois town called Carlyle. Myles Brown had told me that Frank Golata, whom he had met on the trail on his own Stone-sheep hunt, had gone into the outfitting business. On my return from the Yukon hunt I wrote Golata and he gave Dr. DuComb as a reference. We made a date to have dinner together at the St. Louis Athletic Club. In the course of telling me about the hunt he had with Golata he got so enthusiastic that he decided to go with me the next fall.

We met in Fort St. John with our rifles, duffle, and bedrolls. We hired a taxi the next morning after obtaining our hunting licenses and drove to Buckinghorse Creek on the Alaska Highway. Prior to this time, hunting parties that had gone into the head of the Muskwa and gone from Fort St. John by the way of the old Klondike trail, but by taking off from the Alaska Highway three or four days pack could be saved. Ours was the second party to take that route. Two Los Angeles lawyers in a party in which Westley Brown was the outfitter and Don Peck a guide were ahead of us. I am glad they were, as even with them to break trail the going was grim. We packed a day and a half over rolling country of muskeg, willow, dwarf birch, and scrubby spruce before we dropped down into the sharp-walled canyon of Nevis Creek, where we saw our first Stone sheep. We hit the Besa at the mouth of Nevis Creek, camped, swam our horses across the Besa (and got the whole outfit wet in doing so) after a couple of slow days on soft ground and steep mountainsides. We camped at Keily Creek, hunted for a day, then crossed the Caribou Range (a big stretch of rolling caribou barrens far above timberline) to Richards Creek, where we overtook Westley Brown's party and camped with them.

We forded the Prophet and went into camp in a cold rain. By then it was around the first of September. It was cold and clear when we awoke the next morning. There was ice in the buckets and heavy frost on the grass. We could tell that fall had come. The aspens were shimmering gold and the hillslopes were scarlet with dwarf arctic birch, which the natives call "bug brush" or "buck brush." The mountain peaks in every direction were dusted white with early snow.

We climbed up to the Prophet Bench that day. It was not dangerous climbing but it was laborious. First we climbed through a belt of aspens with white trunks and golden leaves. Then we struggled through a belt of head-high willows laced with moose trails. Next we overcame a belt of waist-high arctic birch that showered scarlet leaves like drops of blood. Then we were in slanting pastures of thick rich grass, where we found sheep trails and droppings. Finally we struggled over the rim and were on top of the Prophet Bench. At our left was a high, black, cliffy mountain splotched and streaked with snow. This was rather romantically called the Mount of the Gods because the Beaver Indians thought their gods lived there. Far below we could see the silver thread of the Prophet River and a fleck of white that was one of our tents in the grove of golden aspens. All around were great shouldering mountains with the purple flanks of heavy timber and apple-green sheep pastures above timberline.

We climbed to a little grassy knoll, sat down to glass. Sheep were everywhere. Some were off alone. Some were in bunches of from three or four to a dozen. Some were feeding, some lying down working on their cuds and thinking things over. Most were standard Stones with gray heads and necks and dark bodies. Some had very light gray heads and necks, and Golata called these "Fannins." It has long since been proved that there is no such subspecies as the Fannin and that the specimens which W. T. Hornaday thought were a different subspecies were simply intergrades between the Stone and the Dall. Nevertheless, the myth of the different subspecies still persists. However, the Prophet River "Fannins" would have been called fairly dark Stones farther north. Instead of appearing to be snow-white, their heads and necks were definitely a light gray. Their "saddles" were black-brown.

All of the sheep were rams—but all of them were young or middle-aged. We saw no heavy, close-curl heads with broomed tips. We saw no rams with argali-type horns. I doubt if we saw a head that would go over 37 inches. That day we must have seen in the neighborhood of one hundred rams, not a single ewe. When the sun began to slant down in midafternoon we picked up our rifles and headed back to camp without firing a shot.

We moved camp to Lapp Creek. It was so called because John the Lapp, a trapper from Lapland, had built a cabin there and had trapped the area. We saw his cabin, a simple structure of logs that grew smaller as it went up until the opening at the top could serve as a chimney. It had a door but no windows.

We rode clear to the head of the Prophet from the Lapp Creek camp, saw the little glacier that is its source. We crossed Lapp Creek one day, rode over the high barrens where the world record Stone had been taken. Doc DuComb and I shot a grizzly. Later from the Lapp Creek camp I shot a tremendous moose.

We broke camp, pushed on over the Muskwa pass. When we began to descend to the Muskwa we must have been 2,500 to 3,000 feet above the river, yet it appeared almost directly below. The trail was so steep we led our horses down. The descent took us at least two hours.

We were, I believe, the first party over the Muskwa pass since 1939 and one of the first to hunt sheep in the area. We had rain, a little snow. Most of the time the mountains were clothed with heavy gray clouds. The mountains were very high, very steep, and very tough climbing, since their lower slopes were thick with willow and dwarf birch. We saw a fair number of sheep. All were rams but there was nothing outstanding.

When we got back to our old camp on the Prophet, what had been a bright and lovely country had begun to have the gray, pinched look of winter. The leaves were off the aspens, and the hillsides that had been scarlet with dwarf birch when we left were brown and drab.

But we did get a break in the weather. Before we turned in that night the Northern Lights were sweeping across the sky with great streamers of glowing mist so bright they dimmed the stars.

We left camp on foot in gray dawn the next morning to climb the Prophet Bench again and to see if the fall migration had brought the big old rams down their migration route from west of the Rockies to the lower hills where they wintered and kept their assignation with the ewe herd.

Doc DuComb was guided by Collin McGuire, an Irishman who trapped during the winter. About halfway up the mountain Doc ran out of gas and said he would have to take the climb more slowly. Frank and I said we'd go ahead and because we could cover more territory I would not shoot at any rams on the near side of a big canyon that cut the bench in half. When Frank and I made it to a spot from which we could glass we found rams everywhere, singles, small bunches, large bunches. This time all the rams were old. I don't suppose we saw a ram all that day that was less than ten years old. Before the day was over I counted ninety rams and one ewe. What that one ewe was doing with all those rams I'll never know.

Presently we found two very large rams with light-colored necks and heads about a mile away. One was feeding, the other lying down. We put the 20× spotting scope on them, but by this time the sun was high and the mirage made exact judgment of heads at that distance very difficult. We could see enough, however, to know they were exceptional.

So we started out. Ours was an embarrassment of riches. There were so many rams we were always running into bunches or singles we had not seen before. Since we didn't want to spook them and thereby spook the two big fellows, we had continually to drop down to stay out of sight. I hated to lose all that hard-won altitude but we had no choice. We dropped down about 1,000 feet on the side overlooking the pass through which the Klondike trail ran. Then we cut up to our left, traveling along the side of a canyon. In about a mile we would be in position to stalk the two big "Fannin"-type rams. They would undoubtedly have moved to some spot to bed but they probably hadn't moved far, and since they had not been hunted and we were looking for them and they were not looking for us we thought we stood a good chance of locating them.

Once when we paused to get our wind I started idly using my 9×35 binoculars when on a point well on the other side of the canyon I made out yet another bunch of rams. One looked very good. We set up the spotting scope, got him in it. We both declared him the best yet, a fine fellow with a curl I estimated to be around 45. At the time I had not shot a ram with a curl of 40 inches, although I had come close. I had sworn that I was going to get a 40-incher on this trip or break my neck in the attempt.

So Frank and I set out. We traveled for a half-mile or so up the canyon we had been in when we located the ram. Then we cut up a side canyon to the left. It had been partially filled by a rockslide. Some of the rocks were as large as basketballs, some as large as small houses. The sun was high now. I was wearing long wool underwear, wool pants, two wool shirts. I was very hot and I was also thirsty. At the bottom of the rockslide far below I could hear the tinkle of running water.

We crossed the rockslide. Below us was the canyon that had been filled by the slide farther back. In it a delicious-looking little stream ran through banks carpeted with lush grass and moss. I was tempted to climb down for a drink, but the big ram was more important. We were nearing our goal. All we had to do was to follow the side canyon around, go to the head, climb over the saddle, and the point where we had seen the rams would be in rifle range. We stopped to rest. I found a little patch of snow on the north side of a rock. I ate it.

We had left Doc far on the other side of the bench. Earlier we had heard him shoot three times. We thought he was well on the far side of the big canyon. Suddenly on our side and not over a half-mile away we heard a shot, another, another, and another. Cursing bitterly, I ran up the side of the draw to look at the point where we had seen the big ram. I made it just in time to see the bunch of rams disappearing over the horizon, the big one bringing up the rear, his wide plump rump bobbing as he ran. He looked larger than ever.

I went back to join Frank. He was sitting on the grassy hillside with his binoculars to his eyes.

"Of all the lousy damned breaks," I said. "The big ram has taken off."

"Keep your shirt on," Frank said. "That shooting may run something good our way!"

On top of the ridge on the other side of the canyon up which we had come I could see rams frightened by the shooting headed for the high, rough country around the Mount of the Gods. Some were walking, some trotting, some running. Then I heard rocks rolling and to my left about 75 yards away a handsome ram with broomed horns and a close curl popped up out of a side draw. I lifted my rifle, looked at him through the scope.

"Don't shoot!" Frank said. "We'll see something better! . . . Hey, look at this!"

On the other side of the canyon and just under the crest was a parade of old rams. Some had broomed, close-curl heads, some long horns with perfect points. Most were typical Stones with medium-gray heads and necks and brown-black bodies. Some had light-gray heads and necks—Frank Golata's "Fannins."

"What about the big Fannin in the middle?" I asked Frank.

"Very good," he said. "If I were you I'd take him."

"Will he go 40 inches?"

"If not he'll be awfully close to it!"

That was enough for me. Frank was a good judge of heads but always conservative. If he suspected the head would go 40 inches I was sure it would. The horns looked heavy and heavy horns always measure up better. They came far below the point of the jaw and well above the bridge of the nose. This was the best head I had ever got a fairly close look at.

I laid my binoculars on the grass, picked up my rifle. It was a .270 on an engraved commercial Mauser action that an officer friend in the Tank Corps had liberated at the Kreighoff factory in the German gunmaking city of Suhl when the Americans took the town. It had a 22-inch barrel by the great Phoenix, Arizona, barrelmaker Bill Sukalle and a 4× Weaver scope. Years later I gave the rifle to my son Bradford and he shot his first sheep with it. In 1969 it was stolen enroute to Africa when Bradford was going to Zambia on his first safari.

I switched off the safety, put the crosswires in the scope behind the ram's shoulder about one-third of the way up from the bottom of the chest, swung about 2 feet ahead as he walked to allow for the movement, and squeezed off. I thought I heard the bullet strike. The ram stopped. "You broke his right front leg high," Golata said. I shot again with the same hold. The ram stood there. "Same place," Golata said. I held a bit higher. The ram toppled over.

We toiled over to where the ram lay. Golata looked him over carefully.

"By golly," he said, "I am sure that head's 40." Neither of us had a tape, but when we measured it in camp later the longest horn was over 42 inches and the bases were almost 16. Some heads shrink more than others, as I have explained before. This shrank down to 41½ and 14⅞. It was No. 10 in two record books. The bases are among the largest recorded for Stone sheep.

Not only did the ram have an excellent head but he was very heavy. He measured 22 inches in a straight line from the tip of his shoulder to the bottom of the brisket. This measurement in most large buck mule deer that field-dress 190–210 pounds is 18 inches. My first shots had almost severed the right front leg where it joined the body but had just missed entering the body cavity. My third shot was higher and had gone through the heart.

When we left, I with the head and scalp, Frank with a load of meat on his packboard, it was around two-thirty. On the next ridge we could see Mack and Doc skinning out a sheep head. On the map we were 7 miles on a straight line from camp. We made it while we could still see a little. A half-hour later I had measured the head and was working on my second Scotch and creek water when we heard Mack and Doc stumbling by in the dark. They were within 50 feet of camp and it was so dark down there in that aspen grove that they had not seen it. I had shot one of the two big Fannins we had first seen that morning. Doc had got the other.

Because some of the trail on the way in had been pretty grim, we decided to return to the highway by a more traveled and easier route. Part of the way we were on the Bedeaux trail, about which there is a story. Bedeaux was a Frenchman who had become a naturalized American citizen. He had invented some sort of an efficiency system widely used by businesses. Whatever the system was, it made him rich. He was also, from what I gather, something of a social climber and a publicity hound. With a couple of French counts and a countess as his guests he set out to send an expedition powered by tractors to the head of the Prophet River. To bring supplies and to cut trail, Bedeaux had hired just about every pack and saddle horse and every bushman looking for a job in the Peace River block. Frank Golata, who was one of the packers that went along, told me that there were well over one hundred pack horses as well as saddle horses. The tent camp that housed all those people and supplies was a small city. Gasoline for the two tractors was packed by four 5-gallon tins to the pack horse. Several horses were used to carry an assortment of fine wines. Champagne was cooled for dinner in icy mountain brooks.

Bedeaux and his guests did some hunting but did not take anything more than fair trophies, Golata told me. The objects of the trip were to prove that tracked vehicles could go anyplace a horse could go, to entertain Bedeaux's guests, and to get Bedeaux and his system some publicity. The tractors got about halfway. They bogged down in the muskeg and if I remember the story they eventually sank out of sight. I imagine that Bedeaux charged the whole thing off to promotion.

As I remember it now we were on the Bedeaux trail for most of one day. We enjoyed it. Bedeaux had sent axemen ahead to cut out a trail 12 feet wide so the tractors could get through thickets of jack pine. They had also corduroyed bad stretches of muskeg with felled jack pines. In spite of all the effort and expense the only thing it proved was that the most reliable ground transportation back in the bush and in the mountains is still the good old-four-footed pack horse.

The Bedeaux story has a bizarre ending. Bedeaux was in France when the Germans overran the country. He strung right along with the Vichy regime and cooperated with the Germans. He was on Vichy territory in North Africa when the Americans liberated it. The Free French stood him up against a wall and shot him as a traitor.

We packed twelve days from the camp under the Prophet Bench where we shot the rams to the point where the Beaton River crosses the Alaska Highway. At the trading post there we left "Mack" McGuire with the outfit and caught a bus into Fort St. John. From the farthest point on the trip, the head of the Muskwa, was fourteen days' travel by pack train. On the return trip I am relatively certain that we averaged about 15 miles a day. By trail, then, we traveled over 200 miles coming back. We were out for forty-five days. When we left the highway at Buckinghorse Creek it was late summer. The dwarf birch, the willows, and the aspens were still green. The first few nights we were bothered by mosquitoes. I slept with my down bag completely unzipped. The last few nights on the trail it was so cold that I would awake in the mornings to find that my breath had condensed into a half-inch of ice during the night.

Frank Golata was a very efficient outfitter, one of the best I ever hunted with. As I remember we had only eight pack horses but we suffered no hardships. We had plenty of sheep, moose, and caribou meat, and a black bear that Doc shot was young, berry-fed, and tender.

We were on the trail so long that it almost became a way of life. When the shadows began to lengthen we would stop at a campsite, offload the packs. The kitchen tent went up first and soon Johnny Cooper had a fire going in the stove. If it was particularly cold we might fix a hot buttered rum for all hands. Otherwise Doc and I would do away with a Scotch and creek water, roll out our beds, blow up our air mattresses. Before long Johnny would have a hot meal on the table. We'd eat, talk a little while, and then turn in.

Such trips are today pretty much a thing of the past. Not only are there no sixty- and forty-five-day pack trips any more, but even a twenty-one-day trip is almost unheard of. Instead of spending those long and interesting days on the trail most hunters today want to fly into a lake in sheep country, grab a rifle, go bounding up the hillside, knock off a 40-inch ram, and get back to the Little Woman and the Old Salt Mine as soon as possible.

I love pack trips and I love getting away from people, telephones, the smell of gasoline, typewriters, cocktail parties, television, importunate letters from editors. A long pack trip enables one to get back to basics. On each trip I relearn how important such things as food, warmth, and rest are. A wash pan filled with hot water is an incredible luxury, a seat on a pack pannier with a Scotch and creek water in the hand is contentment. The best sleeping I have ever done has been in a down sleeping bag laid on an air mattress. My Iranian friends tell me that Allah does not count in the total of man's days the time he spends on hunting trips. I think the old boy is right!

The first big Stone-sheep heads came out of the Telegraph Creek area of the Cassiars. Some good ones still are taken there but on the whole the heads seem to be no less massive and consequently do not score as high as heavier heads. In the 1939 edition of the Boone & Crockett Club's *Records of North American Big Game* I see that the Cassiar heads listed have rather small bases, mostly running around 13½. The top five heads in the book are all from the east side of the Rockies. All were shot in the 1930s. Among the Cassiar heads listed, most were shot in the teens and '20s. Looking down the list of record heads, twenty-one heads were taken in the Cassiars. The locality where many of the others were shot is pretty doubtful. One, for instance, is listed as having been shot near Jasper, Alberta, by Helen Lerner. Since the locality is bighorn country and the bases are 16 inches in circumference this is undoubtedly a bighorn. In the 1939 book the trophies were ranked by the length of the longest horn and *not* by a score made up from the circumference of both horns at the quarters plus the length of both horns, as they are today.

In the 1952 record book, the first in which sheep were ranked by total score, the Chadwick head was still No. 1, but a head by T. E. Shillingburg shot on the Muskwa with Frank Golata in 1937 has dropped from No. 2 to No. 5. Of the first fifteen heads in the records, fourteen are plainly from the great limestone mountains on the east slope of the Rockies. One by Col. Wilson Potter, who was the second man to take all species of North American sheep, was probably shot in the Cassiars. The big ram I shot on the Prophet Bench is No. 10.

In the 1958 record book that perpetual champion the Chadwick ram is still No. 1, and from the place names I can tell that eighteen of the first twenty were shot on the east side of the Rockies. Eight are listed as having been shot either on the Prophet or the Muskwa. One head came from the Pellys and only one, which was shot on the Stikine, is from the Cassiars. My own head from the Prophet Bench is still No. 10.

In the 1964 book the heads from the east slope of the Rockies are still more numerous, but heads from the northern Cassiars begin to show up. I notice one head, No. 5, from Colt Lake, where I shot a ram in 1971. For a long time this area was not hunted and just about unknown. It was the territory of a picturesque old Scot pioneer named Skook (for *skookum*—"strong") Davidson. He gave half of his territory to Frank Cooke, who opened it up. This was virgin territory. Rams were plentiful and large and heads long and heavy. The first few years the country was open, almost every hunter who went in and had a little patience came out with a head going 40 inches or better. In the 1971 record book the No. 3 head is from this northern Cassiar area, and now sixteen heads of the first thirty are from the Cassiars. Most of these are from or near the territory of Skook Davidson or Frank Cooke. I think this area is the best bet for big Stone heads as I write these lines in 1973.

The great area around the heads of the Prophet and the Muskwa on the eastern slope of the Rockies has been pounded pretty hard. An enterprising outfitter scratched out a landing strip near the head of the Muskwa, and as a consequence hunters could fly in from Fort St. John in light planes in the morning and be hunting sheep in the afternoon. No more fourteen-day packs to get into the best Stone-sheep country! As I understand it, the outfitter had several camps in the general area. The hunters were flown into the strip near the head of the Prophet. Some hunted out of the camp near which I landed, which incidentally is only a few miles from the spot from where the world record Stone was shot. Others pack a day or two to other camps. It takes nine or ten years to grow a trophy ram, and twelve to fifteen to grow a head high in the records.

In this day of the float plane, most of the Stone-sheep country is very accessible, as the country is heavily glaciated and full of lakes.

The Alaska Highway did much to open up the country. The establishment of charter services where planes could be rented did even more. Packing very far into an area is almost unheard-of today. Hunters fly into Watson Lake by Canadian Pacific Airlines, buy their licenses and booze, hop into a float plane, and are in camp in an hour or two. To show how hard Stone sheep have been hunted in the past decade or so, that fine ram I shot on the Prophet Bench in 1946, that ram that was No. 10 in two record books, is now No. 75! But it is still a handsome head and I value it more highly than if I had flown in and bopped him the next day.

9
The Wild Ram: His Life and Times

The gestation period for the wild sheep is 180 days. Nature has arranged for the lambs to be born at a time when there is good weather for the lamb and food for the mother. Since the bulk of the breeding for most northern sheep falls in late November and December, the lambs are born in late May and in June. In the Sonora and Arizona desert the mating takes place for the most part in August and September so that most of the births occur in February and March when vegetation is greening up from the December and January rains. The breeding season of some of the California bighorns in British Columbia is from mid-September to late October, and the births come in late April and early May. This may be an indication of a southern origin of the subspecies. I understand that the breeding season of the extinct Audubon bighorn was also earlier than that of the northern sheep.

When the ewes are about to give birth they go to very rough country where such soft-footed predators as wolves, coyotes, and bobcats would have a difficult time getting at them. The newborn lamb weighs 7 to 9 pounds. If the lamb's mother is healthy and well fed he gains weight rapidly. Among North American sheep, twins are rare, but they occur occasionally in healthy herds. In some Asiatic species—the urial of Iran, for example—twinning is normal.

The first year of a lamb's life is the critical period. In healthy herds that are on good range, 70 to 80 percent of the lambs survive. In herds on poor range where the ewes are half starved at the time they give birth only 5 to 10 percent may survive, and with such a survival rate the herd barely holds its own if it does not decrease. In the first week or ten days of the lamb's life he becomes stronger and livelier. It is in this initial period of the lamb's existence that he may be taken by golden eagles. On a few occasions eagles have been seen after lambs, but as I have said before, if the lamb can get shelter under the ewe's body he is in no danger. In the chapter on desert sheep I mentioned being in the San Francisco mountains of Sonora one March observing sheep. There were golden eagles in the range, and I found two or three places where there was blood on the rocks. I concluded that the blood may well have marked the spots where eagles had taken lambs. Whether this was a correct conclusion or not I cannot say.

Lambs are subject to respiratory diseases and many die of pneumonia. However, like most other sheep problems this early death of lambs seems to be related to nutrition. If the lambs are born of well-fed mothers that give plenty of good, rich milk and if the lambs themselves have access to good grass early in life, they survive their infantile illnesses. I think that the varying size of adult sheep of the same species is also related to the early nutrition of the lamb. A male lamb born of a half-starved ewe that gave only enough milk to keep it alive and who then has to feed on scant and unpalatable forage will never grow up to his potential. I have seen runty rams among all subspecies of North American sheep. I have also seen extra-large rams among all subspecies. I would guess that not only did these big rams inherit genes for growth, but they were fortunate enough to have healthy well-fed mothers.

The connection between nutrition and stature has been long remarked with human beings. Immigrants from parts of Europe where people grew up on protein-poor diets tend to be short and dumpy as compared to their own better-fed American-born children. The first time I was in Rome a generation ago I noticed that perhaps a majority of native Italian girls were short, dumpy, and had poorly shaped legs. Today Rome is full of native Italian girls with long, shapely legs that would do credit to any American or North European girl. This, I am sure, is a matter of more protein in the Italian diet since the war. Today's generation of young Americans is taller and has longer legs than those of us who were born in the early years of this century and were in college in the 1920s. Before I shrank down under the weight of my years I was a half-inch over 6 feet in my bare feet. I was taller than almost all of my acquaintances. Today, 6-footers are a dime a dozen.

Lambs soon gain strength and follow their mothers almost anywhere. I read somewhere of a very young Dall lamb who attached himself to some human beings and would go with them uphill and down and even across rapid streams. When the lambs are able to follow their mothers nicely, the ewes get together in large bands with the lambs of the past two seasons. I have seen such bands containing over one hundred animals in the Yukon with Dalls and in Alberta with the bighorns. The desert sheep are less plentiful and possibly less gregarious. I have never seen a ewe-lamb band of desert sheep with more than about thirty animals, and usually there are no more than fifteen or twenty.

The mature rams leave the ewes before they lamb. In many cases the rams depart right after the rut and go to a separate winter range. Generally the young rams stay with the ewes until they are three years old. Then they attach themselves to older rams and begin life as adults.

Among all species of sheep I have noticed a tendency for rams to associate with other rams of the same age and about the same horn size. The last ram I shot was a nine-year-old Stone. He was with about fifteen other rams and they were all just about as much alike as peas in a pod. A companion, Gene Cook, and Rawhide, a famous northern British Columbia Indian guide and protégé of the fabled "Skook" Davidson, and I had seen a couple of rams walk over a ridge. We left our horses and followed. On the far side of the ridge near some cliffs we saw three rams, all about eight or nine years old and all about alike, bedded about 200 yards away and below us in some arctic willow.

Rawhide decided to go down and to the left around a bluff to see if he could see any more sheep. I was sitting there with my old .270 Model 70 Winchester beside me looking over the larger of the three bedded rams when about a dozen rams came tearing around the point below and started single-file up a sheep trail through the arctic willow to the left of the three bedded rams. Traditionally, the ram with the largest horns is supposed to take the lead, but after a quick look with my 8× Zeiss binocular I made a fast decision that the second ram in line had a little better head than the leader. I may or may not have been right. At any rate I swung ahead of the second ram and when I shot I heard the bullet hit and the ram turned away from the others into the willows at his right. A second quick shot was a miss over his back as he headed downhill. He stopped and the third shot was through his lungs behind the foreleg. I was using rather heavy-jacketed 130-grain .270 bullets, and the first had struck to the right of the spine and had come out his chest with little expansion. From his actions I thought I had probably gut-shot him, but the bullet had landed just about right. A softer bullet that expanded quicker would have killed him in his tracks.

The ram's longest horn measured 37 inches. I have taken better heads, but a man seventy-one years old and whose legs aren't what they used to be cannot be too choosy. The ram was a big one, fat and heavy. He certainly would have field-dressed close to 200 pounds. Since those hills grow higher and steeper every year I would not be surprised if that 1973 Stone ram was my last—the end of a career of twenty-seven years of the off-and-on hunting of Stone sheep.

In the chapter on the Stone sheep I told how in 1946 Frank Golata and I climbed the Prophet Bench twice. The first time, around the last of August or the first of September, we saw at least eighty rams. All were young and middle-aged rams. There was not a ram there over seven or eight years old at the oldest, and I doubt if the largest head would have gone 38 inches. About two weeks later when the northern fall was well advanced and there was a hard freeze every night we again climbed the bench. Again we found the area full of rams. This time they were all old-timers. I doubt if there was a ram on the bench that day under ten years old. They were old rams with heavy, broomed heads and others with longer horns with perfect points. It was an embarrassment of riches!

On a hunt with Bruce Creake-Dennis in 1967 in the Telegraph Creek area we saw an enormous bunch of Stone rams. All the rams were about the same age and had horns that went from 36 to 38 inches. On the hunt we saw no ewes or lambs but we did see perhaps seventy rams. Not a one appeared to be older than nine. Bruce Creake-Dennis told me that in that particular area it was rare to see a ram larger than the ones we saw. When rams got to be about ten years old, he said, they joined other old rams on what he called Ice Mountain.

On the other hand, the sheep hunter will often see rams of different ages together. The best Dall I have ever taken, a thirteen-year-old ram whose beautiful head is illustrated in this book, was with three other rams, one about five years old and the others about seven or eight. A Stone ram with a very acceptable 38-inch head and about nine or ten years old which I shot in 1971 was with two younger and smaller rams. My best bighorn, another thirteen-year-old, was with a ram about seven years old.

My feeling is that finding small, mixed bunches of rams, old and young together, is an indication that there are not many sheep in the immediate area and that large bunches of rams of more or less the same age indicate that there are a good many sheep in the area. This has worked out for me in many areas, but some observers with more experience than I have had do not agree.

Let's face it. The wild ram is not a very nice guy. He is at once a toady and a bully. He is quarrelsome. He is a rapist and he has strong homosexual tendencies. The head of the pecking order is the ram with the largest and the heaviest horns. Like a gold-plated .300 Weatherby the horns are at once the ram's weapon and his status symbol. Lesser rams defer to the ram with the big horns the way the owners of Volkswagens defer to the drivers of Cadillacs and Rolls Royces. According to Valerius Geist, a new ram joining a bunch is classified by the others by the size of his horns just as the English size each other up by their accents. He may battle with the dominant ram of the bunch in order to establish himself, but the lesser rams defer to him, kowtow to him. He can kick them with his front foot and they will take it. He can even mount them and they stand for it.

Geist says that rams have frequent minor squabbles to determine each other's combat potential and place in the pecking order. These battles occur at all times of year. Geist does not mention this but I have seen rams stand for long minutes with their horns together. These minor combats are between rams of similar horn size.

Dominant rams butt lesser rams to keep them in their places, but being the dominant ram in a bunch is no bed of roses. Lesser rams are always trying to knock him off. Rams are not chivalrous. They butt rivals when they are battling other rams and they bully larger rams who are ill or injured.

Young rams resemble ewes in body conformation and, according to Geist, imitate the conduct of ewes in being passive and allowing the mature rams to mount them. Geist says that a direct stare by one sheep at another is considered an act of aggression and that when sheep bed down they lie in positions where they are not looking into each other's eyes. Rams seeking to impress each other by the size of their horns do so with what Geist calls the "low stretch." Rams thrust their heads forward at an angle toward the animal to be impressed and sometimes advance in a bent-legged crouch.

An alarmed sheep gets to his feet, stares at whatever has caught his attention. He stands as rigid as a statue. The sight of the rigid sheep alarms others. Sometimes alarmed sheep stamp their feet. I once had a young desert ram follow me down the comb of a mountain. He stayed 100 to 150 yards behind me and every time I turned to look at him he stamped his front feet. When I got to camp and sat down on a stool to enjoy a cold bottle of that great Hermosillo beer called High Life the ram was still on the point watching me.

Rams communicate by their actions. Under some circumstances they may blat, but I have never heard one. On the other hand, a flock of ewes and lambs is fairly noisy.

Ewes and lambs commonly band together in large bunches. Oddly enough I have never seen a very large bunch of Stone ewes and lambs—probably because I have for the most part spent my time in ram country. Generally, but by no means always, the ewes and lambs are found lower than the rams and after the lambs are old enough to climb well and get around rapidly they are generally in less rugged country. On two hunts in Frank Cooke's Stone-sheep country around Colt Lake I have seen at least 200 rams but only one bunch of ewes and lambs. I was told that their summer range is a good deal lower. Where I have hunted bighorns in Wyoming and in the Canadian Rockies the ewes and lambs were as high as the rams but in different areas. Sometimes a basin will be full of ewes and lambs and another basin 2 or 3 miles away will contain a big herd of rams. In Alberta once I saw a bunch of about eighty ewes and lambs high on a hill. Two thousand feet below and on a point overlooking a creek were two rams, and about 4 miles away in a basin were about a dozen rams. I have seen many large bunches of Dall ewes and lambs in the Yukon but I have never seen a really large bunch of Dall rams. This, I believe, is a matter of chance. At the head of the St. Clair River once I must have seen a hundred rams of various ages but they were on both sides of the river and in small bands, usually pretty well segregated by horn size and age.

A bunch of rams is not a permanent unit. Large bunches, I believe, are composed of smaller groups that have united in an area of good feed or water. In the chapter on the desert bighorn I mentioned seeing about thirty rams low in a wide arroyo one time. The desert was dry and the rams were breaking open barrel cactus *(bisnaga)* for water. In other times of drought, desert sheep will collect in the neighborhood of open water.

Sometimes two or three rams will go off together. Sometimes two rams together will be an old one and a younger subordinate ram—a knight and a squire. Often they are two old-timers, possibly rams who have been together most of their lives. In the Yukon in 1950, Moose Johnson and I spent an hour or so at a spotting scope watching two magnificent rams. Both were old and thin. Each had a tremendous head. One of the rams had horns with the widest spread I have ever seen. They went out almost like those of a Texas longhorn steer. The other ram had an argali-type head with very long horns. I could not go after the rams since I had previously taken an excellent trophy. Moose and I told Herb Klein and his guide Paddy Jim about the two rams. The next day they made the stalk and took the ram with the argali-type head. The ram was so old that most of his teeth were gone. He was very thin and had not an ounce of fat on him.

In 1963 my wife in an interesting stalk got a thirteen-year-old ram that was with two other rams equally old. The two survivors headed for the high country as if they had been turpentined. Often when one or two young (four-to-seven-year-old) rams are with an older one, the young rams will stand around if the old one is shot and drops in his tracks. They do not seem to know what to do. Most of the rams I have shot have dropped stone-dead, and sometimes the sheep with them have not seemed unduly alarmed. I have been told, though, that if a ram is wounded and flops around, the other rams are terrified.

Now and then lone rams are encountered. Sometimes they are young rams looking for a bunch to hook up with. Once in British Columbia when my wife and I were riding along a high plateau we saw a ram about three years old standing on the skyline watching us. Instead of running away he trotted in our direction. Apparently he thought we were sheep until he got a better look at us or smelled us. Sometimes lonesome rams will join a herd of cattle or a herd of domestic sheep.

In the mating season rams wander widely, often alone. In the Sonora Desert during the late-summer rut, rams will go from mountain to mountain looking for estrous ewes. In the past these wandering rams have often been roped by cowpunchers in Sonora and in Arizona. One of the largest rams ever killed in Sonora was taken by a Mexican farmer near Sonoyta. He saw it bedded down under a peach tree in his little irrigated orchard. He had no gun of any sort, so he walked over to a neighbor's house, borrowed an old .30/30, sneaked up on the ram, and shot it. He and the neighbor shared the meat. My old outfitter friend Charlie Ren bought the head from the *paisano* and told me the story.

Sometimes these old rams simply seem to travel because they are restless. I have seen old rams in Sonora alone in desert flats and on little insignificant hills that are by no means sheep country. I would guess that they had been traveling from one range to another and had stopped to feed and rest. In Arizona, traveling rams are commonly hit by automobiles.

For whatever the reason I have seen a higher proportion of old lone rams in Sonora than anywhere else. I mentioned in the chapter on desert sheep a very old, very large, and very fat ram that had been living all alone in a basin in the Pinacates. In fact, a fairly high proportion of all the old Sonora rams I have seen have been alone. Whether this means that the desert sheep is less gregarious or simply that the desert sheep is a relatively scarce animal and does not have many of his fellows to consort with I do not know.

The heaviest Dall ram with the largest body that I have ever seen was a lone ram shot by Bill Rae in 1956. He was feeding in a big empty basin about 2 miles from the nearest sheep. From the sign it looked as if he had been in the basin for a month or more. He had heavy close-curl horns broomed well back at the tips like those of a bighorn.

Why are these old rams all alone? My theory is that as they get old they get stiff. Younger and livelier rams with horns just as big come along and push them around. Like old men, they don't enjoy this and simply want to be left in peace.

The times of peril to the wild sheep are his youth and his old age. If he survives his first year he has a pretty good chance of living to be from eight to ten years old. If he is on good range and gets the breaks in the weather he may live to be thirteen or fourteen, occasionally older. Jack Atcheson, the Butte, Montana, taxidermist and safari booker, who is also a sheep hunter, tells me that of the sheep heads he mounts he sees a higher proportion of desert rams that are old than anything else. Most of the heads of northern sheep he mounts are from rams around eight or nine years old. Probably this is because the older northern rams at the conclusion of the rut are thin, run down, and exhausted when they go into the severe northern winters.

Once he becomes a young adult the wild ram is pretty well able to take care of himself. On level ground he is not a very fast runner, so he tries to stay fairly close to cliffs and slides. There he can get away from any of the animals that prey on him—wolf, coyote, bobcat, cougar, grizzly bear. He has feet wonderfully adapted to mountaineering. The center pad is soft to stick on smooth surfaces. The outer edge of the hoof clings to rough projections and cracks. He is not the mountaineer the white goat is, but he can cover country much faster than the goat. Actually I have never seen a goat travel faster than a fast walk. The slower, more deliberate goat can go places where a sheep would break his neck. The sheep is a great jumper and bounder in rough country, whereas the goat is a deliberate climber.

Once in Sonora I saw a good ram all alone on a long point that projected out from another mountain. For about 500 yards the cliffs on either side of the point appeared to be sheer except for some inconsequential ledges that did not look wide enough to hold a sheep. A Mexican lad and I managed to get around and climb the hill behind the point without awakening the ram's suspicions. As we walked quietly out toward the end of the point we thought we had the ram cornered. We had gone about 200 yards when the ram's head popped up over a rock. He took one look at us and disappeared. I was so sure he was mine that I felt almost sorry for him.

But we never saw that particular ram again. He had apparently hit about four of those inconsequential ledges, pausing only to break his descent. The talus below the cliffs was composed of small stones, and the marks of his hooves showed he had been traveling fast when he hit it. His escape was a smart, bold, and daring thing and I greatly admired him for it. José, my Mexican friend, and I took up his track to see what he had done. For about 300 yards his tracks showed that he had traveled at a run. Then he had stopped, looked back, and discovered that he was not being followed. Then he alternately walked and trotted toward another rough mountain in the same range. A frightened deer will run around to the other side of a hill, find a thick patch of brush, and lie down. The frightened ram will leave the mountain.

The most accomplished mountaineer I have ever seen is the ibex. He is a cliff dweller by nature, whereas the wild ram is not. In Iran when sheep and ibex are found in the same mountain the ibex stick to the cliffs and crags and the sheep are found in rolling country. They use rough and cliffy country only for refuge. I have a 16-mm. motion-picture film of a bunch of Iranian ibex going down a cliff that looks to be straight up and down, but which, of course, is not. A sheep might hit a little ledge, bounce to another, and make it down, but those darned ibex are taking it slowly. Nevertheless, a sheep can go up a rough and rocky hillside in fifteen minutes that would take a strong and agile man a couple of hours to climb.

Valerius Geist calls the commonly held notion that the eyes of sheep are equal to those of a man with 8× binoculars a myth. I have been writing about sheep and sheep hunting a long time, and maybe I am the guy that started this "myth." I originally based that statement on an experience I had in Sonora. I could see that a ram below me was looking at something with considerable interest on the desert a long way off. I could not see what it was with my naked eye. With me I had an excellent pair of 8×30 Bausch & Lomb binoculars. With them I saw that the ram was watching a traveling coyote.

Sheep are very good at picking up moving objects at great distances, even though the objects are fairly well camouflaged by backgrounds of similar color. They are not much good at figuring out what stationary objects are. Once in Sonora I saw a young, lone ram feeding. I thought I would sneak around to see if I could get a picture of him. I went over a ridge, came up behind him, and climbed up on a boulder that was about 10 feet higher than the ram's head. The ram was busily browsing. A breeze was blowing and I was able to take a couple of pictures of him without his being able to hear the click of the shutter. Presently I sat on the rock with my feet hanging over. He still did not see me. In a couple of minutes he reached for some browse, saw me sitting there, and froze. He knew I looked strange but had no idea what I was. Finally I waved a hand at him and said, "Hi, ram!" He was away around the hill bounding from rock to rock like a rubber ball.

On another occasion, this time in the Yukon, Moose Johnson and I spotted three sheep about a mile to a mile and a half away near the head of a big basin. We set up a spotting scope. The three rams were very ordinary, and we were about to look for another bunch when I made out part of a horn of a ram bedded behind a little rise. The longer I looked at it the more massive the portion of the horn I could see appeared. My hunch was that this largely hidden ram was worth investigating.

The conditions were ideal for a stalk. We dropped down into a ravine, got on our horses, rode until we had to lead them up a very steep, rocky slope. Then, keeping a ridge between us and the rams, we rode above timberline for perhaps a mile. Then we tied the horses to each other, head to tail, and headed for a sharp rock by which we had marked the location of the rams. Moose and I crawled along the ridge to look in the basin. Nothing did we see. We crawled closer and closer. Still nothing. This was strange as we were certain the rams had not been frightened. We crawled still closer, right to the top of a little cliff about 30 feet high. Then we saw why we hadn't seen the rams previously. They had moved 100 yards or so from where we had seen them and were almost directly under us.

The rams were all lying at different angles. The big one had a tremendously long and massive head of the argali type. He lay gazing down into the basin with his rump toward me. Two other rams were lying at angles of about 30 degrees as compared to the big one and they were also gazing down into the basin. Almost directly below me and broadside, the smallest ram of the lot was lying. I knew that there was no way in the world that the big one could get away, as I am a reasonably good shot and there was nothing but open basin in any direction. I could have shot him at once, but if I did I would either have had to shoot him in the neck or in the fanny. One way I would spoil the scalp and the other way a good deal of the meat. I decided to wait to see what happened.

I had been sitting there two or three minutes with my .30/06 across my knees when the small ram near me became aware through his side vision that there was a bump on the skyline he could not remember. He turned his head and looked me straight in the eye. I remained frozen and so did he. I met stare with stare. I knew something was going to happen eventually and I might as well be ready. I had chambered a cartridge and had put on the safety when I started to climb over the crest. I moved my right thumb to switch off the safety.

That did it. Surprised like that, rams often mill about. Sometimes they will run a few yards and stop to look. Not these rams! The small one that had been lying broadside took off the way he was facing the instant my thumb moved. The others did not even look around to see what had frightened the little one. Instantly they were off down into the basin. I had no choice but to put a 150-grain .30/06 bullet into the big boy's fanny. That is the best North American sheep I have ever taken—and one of the easiest stalks. For a time that ram was No. 12 in the record book.

As these two anecdotes illustrate, sheep don't often look up and stationary objects mean little to them. Once in British Columbia I was sitting with my back to a rock glassing when a half-dozen rams frightened by another hunter came tearing up a sheep trail and almost ran over me. I was in plain sight but they did not notice me because I did not move. Geist says that when he was followed by park bighorns which he had taught to take salt from his hand they could not find him if he climbed into a tree even when his feet were not far above the level of their heads.

I have always read that among warmblooded creatures only the birds and the primates can distinguish color. Geist seems to think that goats and sheep can distinguish color. I am sure they are quick at picking up contrast, and all old sheep hunters try to wear clothing of about the same value as the country—gray or brown. White and red are considered poison. My own feeling is that the eyes of sheep, though good, are inferior to those of pronghorn antelope. I know that when I stick my head over a crest, pronghorns spot it quicker than sheep generally do. Nevertheless, it doesn't pay to monkey with the eyesight of sheep. When I first poke my head over a crest I try to make my initial examination from behind a shrub, a bit of grass, through the branches of a tree—anything to break up my outline. I also take off my hat and put a stone on it. The head without the hat is smaller and the wide-brimmed hats I generally wear in sheep hunting look less natural than a head and if the brim is soft may flap a bit in the wind.

Geist says that sheep can distinguish a circle from a square but not from a heptagon. How he knows that he did not say. He also says their eyes are probably astigmatic and see vertical lines better than horizontal ones. He writes that he could spot sheep with an unaided eye before they could spot him. He says he could readily spot them at 2,000 yards away on slopes and up to 4 miles if they were moving on snow. This is with the naked eye.

I am wondering if part of this did not come from the fact that he was looking for the sheep and they were not looking for him, an advantage the hunter always enjoys over the hunted. Sheep on a hill feel safe and generally don't stare at intruders below, particularly if the intruders are more or less familiar and they think they mean them no harm. Particularly in areas where sheep are hunted a good deal I have found sheep with glasses at a mile or more and have seen that they were looking at me—or at least in my direction. This was particularly true in Sonora, where back in the 1930s the sheep were pecked at twelve months out of the year. In wilderness areas where sheep have not been hunted I have had them look at me and then go on feeding. The last large bunch of desert sheep I ever saw was on the side of the largest hill in the Los Mochos range in Sonora. They were ewes, lambs, and young rams. A Mexican *vaquero* named Santiago saw them before I did. I got off my horse, sat down, and began glassing. A couple of ewes looked at me and then went on feeding. A young ram popped up on a rock and stood staring at us. The rest of the hungry sheep paid no attention to us.

Ernie Miller, a guide, outfitter, and dude rancher who has now passed to his reward, did a good deal of sheep hunting in Montana and Wyoming and some for Dall sheep in the Wood River country of Alaska. He always swore that sheep had noses no better than human beings and grew furious if anyone differed with him. As I got it he based that statement on the fact that in Wyoming a ram had once walked up to him upwind and had licked his hand. I think that only proves that sheep sometimes do some goofy and unpredictable things—just as human beings do.

I have had other hunters tell me that sheep do not smell well. I think the reason for this is that sheep live in the mountains, a region of erratic air currents. Sometimes sheep appear to be directly downwind and yet not smell the hunter when in reality an air current is carrying the scent above or to one side of the sheep. I have deliberately given sheep my wind, and they always react. Sheep do not have noses as keen as those of deer, moose, and bears, but they certainly have noses better than human beings, and no smart sheep hunter takes a chance on a sheep's winding him. Another animal that often doesn't pay much attention to what he sees and often appears not to have a very keen sense of smell is the Rocky Mountain goat. I think he both sees and smells well, but he is up there in the rocks and feels safe. He simply does not give a damn. Geist has determined that sheep have a keen enough sense of smell to scent a man at about 350 yards under favorable conditions. That is approximately my own experience.

I would guess that sheep hear quite well but they do not pay much attention to what they hear. They spend much of their lives in places where the rocks are unstable and looking for an excuse to roll. They are so used to the sound of rolling stones that they pay little attention to them. However, they can hear alien noises—the sound of a bolt chambering a cartridge, the sound of a canteen striking rock. When they do they are usually spooked.

Young rams become sexually mature at one and one-half to two and one-half years, as do ewes. At that age sheep of both sexes look about alike. However, ewes keep their appearance and continue to look like young rams the rest of their lives. Rams continue to grow and fill out until they are at least eight or nine years old. From such experience as I have had in the field I think that if given good feed a ram continues to get heavier as long as his teeth hold out. I have seen rams thirteen years old that had good teeth. I have seen others only eight or nine whose teeth were about gone. Such rams usually suffer from what is popularly known as "lumpjaw." This looks like pyorrhea in human beings. The gums recede, the teeth loosen and elongate. Eventually they fall out. Grass gets below the gums. Eating is inefficient and undoubtedly painful. The ram gets thin. Eventually he gets killed by a wolf or simply dies on some cold winter night.

Geist divides rams into four classes. His Class I consists of young mature rams two and one-half years old. The Class II rams are those from three and one-half to six years old, Class III those that are six to eight years old. His Class IV are the old rams that furnish the trophies—those eight years old and older. These are the ones that dominate the groups and that, according to Geist, do most of the breeding. The horns of these old rams are heavy and if close-curled are almost always broomed. Their coats are generally darker. In extreme old age (twelve and up) they often get swaybacked and have hollow rumps. This is particularly noticeable in the desert sheep because of their shorter hair, but it is noticeable with all sheep in the thinner summer coats.

Geist says that the older the ram is the more likely he is to be found alone. Both his Class III and Class IV rams are apt to be found as singles, the Class IV more than the Class III. The Class III rams are the so-called three-quarters curls. These are the ones who do the most fighting among themselves, as they are in the process of establishing their places in the social order. These are the ones that if shot never become old trophy rams. Outside of the mature ewes the Class IV rams from eight to thirteen years old are, unless they have been hard hunted, the most plentiful sheep.

The old trophy rams are usually found with other rams, more often than not of more or less the same age. The younger the ram the greater the chance that he will associate with the ewes.

But there are always exceptions. In my chapter on Dall sheep I tell how I found a fine old ram in the same basin with a bunch of ewes and lambs. He was alone but the ewes were close by. In the Yukon in late August 1956, my guide and I went out one day, climbed a little slope to get a good vantage point for glassing, and the moment we looked into an interior valley we saw a big bunch of sheep below us crossing from one mountain to another right out in the arctic willow and muskeg. There were at least thirty in the bunch and they ranged all the way from lambs of the season to old thirteen-year-old rams. As far as I can remember this is the only such instance I have encountered. Seven or eight were old mature rams from ten to thirteen years old and with horns that ran from 38 to maybe 42 inches. My guide, Sam Williams, and I sat still and watched the sheep. They went by us within 50 yards and climbed the shoulder of another mountain. I did not take one of the rams because I felt this was a good chance for the two hunters I was with to get rams. I did not want to spook them. The next morning we found the ewes, lambs, and young rams, but the old rams had gone off together. Sam and I found the rams lying down later.

Rams come through the late fall–early winter rutting season in poor shape. They have been fighting and chasing ewes for at least six weeks. Geist thinks the better rams fare the worst of all as they have kept the lesser rams away and have done the bulk of the breeding. He says the rams that mature fastest, grow fastest in horn and body, tend to die young because of their exertions.

At the end of the rut the sheep go to their winter range. In some places it is low where the snow does not lie deep. In other places the sheep winter on high ridges where the wind blows off light dry snow. Sometimes winter and summer ranges are near each other and the sheep simply go up and down. In others the winter range may be many miles away. Geist says the sheep have several definite ranges which they occupy at different times of the year.

In the north the winter is a hard time. The ewes are pregnant and are eating for two. The weaker lambs don't make it. The old rams go into the winter thin and tired. Sometimes they have sprained or broken legs, infected wounds. A ram with a broken leg can't paw through down to his feed. Many thin or injured rams die.

When the spring comes the sheep begin to put on weight. The old rams like to go high, find basins where there is good feed, water, soft shale for beds. A bunch of rams may stay in two or three basins through the summer. They do not move much until sharp frosts come and they start thinking of the ewes. They are generally still in the summer range when the August and September hunting season rolls around. If their teeth are good the old rams are very fat at this time. Since their flesh is "new meat" that has been put on since the starving time of winter, it is very tender and good. Generally the rams do not travel much during the summer. I have covered a good deal of territory without seeing a ram track, then have looked into a basin to find from ten to fifteen rams in it.

Just before the actual rut begins the rams start to wander. They move down toward the breeding ground, where they will hook up with the ewes. I have never hunted North American sheep just before the rut, but the habits of all wild sheep are similar. I have hunted Iranian urial at this time and it was a frustrating experience. The late Jack McPhee, who was a market hunter in Alaska during the 1920s and 1930s, told me that the Dall sheep of Alaska before the rut act just like the urials. As I have mentioned, in 1970 my wife and I hunted urials in the Mohammed Reza Shah National Park in northwest Iran as the guests of Prince Abdorreza Pahlavi. Stalking sheep was extremely difficult because the sheep were always on the move. Sheep of all kinds were very plentiful and I suppose we must have seen 2,000 sheep or more each day. The old rams were in bunches of from ten to thirty. They never lay down. Sometimes they could stand in one place for a half-hour or so. Then they would move off.

We would see a bunch of good rams and start our stalk, only to discover that another bunch had got between us and the ones we wanted or that the rams we had wanted had moved and were a mile away. The rams did little feeding. I told my wife that they reminded me of a bunch of adolescent high school girls—they knew they wanted something but they were not sure just what it was. At the end of the second day, when a half-dozen stalks had gone wrong, my wife said that if she got a urial ram it would be one we just ran into. So it happened!

In 1959 I hunted urial in the same area in December during the rut.

I have never seen the sheep of northern North America during the rut but from what I have read and have been told they act about like their distant cousins the white-necked urial. The sheep were gathered in bands of from fifty to onc hundred or more, all over those juniper-clad hills. Big rams were fighting. Some rams moved from bunch to bunch looking for receptive ewes. Several times I saw one big ram chase another away from an estrous ewe and while he did it a young ram came in and covered her. Rams chased ewes that were not ready. Rams went from ewe to ewe, smelling their sexual organs. Rams sniffing ewes curled their lips, exactly as I have seen stallions do when they were around mares in heat.

Hunting sheep during the rut is difficult. This is not because the rams are particularly wary. Actually they are so sex-crazed that I believe that if there was nothing but rams around they could be killed with clubs. It is the ewes that are the problem. Those who are not in season are always wandering around to feed at the edge of the bunches where the large rams are. Then when the hunter approaches they run and alarm the bunch.

On my last hunting day my guides and I saw a bunch of around one hundred sheep that had a group of from seven to nine big rams in it. They were on a hillside about three-fourths of a mile away and on the far side of a deep canyon. On one side of the big bunch was a draw thick with junipers. My guides wanted to cross the canyon, go up the draw, and then shoot. I was afraid that if we went up the draw we would bump into a ewe and she would spook the bunch. Instead I wanted to go clear around, cross the deep canyon near the head, and come on the rams from above. Against my better judgment we went as the guides suggested.

Just as I predicted we bumped into a feeding ewe just as we got to the top of the draw. She left at a dead run for the big bunch. I ran after her as fast as I could travel. I made it just in time to see the whole herd take off, the big rams all bunched together and running to the right. I had about four seconds to pick the largest and try to hit him before the lot of them disappeared over a rise. I swung ahead with a .270 I had borrowed from Prince Abdorreza and shot. The rams disappeared. I had seen no sign of a hit. At the moment I was probably the world's gloomiest sheep hunter, but in a few minutes one of the shikaris (guides) came running up to tell me I had hit the ram and he was down. The 130-grain .270 Silvertip had landed a bit too far back.

The ram had run about 100 yards and had fallen over a little cliff. He was a handsome creature with reddish body, snow-white neck, and 38½-inch horns.

The concupiscence of the ram, wild or domestic, is legendary. The testes of the wild ram are extraordinarily large, many times larger than those of the much bigger grizzly bear, for example. Anyone watching wild rams fight, frisk, and fornicate cannot help being awestruck. The domestic ram may well be the wild one's equal. I once knew a sheep rancher who had 150 domestic ewes in a tightly fenced pasture. They were estrous but he did not want to breed them that early. He had planned to wait until they came in season once more. But a ram somehow forced his way into the pasture. He was discovered the next morning and booted out, but the rancher had about 80 early lambs that year. Or so he says. It is a good story. At any rate that is not a bad night's work.

Many people hold that the eating of the "mountain oysters" of the old ram is a great restorative for lagging male sexual ardor and fertility. Ernie Miller, who was my outfitter on a sheep hunt in Wyoming, told this one: A forest ranger who had been married for ten years but who had been unable to produce an heir came into one of his camps high in the Wyoming Rockies, where he was going to spend the night. That day one of Miller's hunters had shot a ram and the guide had brought back not only the head but the meat and the mountain oysters. Half-jokingly, Miller suggested that the forest ranger eat the mountain oysters and told him they might be the answer to his fertility problem. The forest ranger did so, went back home, and immediately got his wife with twins.

Knowing that my friend Myles Brown was a very persnickety guy when it came to food, I once brought back the testes of a Dall ram, peeled them, sliced them, dusted them with flour, and fried them in bacon grease. I offered a share to Myles. Not only did he refuse to eat them but for the entire trip he wouldn't eat anything cooked in the frying pan I had used. I have eaten my share of mountain oysters. I am inclined to believe that their restorative powers are a myth.

Charles Sheldon spent the winter of 1907–08 in Alaska around Mt. McKinley observing sheep. In his book *The Wilderness of the Denali,* writing of the week of November 30–December 7, he tells how four friendly rams were sharing the favors of the ewes in five herds numbering from five to sixteen sheep. He wrote:

> Each ram served only one or two ewes in a band and then went on to the next. After leaving one band, a ram would walk and trot toward another. Sometimes . . . the head was held in a natural position. At other times it was extended forward, the neck stretched straight out, the horns apparently resting on it. [This is what Geist calls the "low stretch."] One ewe was served twice at different times by different rams. None of the rams fed at all during the hour they were observed . . .
>
> But the undisturbed friendly possession of the ewes by these rams was soon disputed, for from afar came a single ram with large horns, much larger than those of the rams present, head drawn back, neck swelled, walking with springy steps in a majestic strut. None of the active rams noticed him. Straight toward them he came, nearer and nearer, without quickening his pace or changing his attitude. . . . One of the rams having just served a ewe appeared to take no notice whatever of the approaching rival, which was then within twenty feet, and had not yet changed either gait nor attitude. . . . As if he had been watching the approaching ram all the time and had been planning to meet him, he suddenly backed off and slightly lowered his head. At the same time the other also slightly lowered his head. They rushed at each other at top speed, lowering their heads still more as their horns met squarely, butting together with a sharp knock. The smaller ram was knocked backward and a little sidewise, but recovered at once. Both backed about fifteen feet and again rushed together. This time the smaller ram was pushed well back, vanquished. He quickly turned and trotted down the slope, the larger ram trotting after him to the edge.

Sheldon goes on to tell how this knight errant, this heavyweight champion among rams, went on to vanquish ram after ram and then have his way with the ewes. Sheldon was not a professional writer. *Wilderness of the Denali* is better written than *Wilderness of the Upper Yukon*, but he still has the habit of stringing complete sentences together with commas. When I was taking and teaching freshman English in college this was considered a crime almost as serious as desecrating the flag or ravishing a Red Cross nurse.

Wild sheep are neither monogamous nor polygamous. The ram does not collect a harem and try to protect it from the inroads of other rams as does the bull elk with his cows or the buck mule deer with the does. Incidentally, neither the bull elk nor the buck mule deer is anything like 100 percent successful in this endeavor. In both species I have seen young males rush in and serve females while the master of the herd was chasing off another rival. I have likewise seen rather young desert bighorns cover ewes.

However, Valerius Geist says that eight-to-twelve-year-old rams do most of the breeding. I have no doubt that he is right, but this is because the rams this age are larger, heavier, and have bigger horns and try to keep the younger ones away. James Morgan, a biologist who studied the Salmon River herd in Idaho, thinks young rams chase and chivy the ewes excessively during the rutting season and that if the bulk of the breeding is done by the young rams the ewes are so harassed that they go into the winter in poor shape and may die. Morgan, who is a very belligerent guy, incidentally, says that the hunting of big rams is bad for the sheep herds for that reason. Others say that shooting off the rams with large horns will mean that lesser rams will do the breeding and the herds will deteriorate. In Rhodesia it is against the law to shoot bull elephants with tusks weighing over 40 pounds. The big 50-, 60-, 70-, 80-, and 90-pound bulls should be saved for breeding. To me this is about as logical as doing away with the enthusiastic and potent twenty-one-year-old human males and having the race perpetuated by nasty old men with long white beards. Geist says that females prefer heavy-horned rams and accept more mounts from them. A cynic might observe that this is to some extent true of the human race.

Valerius Geist calls real knock-down-and-drag-out battles between rams "clashes." The clash, he says, is an exaggerated form of the butt, and two rams take part. Often both rams rise on their hind legs. The legs propel the body forward as it straightens out and begins to fall. The ram tries to concentrate all the force on the keel of one horn from the forward motion of the hind legs, the fall of the body, the forward and downward movement of neck, head, and horns. Geist says smart rams try to clash with another from uphill.

The British Columbia game department estimates that two rams come together at a combined speed of 50 to 70 miles an hour and with an estimated energy of 2,400 foot-pounds.

Rams possess specially structured skulls to withstand such blows but nevertheless they often suffer injuries. Horn tips are often splintered.

Chunks of horn are knocked out. Occasionally a horn core is broken off. Rams get nosebleeds, broken ribs, undoubtedly internal injuries. In the spring and summer when the horn is growing out from the base the battering often makes the horns bleed at the point where horn meets scalp. Then as the ram feeds or walks through brush the blood is smeared on the horn. This mixed with sap from forbs and bushes attracts dust, dries in the sun, and often makes the otherwise light-colored horns of Dalls and some Stones almost as dark as those of bighorns.

In *Wilderness of the Denali,* Sheldon describes a Dall ram which he shot in December, right in the middle of the rut:

> The horns were large and massive, with ten rings, and were freshly chipped at the tips, the end of the right one having been cracked and slightly splintered. He carried evidence of recent combats: two flesh wounds on his face, one on his cheek, and a cut below the left eye. His face was very dirty and his long silky winter coat was stained brownish. The lachrymal glands were greatly enlarged, the areas around the eyes much swollen, the testes enlarged, and a strong odor emanated from his body. . . . I cut off the head and examined the stomach, which contained exclusively grass, some of it green at the roots.

Apparently this ram was not so much in love that he could not eat.

Sheldon's comments about the battles between rutting rams are worth recording in any book about sheep:

> Dec. 9–13.—Watching the rams among the ewes I often witnessed many short battles, all single combats. Friendly rams remained among the ewes, serving them indifferently. The fights always occurred when stranger rams attempted to enter the bands. At times new rams intruded among the ewes and shared their privileges without apparent objection on the part of the rams already in the bands. My observations during the rut led to the conclusion that most, if not all, combats among rams at this period are between members of bands occupying different areas during the summer. Rams that have run together in the same band, although they may separate and travel widely, do not fight when they meet seeking ewes at rutting time. In fact, I twice recognized rams joining a ewe band that was being served by

> rams (one in one case, three in another) of the same band and no antagonism was shown. . . . From early November to January new ewes kept entering their periods and the rams were constantly traveling to find those that were receptive.

My only observations among rutting sheep have been of the desert bighorn and the Iranian urial. What Sheldon writes confirms my own impression—that sheep are neither monogamous nor polygamous but promiscuous. A ram, or several rams, will follow, and sometimes chase and corner, an estrous ewe, but once the ram has had his way with her he seems to have no objection to sharing her favors with a pal. But if a guy from the other side of town shows up that's another story.

From what Sheldon says, the rut of the Dall sheep must last at least two months. In *The Desert Bighorn Sheep in Arizona* John Russo says he had found sheep rutting as early as July and as late as October. From my own very limited experience I would have thought that the rut of the Sonora sheep was fairly well concentrated in the four weeks from August 15 to September 15 because it was during that time that I saw considerable activity. However, that was the time when I myself was most active. In those days I was a professor at the University of Arizona. I could prowl the deserts in August and early September but by the middle of September I had to be back to guide the young to wisdom and virtue.

When the rut is over and the big rams lose interest in the ewes they drift off by themselves, usually in small bunches of from two to seven. The rams that remain with the ewes are usually young ones. A few times, however, I have seen big desert rams running with ewes as late as February 1, not far from the time the first lambs begin to appear.

When the old breeding rams go off by themselves they are in bad shape. They have used up their fat in fighting and frolicking and they are thin. Sometimes they suffer from broken ribs and internal injuries. In the north the snows and bitter cold have come. Deep-crusted snow can now cause many deaths among weakened rams with no reserves of fat. If a ram has a badly sprained or broken leg he cannot paw away the snow to get at the feed. Geist describes the last days of Old B Ram, a thirteen-year-old who went into the winter thin and with an infected hind leg. He spent his last days in solitude and misery. A wandering wolf finally ran across him bedded alone in the snow and put an end to his life.

The desert rams do not have to battle the snow and the cold nor dig through snow for their food. How long it takes them to recover their condition I cannot say. I once shot a ram in Sonora right about the first of December. He should have had at least a month to recover from the madness of the rut but although healthy he was very thin. The only tender meat on the carcass was the backstraps. On that same trip the members of my party took whitetail bucks and desert mule deer, neither of which had as yet gone into the rut. Everyone remarked at how much better the venison was than the sheep meat.

In the Arizona and Sonora deserts the winter rains generally start about December 1 and continue off and on until the end of January or the middle of February. When the rains are good the desert comes alive. Stretches that had looked as bare as the face of the moon miraculously become green. The prickly-pear leaves plump up with water. Leaves appear. Grass and forbs spring from the ground. It is following the rains that the desert lambs are born and the old rams fatten up. By the first of April the rams are fat and their meat is tender. The old-time sheep hunters in the bad old days in Sonora liked to go sheep hunting then. The shootable rams had left the ewes and hunting rams did not disturb ewes or lambs. Nights were pleasantly cool, days not yet too hot. The paloverde trees are clouds of golden bloom and filled with swarming little striped desert bees after the sweet nectar. The ocotillos are in new leaf and flaunting scarlet blossoms. The desert rams feed early in the morning, late in the evening. Now is the time to skirt the hills as soon as you can see to catch the old rams out on the flats, in the arroyos, or going up the hills to bed. A pal and I used to buy a 300-pound cake of ice in Ajo. Then we would dig back into the cut bank of an arroyo, keep our beer and our food cool with the ice, have ice for our Scotch and soda when we came in tired and dehydrated from the rocky hills.

In the north as snow goes and the country greens up, the rams, be they brown, black, or white, move to their summer range. In some places they have wintered high on ridges where the wind has blown away the light, dry snow and revealed the life-giving grass. In others they may travel 30 or 40 miles between winter and summer ranges. A favored place to spend the summer is a big basin. Often throughout the summer there is an old snowbank at the head. In some places there is the decaying remnant of an ancient glacier. In either case there is a little stream of pure icy water running through the basin and the grass is fresh and lush.

The rams get up at first light, graze lazily, drink perhaps, go back around nine or ten o'clock and lie down to doze and dream. Generally they get up during the middle of the day, eat for a little while, and then lie down until the shadows begin to lengthen and the cool air starts running down from the heights. The big old Dall ram I shot in 1950 was in such a basin. We would never have found him except that we met an old Indian who had trapped there in his youth. "See big peak?" he said. "Call-um Pilot Mountain. Go left side. Big basin. Always rams there. Usually one, two great big ones. No white man ever hunt there, only Indian. Not much time Indian kill sheep. Moose better. Sheep too little, too far away!"

So we went in and camped at a site the old Indian had suggested, in the last timber at the foot of Pilot Mountain. I don't think the Indian was kidding. We were the first party of white trophy hunters there. Around the camp the stumps of the trees showed that they had been cut with stone axes.

Spooky old rams that have been shot at like these basins particularly. Then they pick a spot about halfway between the top and the bottom of the basin. They are almost impossible to stalk. The last good trophy bighorn I have seen was a fine old ram with a close-curl, heavily broomed head. He was in a big Alberta basin with four companions. When we saw him he and the lesser rams had been down to a creek to drink. We first spotted them as they walked slowly in single file up a sheep trail that emerged from the dense timber of the creek bottom. They slowly climbed the hillside, paused for a while to think things over. Then they headed for a dense patch of what the Alberta guides call "shintangle"—arctic fir that grows low and thick right at timberline. They went into the patch and lay down. They were almost completely concealed. The guide, my daughter, Caroline, and I were not much over a half-mile away and had 9× and 10× binoculars, but the only evidence we could see of the four rams was part of one horn. If we had not known the rams were in that patch of shintangle I don't think we would have detected even that. The rams, however, could see out.

We waited about twenty minutes to see if the rams were settled down. We then decided that they were. It looked as if we could go down into the stream bed about 1,000 feet below, work around the slope to our left out of sight of the rams, then up a ravine cut by another stream. Then we would be above the rams. We could sneak around above them and get a shot. Because the rams would be concealed by the shintangle chances were that they would see us before we got a good look at them. But I figured at the worst they would be in sight for several seconds. But, alas, those were very smart rams, and the big old boy with the massive horns could count. They had apparently spotted us as soon as they lay down in the shintangle. We left one guide there, and he later reported that a few minutes after we had headed down the hill for the stream, the old ram had stood up and looked fixedly in his direction. The old boy could apparently tell the difference between four people and one person and suspected that there was some hanky-panky afoot. Finally he had turned and had led the other rams up the hillside, over a saddle, and into the next basin.

I remember another time, on this occasion in the Yukon. The country was very rough. I was out with Field Johnson on a jack camp. We had left our horses hobbled near camp and had hunted entirely on foot. We made it up a rocky creek bed where I remember seeing the weathered skulls and horns of a couple of ancient rams. On the other side of the saddle about 1,500 feet above camp we were on the edge of an enormous basin. Right in the middle of the basin and far below us was an outcrop of black lava about 30 feet high. On it lay about fifteen good Dall rams. The grass around the outcrop was green and tender. A little stream that originated in a great snow cornice to our right trickled past the outcrop. The rams were about 600 yards away. There was no way we could approach them without being instantly detected. On that basaltic outcrop the rams were safe from wolves. Eventually the rams spotted us up there on the ridge above them. They didn't even do us the honor of appearing agitated. They simply went on chewing their cuds and staring out below them.

Incidentally, bedded rams always fold their front legs under their bodies when they lie down. If a ram does not do so it is because he is injured. Once a writer peddled a sheep story to the editor of a prestigious outdoor magazine. One of the pictures was of a ram lying down. The author told how he had cunningly crept up on the ram and had photographed it within a few yards. (As *Time* used to say: A veritable Leatherstockings, he!) I told the editor that he had been conned, that the ram either had a broken back or was dead. Now editors, like anyone else, hate to be told that they have been made chumps of. The editor was sore as hell. He said (a) that he doubted if I were right, (b) that it was none of my damned business, and (c) that none of the 2,000,000 boobs that read the magazine would know the difference anyway. I knew the writer's guide and just for the hell of it I wrote him and asked him about the bedded ram. It was dead, he told me, and he and the writer had cunningly propped it up with stones. The editor was right about one thing. He did not have a single letter about the propped-up cadaver of the ram. The only other person I ran into who noticed the phony picture was my sheep-hunting son Bradford.

I think rams are getting smarter. When I first started hunting sheep, rams often bedded just under ridges and high in basins and the hunter could make a circuit, come around above them, collect them at short range. More and more I now see them bedded in big basins about half-way between top and bottom. Then they can be approached neither from above nor below. In such cases one of the fun ways to collect a ram is by a stake-out. The hunter goes somewhere and waits out of sight until a ram moves within range. Another way, but one much less ethical, is by a drive. The hunter conceals himself above the rams and a guide or someone else comes at them from below. The rams run up and the hunter gets a shot.

Old rams these days are also staying out of sight more. It used to be the rule that rams bedded down on points or on hillsides and depended on their keen eyes and strong legs for safety. Now more and more they are staying out of sight. I first ran into that phenomenon on the Middle Fork of the Salmon River in Idaho. Ewes, lambs, and young rams would bed down in plain sight and feed on open hillsides. The old rams pretty much stuck to the timber on the north sides of the hills. Jack Atcheson, Montana taxidermist, hunting-trip and safari booker, and sheep hunter, says this business of rams taking to timber when hunted is now common. Frank Cooke, Sr., the northern British Columbia outfitter, tells me that in areas of old burns in his territory the grass and brush have come up and Stone sheep have moved in. Then, he says, they must be hunted like deer.

On my last two sheep hunts, both with Frank Cooke, I have noticed sheep bedding down in brush. Once Frank Cooke and I watched two good rams bedded in shintangle most of the day. We could not have seen them if we had not been above them. The bunch of rams I shot my last Stone out of had been bedded in 3-foot-high arctic willow.

If sheep make an adaptation to brush and timber it would be a surprising thing. Sheep are by nature open-country animals. The only brush-dwelling sheep are the Sardinian and Corsican mouflon. The urial in the Mohammed Reza Shah National Park in Iran inhabit a country of rolling hills clad with low junipers. It looks for all the world like Upper Sonoran Zone country in Arizona, New Mexico, and Colorado. These beautiful sheep, however, do not hide as do true brush dwellers like deer. They escape their enemies by running. The animals that prey upon them are principally wolves and leopards, but in the old days the country also contained Caspian tigers.

A bunch of California bighorn rams in British Columbia. Their ears are long and pointed, not short and rounded like those of the Rocky Mountain bighorn.

A herd of Montana bighorn rams. The two rams on the left are excellent. If I had to make a quick choice I'd take the second from the left because I like the broomed, close-curl heads typical of the bighorn. Photo by Jon Cates.

The author being congratulated on his best Rocky Mountain bighorn. It was shot on a bare ridge in the fanny, ran downhill, and was stopped here by a shot in the lungs.

Bert Rigall (now deceased), an Englishman who was dean of the sheep guides and outfitters in southern Alberta. Rigall used a loop of rope around his knees to steady himself when glassing or shooting.

The author with two Alberta bighorn heads. The one on the left has the typical close curl, the other has a rather wide spread.

Mule deer above, bighorn sheep below on the same winter range.

Part of a ewe herd in a big Alberta basin. Note the lamb nursing.

A rare sight—a mixed bunch of Dall ewes, lambs, young rams, and old rams. This was taken before *the rut; the next day the old rams had gone off by themselves.*

Two Dall rams climbing out of a canyon. It is rugged country.

Packing in the trophy of a lifetime—my wife's 44-inch Dall head.

Yukon guide Sam Williams with a 40-1/2-inch ram I shot on Prospector Mountain in 1946. The ram was small and I thought the head was larger.

Maybe this photo doesn't belong in a sheep book, but the little guy on the left is the late Gene Jacquot, chef, placer miner, trader, outfitter, and famous Yukon character. With him is the late Myles Brown, sheep nut and pneumatic-tool tycoon from Cleveland, Ohio.

Herb Klein and his Yukon guide Paddy Jim with a tremendous Dall. The longest horn of this argali-type head went almost 47 inches.

The author in 1945 with Louie Jacquot at Jacquot's cabin at Burwash Landing on Kluane Lake. Jacquot and his brother Gene packed their outfit and grub over the Chilkoot Pass in 1898.

Bill Rae, former editor of Outdoor Life, *with a very heavy Dall. The close-curl head is broomed well back.*

My best Stone ram, taken on the Prophet Bench in 1946. It was 14-7/8 x 41-1/2 and was No. 10 in two record books.

A young Stone ram of the dark variety. The head is almost as dark as the neck and body.

James C. Rikhoff, Winchester public-relations chief, glasses while he brings a head in. He got this light Stone in the Cassiars of northern British Columbia.

Herb Klein, Texas tycoon, with a "Fannin" Stone with light-colored head and neck.

The guide takes the cape off a 38-inch Stone shot by my son, Bradford.

Jay Mellon with a typical Stone ram about nine or ten years old and with a complete curl.

These great desert rams were both taken in Arizona. The horns are of the argali type and have definite overhanging ridges on the outer edge like the horns of Stones and Dalls. Since they do not block side vision they are only slightly and accidentally rubbed.

Here is a close-curl Sonora desert ram head from my collection. Both horn tips are rubbed well back.

This old Alberta bighorn from my collection has broomed his right horn clear back to the core.

I took this Stone ram in 1971, with my old .270 Model 70 Winchester that I have used all over the world.

10
The Art of Sheep Hunting

The outfitter and the guide were making camp by the last stunted trees at timberline that chill September day high in the Wyoming Rockies. While they were taking off the pack and riding saddles, hobbling the three saddle horses and three pack mules, and pitching our two little tents, I volunteered to climb up above the timber to a little lake and bring back a bucket of water.

A game trail covered with the tracks of bull elk snaked up through the last stunted trees and came out on the flat top of a lofty plateau. I was in fairly good condition but the climb made me puff. Timberline there was between 10,500 and 11,000 feet. Beyond the far side of the plateau, dead white against the blue sky and the brown earth and rock, the sharp peaks of the snowy Teton Mountains thrust up stark and cold. Far below I could see an enormous canyon purple with timber, misty with distance, and at the bottom lay the wandering silver thread of a creek. A little breeze was blowing. The air was icy with altitude, fragrant with the breath of the stunted Alpine firs and white-bark pines.

Ahead on that barren plateau I could see the sheen of the water in a shallow little "lake" that was hardly even a pond. As I drew close I could see that the edge was all tracked up by mountain sheep—and that every track had been made by a ram. Some looked as if they were not over a couple of hours old. My outfitter, the late Ernie Miller, had told me that this lofty plateau was a favorite summering ground for rams—and it looked as if he knew what he was talking about.

It was the day before the Wyoming sheep season was to open, and I decided it wouldn't hurt to take a look at some of the rams that had made the tracks if in the process I did not spook them. I carried the bucket of water back to the camp. The saddle pile was covered with a tarp. The grub boxes were laid out side by side. A frying pan, a coffee pot, and a bucket stood beside a crackling fire. Miller was erecting a tent and the guide was hobbling the livestock.

"While you guys make things shipshape, I am going to take my glasses and look around from on top," I said. Ernie grunted. I picked up my binoculars, puffed up the trail again, and worked up toward the end of the long, narrow "peninsula." There were sheep tracks and droppings everywhere.

The first game I saw, however, was a bull elk. He was a quarter of a mile away and far below me. I picked him up with my 8×30 binoculars as a movement behind a whitebark pine. From the color I knew it was an elk. When he walked out he stood in the open, a big six-pointer. As I watched he battered a tree with his antlers, and a moment later I heard his bugle ring through that lonely canyon. Then he moved slowly through the scrubby trees angling downhill. He was looking for company.

I went on. Every time I came to a new prospect I stopped to glass to make sure I didn't blunder into anything. In the second canyon after the one in which I had seen the bull elk, I sat down to look things over carefully. I was right on a well-used sheep trail, and in every direction there were sheep beds where the rams had scratched out little hollows in the soil and had got rid of the large stones. I could smell the characteristic odor of sheep urine. I picked up a couple of pellets in a bed beside me and squeezed them. They were still soft.

Below me the side canyon fell away thousands of feet into a great darkling valley below. There were scrubby trees, little slanting meadows filled with grass and the little tender plants that wild sheep love. Resting my elbows on my knees to hold the glasses steady, I went over the canyon foot by foot. Sheep trails across rock and shale told me it had long been used, but right away I saw nothing. Then I made out something concealed by the branches of a whitebark pine. It didn't quite belong. I watched it carefully. Presently I became convinced it was part of the horn of a bighorn ram. Then it moved—and I knew it was. I kept watching and presently I could make out other parts of a bedded ram. Then I became conscious that not far away another ram had got up and had started to graze. The sun was slanting down in the west and it was now mountain-sheep dinnertime.

In a few minutes seven rams had materialized out of their beds behind the scrubby timberline trees and had started to graze. All were shootable. Watching them carefully so I could freeze if one looked my way, I worked my way slowly back up to the top of the plateau out of sight and hiked back to camp. The next morning the guide and I were back there early. The rams were feeding almost exactly where I had left them. We went down on the far side of the ridge to the left until we were opposite a cliff by which we had marked the sheep. Then we worked up over the ridge. When I got through the scrubby trees into the clear, I dropped into a sitting position and shot the ram I had picked. He was across the canyon between 150 and 200 yards away.

This short and simple tale illustrates most of the principles of sheep hunting. Most elementary is that it is exceedingly helpful to know where ram country is. On that occasion Miller told me that during the summer and early fall the rams over a wide area concentrated on that one long flat-topped "point," bedding down at the heads of the side canyons, feeding along the sides and on top. Many other areas looked just as sheepy and a hunter might find ewes and lambs in them, but for some reason the rams always came back to that one lofty plateau. Miller's dudes had taken a ram or two out of there each season for many years. He said that if we had hunted the entire plateau carefully we probably would have located about thirty rams.

Another principle this tale illustrates is the importance of seeing the ram first and then staying out of sight. None of those rams saw me until I had pushed my way through the stunted timberline trees on top of the ridge across the side canyon and was ready to shoot. Another lesson we might draw from the experience is the wisdom of stalking as close as possible for a sure shot. When I first saw the rams I was somewhere around 400 yards away. I could have started shooting them up right then. I might even have killed one. However, at best it would have been a sloppy performance and chances are that I would have missed or wounded. It is a commonly held notion by people who don't know much about sheep hunting that shooting rams is a long-range proposition. I have been hunting sheep with a fair degree of regularity since the early 1930s. I can remember very few sheep I have taken with long shots but a good many that I have taken at less than 100 yards, two or three at less than 50 yards. The good sheep hunter never bangs away in hopes that he will hit something—he waits until he is sure!

Wherever they are found, wild sheep have about the same habits. The rams prefer their own company to that of the ewes and the bleating pestiferous lambs. They join the ewes, however, at the time of the annual rut. For the desert bighorns with which I am familiar this is in late August and September, so that the young can be born at the time of the winter rains in February. The northern sheep, whether Rocky Mountain bighorn, Stone, or Dall, mate in late November and into December, so that the lambs are dropped in the spring. From the time of the rut on the rams are apt to be with or near the ewes, but as the lambing season approaches they drift apart. The rams go off in bunches. Sometimes there will be only three or four rams together. At other times there will be a dozen or more. For whatever the reason it seems to me that I have seen seven rams together quite commonly. I can remember seeing bunches of from fifteen to twenty rams and once in Sonora I saw somewhere around thirty desert rams together. But for desert sheep this a very rare happening.

I am convinced that rams like to associate with other rams about their own age, and that if there are plenty of sheep in the country the rams tend to sort themselves out in age groups. I also feel that if I see a bunch of rams with one old-timer twelve or thirteen years old, a couple of four-year-olds, a seven-year-old, and one about eight or nine, it is generally a sign that there are not many rams in the area. (This is my observation. Frank Cooke, Jr., my guide on my 1971 Stone-sheep hunt, does not agree with me.)

In 1967 my wife and I hunted sheep in the Cassiar district of northern British Columbia. We saw a great many rams. Most were in an enormous bunch that contained at least fifty. Every one that I saw was from seven to possibly ten years old, and I am quite sure there wasn't a head in the bunch that would go more than 38 inches around the curl. Later in this chapter I shall tell how we collected a couple of these. In 1963 in the Yukon we passed up some rams of that age, but toward the end of the trip we found three old grandfathers together. After an exceedingly interesting stalk, which I shall describe later, my wife got one of them with a 44¼-inch head. I told her she would win a

Boone & Crockett award with it and she did. The horns of her ram showed thirteen annual rings and I am sure his companions were about as old.

Sheep get out of their beds and start feeding as soon as it is light. Sometimes, as was the case with that bunch of seven Wyoming rams, they begin to feed near their beds. The sheep choose their bedding grounds for safety, and often it is a considerable distance from where they feed. Desert bighorns, for example, often bed high on a mountain and then come down to feed in the valleys. After they have filled up they work slowly back to their bedding grounds and take it easy until late afternoon, when they get up and begin their serious feeding once more. Sheep are dry-country animals and under ordinary circumstances do not water very often. In some areas they get along indefinitely without water. I have not seen many sheep watering, but those I have seen at water have gone there after their morning feed or before the evening feed. The last desert ram I saw came to an Arizona water hole about three o'clock in the afternoon. The last Rocky Mountain bighorns I saw water came in along about ten-thirty or eleven. In desert mountains where sheep must have water because there is little dew and not many water-bearing cacti, lying in wait for sheep in rock blinds at water holes was a favorite method of meat-hunting.

Sheep, and indeed most herbivorous animals, get hungry along in the middle of the day, get up and browse or graze for a few minutes or a half-hour or so, and then lie down again. Often I have glassed all likely spots hoping to find bedded rams without seeing a hair. Then between twelve and one o'clock I would see a ram feeding where I had seen nothing before. Instead of snoozing away the midday hours the sheep hunter should be plying his binoculars!

The tendency among beginning sheep hunters is to be too impatient. If they see sheep, away they go on the stalk. Or if they think they are within possible rifle range they start blazing away. They barge ahead without looking each new piece of ground over. Many a stalk has been ruined because since the sheep were last seen they had moved—from feeding area to bedding ground, from a spot where the sun was hot to one in the shade, to a place where the wind kept the gnats from bothering them. I once went on a stalk carrying only a camera and bringing up the rear. Two companions of mine were to do the shooting and the party was led by a rattle-brained guide who had done little sheep hunting.

We had seen a couple of good rams from camp about 2,000 feet above us and perhaps 2½ miles away as the weary sheep hunter scrambles. I suspected there were more. We were finally near the spot where we had marked the sheep, when, instead of stopping to see what was before him when we came to a grassy bench ideal for sheep beds, the guide charged ahead like a bulldozer right into a herd of about ten good rams. The rams exploded in every direction. My two companions, startled half out of their wits, got buck fever. The only results of the encounter were some badly frightened sheep that were cleared out of the country and a lot of wild shooting. We never saw that bunch of rams again. Shoot at a deer and he'll run around on the other side of a hill and lie down. Shoot at a ram and he'll find himself another mountain. He will come back eventually because the place where he got shot up is his home range, but he'll wait for it to cool off!

I first started hunting sheep in Sonora long before sheep hunting became fashionable. At first I did not realize that a good binocular and the ability to use it is more important in sheep hunting than the rifle. I also spoiled some sheep hunts with some wild shooting at long range. I spoiled others by starting my stalk too early and then finding the sheep gone when I had got to the place where I had marked them.

I think it is wisest when feeding sheep have been located to wait until they have bedded down unless the stalk can be completed quickly. When that happens they will generally stay in the same spot for several hours except for a brief period in the middle of the day when they get up for a snack. Sometimes sheep will move after they have bedded down, but they seldom move far. The sun may get too hot, the wind too strong, or the sheep may decide that the shale around the point is a little softer. For whatever the reason they sometimes move, and during the last stages of the stalk, the hunter should exercise the greatest caution every time he sticks his head over a ridge or comes around a point.

I remember one bitterly cold day at the head of the St. Clair River in the Yukon. Along in midafternoon my old guide Field Johnson and I located a band of rams far across the valley near the top of the opposite ridge. They were about 2 miles away on an air line and at least twice that far the way we had to travel. They were so far away that we knew they were rams only because they were all the same size and "looked" large. We took off our hobnail boots and our socks and waded the bitterly cold river. When I got to the other side I could have amputated one of my toes and I would never have felt it.

About the time we started up the mountain the wind came up. Dark, dirty-looking clouds swept in from the glacier at the head of the St. Clair and snow began to fall. When we finally made it to the spot we had planned to shoot from the rams were gone. For a panicky moment I was afraid we had lost them. But Field kept his head. "They go to get out of wind," he whispered. Presently we found them. They had moved only about a hundred yards and had bedded down on the lee side of a point. As is generally the case after a well-executed stalk the actual shooting was anticlimatic.

As long as I live I'll never forget the aftermath of the stalk. In those days there was a two-ram limit in the Yukon. I had a rifle, a camera, binoculars, and a ram head. Field went before me with a head and a load of meat. On the way down I shot a couple of pictures of Field and his burden, then sat down to change film. When I got to my feet and picked up the head I heard a growl behind me. An unsophisticated grizzly that apparently did not know what a man smelled like had been attracted by the sheep blood. When I stood up he was puzzled at the strange sight and growled to see what developed. Plenty did. I let out a yell that echoed from peak to peak and that grizzly took off. This incident happened in 1945 and there had been no hunting in the area during the war years. A whole generation of grizzlies that had never smelled a man had grown up. Late on the same trip I had another grizzly come to the smell of fresh blood, this time to that of a bull caribou. On that occasion I nailed the inquisitive bear.

But to go on—all the way down the mountain the fresh-fallen snow was 6 or 8 inches deep. By the time we got to the Sinclair we were so wet and cold that we waded the icy stream with our boots on. When we got to camp we found that the wind had blown the flap of the tent open and our sleeping bags were covered with snow. While Field got a fire going I got into dry underwear and a pair of dry pants and boots and dug out a quart of rum so strong it would singe the whiskers of Satan himself. Presently we had got on the outside of a couple of heroic hot buttered rums. The snow seemed less cold and the wind slightly less bitter.

Deer are born suspicious. They are afraid of everything until it has been proved harmless. They are instinctive skulkers and hiders. Sheep have to learn to be afraid of things which have not previously threatened them. If they are in their chosen escape territory, they know they can outrun and outclimb bears or wolves. They have to learn that men with rifles can kill at a distance. I have seen sheep do some strange things. Years ago in the Alberta Rockies, Jack Holliday and I walked slowly up to within 50 yards of a herd of eighty-seven bighorn ewes, lambs, and young rams. We approached at an angle, never made any sudden moves or threatening geqtures, stayed in sight. At first the sheep watched us suspiciously. Then they apparently decided we were harmless and from that time on they paid no more attention to us than if we had been a couple of grazing caribou. We took some stills and some movies of the sheep. I got some pretty fair shots of a lamb nursing. Once a young ram overcome with curiosity came up within 20 yards and gazed at us with innocent wonder as if he thought we were the damnedest looking creatures he had ever seen.

On another occasion I shot a ram at about 150 yards. The other rams did not panic but stood around their fallen companion wondering what had happened. When I walked over to the dead ram the others moved slowly away, but all the time I was dressing the ram and skinning out the cape they stood in a row about 100 yards away and watched. These rams had apparently never seen a man before.

Sheep have wonderful eyes but only for moving objects. Often I have found sheep with 8× and 9× glasses only to find they had discovered me first. But a stationary object doesn't mean much to a sheep. I have had sheep stare at me a few yards away and not know what I was.

Some sheep hunters insist that sheep have poor noses and pay no attention to what they smell. I think they believe this because sheep live in areas of shifting unstable winds and often they appear to be getting your wind when they are not. To see how sheep smell I deliberately have given them my wind. When they get it they always react. Because sheep usually dwell in an area of unstable rock where stones are always rolling they don't pay much attention to what they hear. Their eyes are their principal warning system, their wonderful legs their defense, but they should always be stalked upwind or crosswind.

Sheep usually bed where they can see a long way—on a point, on a ridge, in a shale slide at the foot of a cliff, at the head of a basin. They watch for danger from below and seldom look up. They should be approached out of sight and if it is possible they should be approached from above. Some believe they always post sentinels. I do not think so as I have seen bunches too many times with no outposts whatsoever. Often the "sentinel" is simply a sheep that has got hungry and wandered a little way off. Or maybe it is a nervous sheep that has once had the hell scared out of it by a wolf. However, often when rams bed down one of them will come back to take a look over a ridge to see if anything is on their backtrack.

Fortunately sheep can't count and on several occasions I have taken advantage of this to collect some mutton and a trophy. The last time was in 1963. My wife and I were hunting Dall sheep in the Yukon when on a shale slide about 500 yards away and below us we saw three magnificent rams. They had seen us first and there was no chance to stalk them where they were. They looked us over, then got slowly to their feet and with great dignity paraded downhill until they stopped on a point above a creek and just above timberline. They stood there watching us. Along the creek bottom the timber was thick and apparently the rams were reluctant to enter it, and anyway the mountain where we were was their home.

To our left was a sharply cut draw that led down to the creek and passed within 50 yards of the point where the rams were. I asked my wife if she were game for the stalk. She said she was. I told her guide to take her down the draw while the other guide and I stayed with the horses and walked up and down to keep the rams interested. The scheme worked. Those rams kept staring at us while my wife and her guide ran and scrambled down the draw to within 50 yards of the rams. It was an exciting thing to watch with binoculars. I could see the hunters and the rams at the same time. I saw the hunters pause to catch their wind. Then the guide handed Eleanor her 7×57. I saw her bend over, sneak up the point. I saw her lift her rifle and the rams start to run. Then one of them went down. A moment later I heard the distant crack of the rifle.

Most of the brains have been bred out of domestic sheep but I am sure wild ones rank fairly high on the scale of animal intelligence. Young rams do some very stupid things but old rams that have been chivied around and shot at are as smart as anyone could wish. I think the smartest sheep I have ever run into are the little red sheep of Iran that have been hunted by human beings for 25,000 years. Right behind them come the old desert bighorn rams I used to chase around in Sonora. Rams don't survive this vale of tears for twelve and thirteen years and grow heavy and massive heads by being dumb.

One stunt that smart rams sometimes learn after they have been shot at is to bed down on big open hillsides or in big basins so that nothing can approach unseen within 500 yards or so. If the hunter tries to come at them from above, he will be seen as many of these smart sheep have learned to look up for danger now and then as well as to look below. If the hunter tries to approach from below he is whipped from the start. Rimming around on the same level with the sheep won't work unless there is cover of rocks or trees. When rams choose beds like that a patient man may get one by making a stake-out, watching until they can be taken at a disadvantage—going to water, for example. Or the only solution may be for one hunter to stay out of sight above the sheep near a notch or saddle where the sheep might pass. Then another hunter can show himself below. The instinct of mountain animals is to run up when danger threatens, and if the concealed hunter has guessed right he may get a shot. This, however, is nowhere near as sporting as stalking.

The only time I ever shot a driven ram was in the Telegraph Creek district of the Cassiar Mountains in northern British Columbia in 1967. While our son Bradford was off on a jack camp my wife and I went out from a lovely timberline camp with Bruce Creake-Dennis. Our ram country was a big plateau with a top as flat as a billiard table. On some parts of the plateau where the rock had broken down into soil, there was grass, but for the most part the top was hard, flat, *solid* rock. Sign showed that the sheep crossed over the top from one side to another but there was little to eat on top and they fed and bedded on the hillslopes below the rims.

Except for occasional gusts of wind that could get pretty chilly, our first day was warm, bright, and beautiful. We were probably about 7,500 feet in elevation there on the top of the plateau. Our camp was at timberline, probably about 4,500 feet. We made it to the top after a long, hard scramble up very steep, trailless slopes, sometimes riding, sometimes walking and leading our horses. We saw a few billy goats spotted around on isolated shelves on distant mountains. Once when we paused for breath we could see far below us a couple of caribou bulls. We saw one long young ram that had apparently lost his bunch. He came trotting toward us until he realized we were not sheep. Once we got about 200 yards above a dozen rams with heads in the 35- to 36-inch class. We watched them as they dozed and chewed their cuds but we went on without disturbing them.

Along about midafternoon and about 15 miles from camp we found an enormous bunch of rams—the largest compact bunch of rams I have ever seen in North America. I have on occasion seen as many as one hundred rams on a mountain but these would be in scattered groups. These rams were in a group no more than 150 yards wide and about that long. They were about 700 yards below us and below the rim, about as far from the creek at the bottom of the basin. On either side the hill was smooth grass. The opposite hillside was also grassy, but above there was a big snow patch and the remains of an ancient glacier.

Here was a problem. What was to be done? There was no way we could approach within evel gambling rifle range without being detected. Once before in Alberta I had encountered a small bunch of spooky bighorn rams in a basin. There was no way to get at them. I found that they fed in the open basin, came down into the wooded creek bottom to drink every two or three days. One way to get a shot would be a stake-out. The hunter could take a bedroll and some food and watch the rams until they moved into a stalkable position. I decided that they also might be driven, but I didn't try this.

In this case here in the Cassiars there was no chance for a stake-out. We would have had to stay at 7,500 to 8,000 feet on solid rock with no fire and no water in wind and cold. The only other chance was a drive.

I turned to Bruce Creake-Dennis. "What would happen if we got the cook and horse wrangler to come in below the rams and show themselves tomorrow?" I asked.

"They'd run uphill," he said.

"That's what I thought," I said. "Don't you think they would come up here through the notch?"

"Probably," he said. "A lot of them anyway!"

It looked to me as if the country on the other side of the canyon was so rough and cliffy that it was unlikely that the sheep would go that way.

"What do you say we try it tomorrow?" I said.

"OK by me!"

Bruce, Eleanor, and I parted with the cook and the horse wrangler not far from camp. We were to go back to the spot where we had seen the rams the day before and wait. The cook and the horse wrangler, both young tough lads, would go around and come at the rams from below. Chances were that they would be on the same hillside.

We had just got well on the top of the plateau when far over in the west I saw big black clouds trailing white veils of snow. My wife hates cold, so I said nothing. It is her luck that every time she gets on a sheep mountain she freezes. I watched the clouds. They seemed to be drawing nearer.

Around one o'clock we were back where we had been the day before. The rams were still there. Most were lying down. A few had got up for their midday snack and were feeding. Bruce and I set up the spotting scope and looked them over. All were about the same age—nine- and ten-year-old rams with heads that looked as if they would go from 36 to 38 inches. All I got to look over carefully were the standard Stone type with gray-black bodies and gray heads and necks.

We got out our sandwiches and a couple of cans of fruit juice and ate. Now and then I looked below with binoculars. I looked at my watch. It was nearing two o'clock.

I was taking a gulp of fruit juice when Bruce said, "I see the cook."

I got to my feet, picked up my old .270. My glass showed me the cook far below the rams.

Then suddenly that whole mass of rams started to move. About twenty-five of them headed to the left and it looked as if they would go through a narrow and difficult notch about 200 yards away. I ran toward it. When I got to the spot from which I planned to intercept them I barely had time to switch off the safety and sit down when about ten rams came tearing up the broken rocks in single file headed for the notch. They were about 100 yards away. The leader looked to be as good as any. I fired. He took a couple of steps, then paused and rolled over sideways stone dead.

Just then the storm hit. A bitter wind howled and plastered my glasses and the front lens of the rifle scope with snow.

Then I heard my wife's 7×57 crack—once—twice—three times. Through a rift in the storm I could see my ram lying below.

I climbed back to the level plateau from the point from which I shot. The snow was falling so hard that I could not see over 20 feet.

I picked my way over in the direction where Eleanor and Bruce should be. Presently I saw them on a point about 100 yards away looking down.

"Any luck?" I asked as I neared them.

"Yes, I got one," Eleanor said.

"The ram was running and she was right in line every time but she was just over the top of his back on the first two shots. I yelled for her to hold low and she did on the third shot."

"He was below me and he looked awfully tiny!" Eleanor said. "Boy, am I cold!"

After she had shot her ram about thirty others had come boiling through the notch and across the top of the plateau within 50 yards of Eleanor and Bruce. They had almost run over the horses and had frightened them badly.

Eleanor put on her extra sweater, her gloves, and her rain gear. Snow fell and the wind howled. Bruce went down the cliff, skinned out the head of Eleanor's ram, and brought it up. It measured 37 inches around the curls. It was a respectable mature ram, no record but a good trophy that was the result of a good shot. Eleanor looked at it, her face stiff with disappointment.

"For Heaven's sake!" she said. "Why didn't someone tell me it was just a little one?" This was her second ram. Her first was 44 and 44¼ inches around the curl and won her a Boone & Crockett medal, as I've recounted. The Stone I took that day was slightly smaller.

So this is an account of the only time I ever took part in a drive for rams. It was not without its quota of excitement but as sport it does not compare with the classic stalk. It is not illegal but I am not sure about the ethics. A bad thing about the drive is that if there are more than a few sheep it may be difficult to select the best head. Also the shooting is more difficult, as a running ram is harder to hit than one standing or lying down.

Driving on big game is not common in North America. It is very common in Europe and Asia. Tigers have long been driven in India. Deer and wild boar are commonly driven in Europe. In Spain the *monteria*, a drive for red deer and boar, is a great social and sporting occasion.

Sometimes a very old ram will go off and live by himself. A solitary sheep is generally an old sheep with an exceptional head. Maybe these old rams get so cranky that other sheep cannot stand them. Or possibly they are weaker and less agile than the other sheep and the younger rams bully them. If their teeth are in good condition they get very fat.

These old rams are often very smart, but the fact that they have only one pair of eyes makes them easier to stalk than rams in a bunch. The greater the number of rams the better the chance that one will be looking at you at the wrong time.

In the fall of 1956, Bill Rae and I made an interesting stalk on an old ram all alone in the middle of a big basin with no cover. He was feeding and every time he had his head down to eat we would crawl forward. When he lifted his head up to look around we'd lie still. We must have crawled for an hour, a few yards at a time. When we were about 200 yards away the ram became conscious of a couple of funny bumps he hadn't noticed before. He stared at us long and fixedly. I whispered to Bill that I thought the jig was up. He collected the ram.

One of the hardest things to learn about sheep hunting is the proper and patient use of binoculars. These should be of high quality and of 8× or 9×. The glass I have used more than any other is the Bausch & Lomb 9×33, now unfortunately no longer made. I have also used an 8×30 Bausch & Lomb, an 8×30 B Zeiss, and an 8×32 Hensold Dialyt.

The glass should be in perfect collimation (both tubes aligned perfectly at all interpupillary adjustments), because if collimation is not perfect and the glass is used any length of time a bad headache results.

To search a country for sheep the hunter should first look it over carefully with his naked eye. Often the hunter will start to glass a distant basin when sheep are lying near him in plain sight. I have had that happen.

The hunter should look for sheep trails and beds. If he sees them he knows the country is used. He should look all likely spots for beds over carefully—points, shale slides, saddles, grassy benches, slides of small rock under rims. It doesn't hurt to look first right at the skyline where sheep are easy to see. It is entirely possible that when you see a sheep on the skyline he is looking at *you!*

Look carefully at all objects that could be sheep or portions of sheep. Once I watched for what seemed like a half-hour but was probably about ten minutes what looked like the rump of a sheep. I could see the black tail, the black line joining it to the frame of the body. It did not move and I was about to decide I was looking at a rock. Then a ram stood up. It had been lying down facing away from me and apparently with his chin on a stone to rest his neck muscles tired from carrying heavy horns around. Otherwise I would have seen the head.

Even if a suspicious object does not move the hunter should return to it later. Once when I was hunting bighorns an Indian guide and I found in a shale slide a long way off a collection of brown objects distributed like a herd of resting rams. But they did not move. I put my 8×30 binoculars on a stone so they would not shake, focused them within a gnat's hair, and watched. I had about decided that they were stones that had fallen off the cliff above the slide when one got up and walked.

The sheep hunter should use his glass in the steadiest possible positions. If the glass wobbles around he will get a headache. I sit down and rest my elbows on my knees, or lie down with the glass in my hands and the weight on my elbows. It drives me nuts to see the jaunty way hunters in advertisements and even in some hunting stories hold binoculars in *one* hand.

Look, look, *look!* Come back to all suspicious objects. Be patient. Spend an hour with the glass for every hour walking, maybe for every half-hour.

A spotting scope, which I discuss in the chapter on equipment, saves a lot of wear and tear on the legs. It can distinguish a sheep from a stone at great distance, a ram from a ewe, a shootable ram from an unshootable one. Before I got a spotting scope I made many unnecessary stalks on rams I didn't want when I got up to them. A 20× or 25× spotting scope will enable the hunter to evaluate heads at ranges impossible with excellent binoculars. Incidentally, the spotting scope should always be used from a tripod.

Once the hunter has decided he wants a ram and has decided the ram will stay put for a sufficient length of time for him to make the stalk, he should pick a route that will keep him out of sight. He should also pick out a conspicuous object near the sheep so he will know where the sheep is when he gets there—a peculiar tree, a certain stone, a well-marked rock stratum. Often country looks quite different from one point than from another.

The hunter should neither bang away at long range nor try to get within a few yards. The long-range "hope" shot is apt to miss. The hunter who tries to get too close may spook the sheep. Many guides are pretty sour on their hunters' marksmanship and try to get their dudes too close.

The hunter should take his ram at the first good spot where he is *absolutely* certain he can make a one-shot kill. Then he should take the steadiest possible position and squeeze that trigger. I have shot a good many sheep from prone with the fore-end of my rifle resting over a hat on a stone or moss hummock, a rolled-up jacket—even once with it resting across my guide's fanny.

The successful stalk, the pause to get the wind back, the steady position, the squeezed trigger. This all adds up to the clean kill and the happy hunt. There is nothing so good to cure buck fever and flinching as the crosshairs resting rock-steady on the ram's shoulder. When you know you can't miss, you don't.

A couple of years before I wrote these lines a man called me and told me he had drawn a Washington permit to take a California bighorn ram from a herd planted in the Blue Mountains near Pomeroy, Washington. He wanted me to tell him how to hunt sheep.

My advice was about as follows: Get a light but accurate rifle of .270, .30/06, 7-mm. Magnum, or some such caliber with a 4× scope and a sling. Get a good pair of 8×, 9×, or 10× binoculars. Use them in known ram range carefully and more than you walk. When you see the ram you want, make a careful stalk out of sight, get as near as you safely can, shoot from the steadiest possible position, a rest if possible. I told him to let me know how he came out.

A couple of months later he called. He hadn't exactly followed my instructions, he said. He saw the sheep at about 400 yards, got excited, and started shooting at it offhand. He shot almost a box of cartridges. He said he thought he hit it once because the ram acted "funny." He went over to the spot where he had last seen the ram, looked around, and found some blood. He couldn't find the ram. He came back next day and looked. Still no ram. Since he still had a valid permit he went on hunting. About a week later he ran into some trout fishermen who told him they had seen a wounded ram right down in the creek bottom. Following their directions, he discovered his ram. It was still alive, he told me, but "it stunk awfully bad." It was so weak it couldn't get up. It just lay there looking at him when he shot it. He was disappointed that he couldn't use the meat!

The wild ram is a fine game animal and deserves a better fate.

11
Stories in Sheep Horns

Members of the deer family—elk, moose, mule deer, whitetails—shed their antlers every year.

The mountain sheep, like all the horned animals except the American pronghorn, keeps his horns as long as he lives, and on them he writes his autobiography. He records his age, his battles, his species, his good years and his bad. Superficially, the horns of all mature mountain sheep look much alike, but no two sets of horns are identical, and actually each set of sheep horns is as individual as a set of human fingerprints. An ardent sheep hunter with a good eye and a good memory can recognize sheep heads he has not seen for years.

Horns of two species of wild sheep—the brown bighorn and the so-called "thinhorns," the Stone and the Dall—are somewhat different, as I have explained in earlier chapters. The horns of the bighorn average larger in basal circumference and have more mass generally than do those of the Dalls and the Stones, but some of the northern sheep have horns that often compare favorably in mass to those of good bighorns.

As we have seen, some European zoologists lump all North American sheep and those of eastern Siberia into one species—*canadensis.* All these sheep have rather smooth horns as compared to the heavier-ridged horns of the argali-type sheep *(Ovis amon)* found farther west in central Asia. The average sheep hunter would have difficulty telling the horns of an Asiatic Kamchatka bighorn, for example, from those of a Dall or Stone. On the other hand, he would know instantly that the horns of the argali, or any other member of the *amon* group, with their more pronounced ridges, came from some other sort of sheep.

In North America, and in general wherever sheep are found, there are four principal types of sheep horns—the close-curl, the medium-curl (the type most often seen), the wide-spread, and what I call the "argali-type" that pinches in close to the cheeks and then flares out. For reasons which I shall go into later, many of the record North American heads are of the argali type. Generally speaking, the close-curl type of head is more common among the Rocky Mountain bighorn and the desert sheep and the wide-spread and the argali-types more common among the northern sheep. Medium-curl heads are found among all subspecies. Also, the Rocky Mountain and the desert bighorn have horns that are more nearly oval in cross-section, whereas those of the northern sheep tend to be triangular with an overhanging outside ledge. However, it is possible to see heads of any type in any species. I have myself never shot a desert sheep with an argali-type head or with triangular horns. Nevertheless, an occasional desert sheep is shot with an argali-type head that except for color looks as if it had come from a Dall.

Among my sheep trophies I have the head of a Stone I shot on the Prophet River a generation ago that is oval in cross-section, close-curled, broomed, and except in color is the spitting image of an old Alberta bighorn head. The famous James Simpson head, which is now No. 3 in the world bighorn records, but which was formerly No. 1, is an argali-type head that pinches in and then flares out. However, there is no doubt that the very close-curled, broomed horns are far more common among the brown sheep and the two other types are more common among the sheep of the north.

Of the four types of heads, the rarest, I believe, is the one with the wide-spread horns. I have never taken such a head myself. I believe such heads are most common among the Dall sheep. One day in the Sifton Range in the Yukon back in 1950, I watched for over an hour a fine Dall ram with tremendously wide-spread horns, by far the widest I have ever seen. The head would have made an interesting addition to anyone's trophy room, but on that hunt I had already taken an excellent ram so I of necessity passed him up. A ram with such a head

A battered old head with a complete curl and heavily broomed. This is the record of a long and pugnacious life.

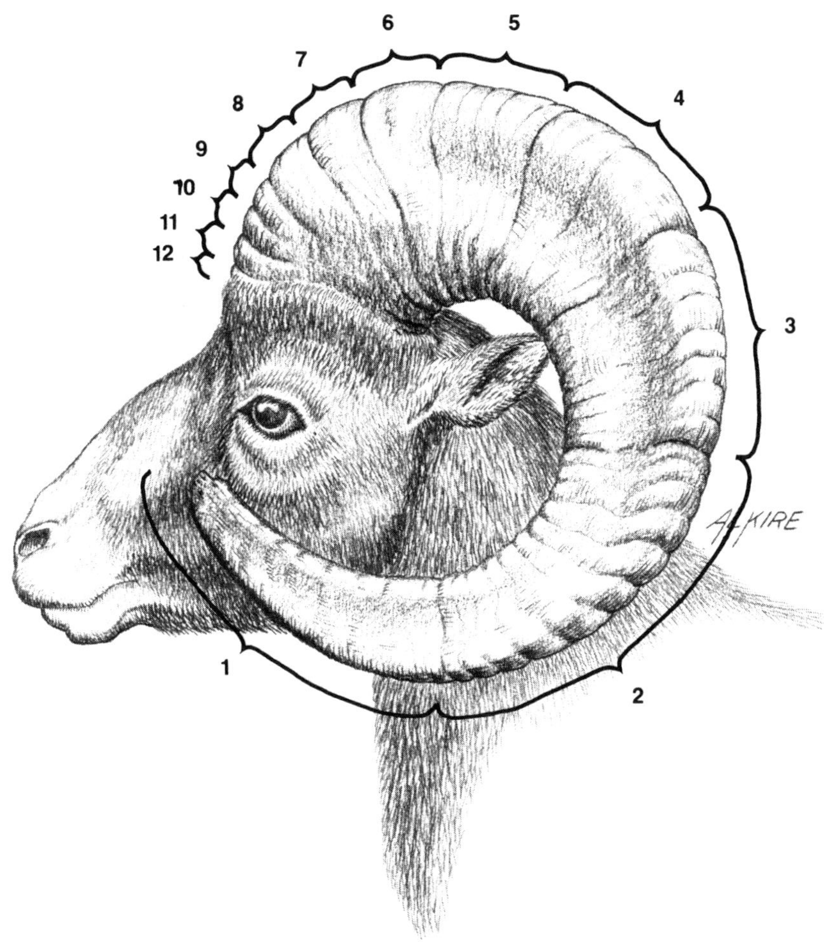

The age of a ram is determined by counting the annual rings of the horns, though it is not always so easy to do as the drawing here suggests. The older the ram is, the smaller the amount of growth each year and the more difficult it is to tell annual rings from seasonal rings.

would be greatly handicapped if he had to get around in rocks or brush or had to travel on narrow ledges.

The horns of a mountain sheep grow as long as he lives, with the horn growth pushing up from the base. When the ram is young, the horn grows several inches in a year. As the ram ages, growth slows down, and in the ram's final years, the annual growth is less than an inch. Major rings on the horns are formed during the breeding season and the following winter months when horn growth stops. The breeding ram feeds little if at all, as his mind is on more important matters. Then right after the breeding season—which with the Rocky Mountain bighorn, Stone, and Dall begins in late November and runs well into December—the rams go into the time of great cold and little food. All of their energy goes into staying alive instead of growing horns. The desert sheep mate in August and September. Since the rut is not followed by a starving time, the annual rings on the horns of desert rams are generally not so pronounced.

The age of a ram cannot be told with 100-percent accuracy because the rings near the base put on in the ram's old age are difficult to tell from seasonal rings, and also because several inches are often broken off the points. A ram does not have a head that is a decent trophy until he is eight or nine years old, and generally the head is not a top trophy until the ram is eleven or twelve years old. A ram that has reached the age of twelve is an old one. Apparently, few rams get beyond their thirteenth year. I have shot several rams with thirteen annual rings, but I have seen only one head that I was sure had fourteen annual rings. I have heard of rams with from fifteen to eighteen and even more rings. I have never seen one and I wonder if such heads were accurately aged.

The color of the horns of the North American mountain sheep varies with the color of the hair on the ram's head and neck, as horns, like claws and hooves, grow from the skin and are composed of a material called keratin. The horns of the Rocky Mountain bighorn and the desert bighorn are a dark mahogany brown, not too different from the hair before it has been faded by sun. The horns of the snow-white Dall are when clean the yellow of dried lemon peel. The pelage of the Stone sheep varies enormously, and consequently the horns vary in color from fairly dark to almost as light as the horns of the Dalls. I remember watching one Stone through a spotting scope. He had a white face, a neck and body that were black-brown. His horns were light yellow. Some taxidermists put oil, varnish or even stain on horns. This changes the appearance and to my way of thinking ruins the trophy. Taxidermists who do this and also those who lengthen horns with fiberglass or plastic wood are barbarians who should be tossed into a pit with vipers.

A high percentage of mature ram horns are "broomed" or "rubbed." Often the horns of an old ram will have lost several inches at the tips. Sometimes the sheath of horn is broomed off down to the bony core. Various explanations have been given for this phenomenon. One writer has said that the horns are broomed off because the rams dig for roots, a statement about which I am skeptical. I have watched many hundreds of feeding rams but I have yet to see one digging for roots. In a recent article in another magazine, a writer who was apparently familiar only with bighorns wrote that the horns were broken and broomed off from fighting. Some believe the rams broom them by bumping them against rocks when they are feeding or traveling. Yet another theory is that the rams deliberately rub the points off their horns when the horns interfere with their side vision.

I think the rams broom their horns because of a variety of reasons. Sometimes the brooming is caused by a fall. I have mentioned the tremendous Dall ram my wife shot in the Yukon in 1963. One horn was 44 inches around the curve, the other slightly longer. However, the ram had apparently had a bad fall a few days before. About 4 inches of one horn was so badly broken it was about to fall off. When I saw the ram, the first thing I did was to wrap the end of the horn tightly with a handkerchief to prevent the break from being completed before we got the head to camp. That old ram had really taken a tumble. On the side where his horn was broken, the ram had some cracked and broken ribs, and the flesh on the shoulder and over the ribs was terribly bruised and discolored. Rams are surefooted animals but they live in rough and dangerous country, take many tumbles, and sometimes break legs or even fall to their deaths.

The fights the rams have certainly leave their marks on horns. I have seen many heads where the violence of the contact had knocked big chips out of horns. I have one head broken so badly about 12 inches up the horn from the base that the bone core shows through. I have also seen horns that had points plainly frayed and damaged by the vibration of striking heads. I am also sure that running rams often bump their horns against rocks and damage the tips.

However, I have seen many heads with horn tips rubbed off as smooth and round and even as if the job had been done with a file. There is no possible way the tips could have been smoothed off by fighting or by bumping accidentally against rocks. The writer who says the horn tips are always damaged by fighting also says the theory that a ram deliberately rubs his horns against rocks in order to improve his side vision gives the ram credit for more intelligence than he has. He adds that he knows no one who has ever seen a ram rubbing his horns against a rock.

I have seen this once. Back in the 1930s, I sat on a hillside in the San Francisco mountains of Sonora and watched an old ram below me and about 400 yards away rub the point of one horn against granite rock for fifteen or twenty minutes. The late A. A. Nichol, a University of Arizona professor of ecology who made the first survey of Arizona's desert sheep back in the 1930s, told me he had on several occasions seen rams rubbing their horn tips on rocks. So did the late Charlie Ren, a friend of mine who outfitted for desert sheep back in the 1930s. Old Charlie had spent years among the desert sheep and knew them as few men have ever done. Bob Housholder, Arizona sheep guide and writer, says he has seen rams rubbing the tips of their horns many times.

In my trophy room is a fairly extensive collection of sheep trophies of the four varieties of North American sheep recognized in the *Records of North American Big Game.* A couple of them, one a desert ram and the other a Rocky Mountain bighorn, have very close curls. Three, all Dalls, have heads of the argali type that pinch in close to the cheeks and then flare out. Another Dall has a rather close curl, as does one of the Stones. Others have what might be called medium curls.

Something that an observant person will quickly notice is that in every case where the ram's side vision has been blocked by the horn growth, the horn has been "broomed" or "rubbed," call it what you will. The close-curled horns of both the desert ram and the Rocky Mountain bighorn are rubbed down to make side vision possible. The Stone with the close-curled horns has likewise rubbed them off, as has the Dall. On the other hand, two big Dalls, one with 44-inch horns and one with 43⅝-inch horns, are of the argali type. Most horns of this type allow unobstructed side vision. In both cases, the horns of these thirteen-year-old rams have perfect points. Another Dall with 40-inch argali-type horns has one damaged point, but it was plainly done by striking a rock or by some other accident. There is no sign of deliberate rubbing. The closer the curl, the more the horns interfere with side vision, and the more the horns are rubbed.

Roy Hargreaves, the Alberta and British Columbia guide and outfitter with whom I shot my first Rocky Mountain bighorn, also told me he has seen rams rub the points of their horns. He said rams try always to keep the side vision of one eye clear. He spoke of "right-handed" and "left-handed" rams, depending on whether they had rubbed the right or the left horn down to clear the vision. This brooming or rubbing of horn tips to clear side vision occurs among Asiatic sheep as well as among North American sheep. Some varieties of *Ovis amon*, the big central-Asian argalis, have close-curl horns, and when these block the side vision, they are always broomed. On the other hand, the varieties of *amon* which have the characteristic argali-type horns usually have perfect points because the side vision is not blocked.

Back in the days before World War I, bighorn heads were judged to a great extent by the diameter of the bases. Hunters spoke of 15-inch, 16-inch, 17-inch, and even 18-inch rams. A ram that didn't have at least a 16-inch base was not considered much of a trophy. Many were the stories I read in my youth of those massive heads with 17- and 18-inch bases. However, they do not show up in the record book, and I can only conclude that they were incorrectly measured. I believe the hunters got those measurements by following the bases of the horns around, instead of going straight around with the tape. The current *Records of North American Big Game* shows one Rocky Mountain bighorn head with a 17⅛-inch base, another with a 17-inch base, a good many are 16 inches or slightly over. Some in the bighorn records are only 14 inches or even less. There may have been bighorn heads with bases that measured 18 inches when thoroughly dry, but I have never seen one. The largest base I have taken was on a desert ram. When fresh, the base was 17 inches. Now, more than thirty years later, it is 16¼ inches.

Today the most important measurement is the length of the horns. Instead of classifying horns by the bases, most sheep hunters classify by length and speak of 38-inch, 40-inch, or 45-inch heads. In the record book, heads are ranked by their scores. These are arrived at by adding the total of the length of both horns around the curls to the measurements of the circumferences of the quarters. A 40-inch head, for example, would be measured at each base, then 10 inches, 20 inches, and 30 inches from the bases. Some of the younger and possibly more scientific trophy hunters speak of heads according to their scores—a 185-point head, a 175-point head, etc.

To me, the most desirable feature in a Rocky Mountain or desert bighorn head is massiveness. I like broomed horns with the mass carried far out toward the tips. This is the classic and typical head for these sheep. The handsomest Stone and Dall heads are those of the argali type.

Some sheep heads shrink noticeably, some do not. Apparently, the shrinkage comes from the age and condition of the animal. This is true of all horned trophies. A greater kudu I shot in Tanzania in 1953 has shrunk from 54¼ inches to 52½ inches, but a 44¼-inch sable I shot the same year has not shrunk at all. One big Stone ram I took in 1946 had a 16-inch base and a 42½-inch curl when shot. It has shrunk down to just under 15 and 41½ inches. On the other hand, my best bighorn has hardly shrunk at all. But most horns shrink as they dry. That is why Boone & Crockett Club regulations require that a head be three months old before it is measured for the records, and also why some shifty fellows keep sheep heads in cold storage for the three months before they are measured.

I have been hunting North American sheep from Sonora to the Alaskan border off and on for nearly forty years, and I am not a bad judge of ram heads. I can generally judge a head to within plus or minus one inch. However, I have on occasions been fooled. A really big trophy head always looks big, and anyone who sees a ram with horns over 40 inches in length knows he is looking at a whopper.

When I am sizing up a head, I first notice if the horns seem massive. Then I check to see if the horns curve down below the jaw. If they do and if at the same time the points go up above the bridge of the nose, the head is well into the trophy class and well worth taking. If, in addition, the horns are heavily broomed and carry the weight out toward the tips, it is a hell of a head, well up in the records.

The popular terms a "complete curl" and a "three-quarters curl" do not mean much. I have seen many heads with complete curls that were not worth taking. The points may come up above the bridge of the nose, but the lower part of the horn above the point of the jaw means that the horns are short. On the other hand, there is a type of horn seen now and then among both desert and bighorn sheep that comes far back and makes a shallow curve. Such heads can go 40 inches, and yet come nowhere near the bridge of the nose. Now and then an experienced sheep hunter is fooled by a stunted ram. Once in the Yukon I shot a lone ram with a close-curled, broomed head which I thought would go about 38 inches. It went less than 35, but the ram was a small animal with a skull about 1½ inches shorter than that of a normal Dall. On another occasion, also in the Yukon, I shot a beautiful ram with horns of the argali type that came down below the jaw and went well above the bridge of the nose. I would have guessed 44 or 45 inches. Actually, it went less than 41—another small sheep. On the other hand, I have made many right-on-the-button estimates. One fine ram shot by a friend measured 46½ inches. I had guessed it as 47.

Most sheep hunters consider 40 inches as the dividing line between the good trophy head and the head that is in the top class. Horns of that length are much more common among the Stones and Dalls, but any head that scores 170 or above is an absolutely first-class trophy. Likewise, any head that is 40 inches around the curl, even though it does not score 170, or any head that measures 37 inches and is broomed. Actually, the head of any old ram is a good trophy.

Most game departments make legal the taking of any ram with a head that makes a three-quarters curl. The three-quarters rule, though enshrined by tradition, means almost nothing. I have seen many heads that could be considered to have three-quarters curls that come from immature rams that should never have been shot. I have also seen excellent heads of what I call the droopy type that would go 40 inches or above and not make a three-quarter curl.

The rule of the three-fourths curl has been responsible for shooting hundreds of rams as young as three and a half years. It has also resulted in a heavy take of rams in the prime of life—those from four to ten years old.

Sheep, particularly the desert and Rocky Mountain bighorns, are rare animals. I think they should be taken only for trophies and that only the old-timers should be shot. Rams over ten years old have done their breeding and have pretty well lived out their lives. Their broomed and broken old horns might just as well adorn the walls of someone's trophy room.

The head of any old ram is a trophy to be proud of—whether it measures 35 inches around the curl or 45. My own feeling is that mountain sheep should be put into a special category and that no ram under ten years old should be shot. I also think that no one should be allowed to hunt sheep without a guide, and that if a guide allows a hunter to take a ram less than ten years old, he should have his license revoked.

Idaho has found out, to its sorrow, that seasons on rams with "three-quarters curls" cannot be thrown open to all comers. That regulation means that almost anything can get by as a "legal ram." All manner of hunters, residents and nonresidents, swarmed into the sheep country centering around the Middle Fork of the Salmon River. Many of them were pretty eager and pretty green. Many simply wanted to be able to say they had shot a ram. One hunter I know is young, tough, enduring. He used to backpack into the sheep country, shoot the first ram he saw that he thought would pass as "legal." All have had curls that could be interpreted as "three-quarters." All were very young rams whose lives should have been before them and not one of them could be by any stretch of the imagination called a trophy. I fancy that many of these green hunters likewise shot ewes. At any rate, during the period when anyone who bought a sheep tag could hunt sheep, the Idaho herd was reduced 50 percent. Part of this can well be blamed on too much shooting of young rams, too much disturbance in the hills. The rule of the three-quarters curl has resulted in the average ram taken being about four years old!

The size of a ram's horns determines his status in the herd. Valerius Geist says that the ram with small horns gives way to the ram with large horns even though the ram with the large horns may be younger. As I have already recounted, Dr. Geist also says that the ram with large horns has a shorter life than the ram with smaller horns. His explanation is that the ram with large horns does more breeding, expends more energy in fighting and chasing other rams away from ewes. Consequently he enters the lean and hungry winter months thinner, more exhausted, and less able to survive cold and scanty fare. The ram with the largest horns will generally lead the bunch, and Geist says that the instinct of sheep is to follow the ram with the largest horns.

Geist quotes another study which says that the average set of horns and upper skull of mature bighorn rams that were winter-killed in various parts of the Rockies weighed 25 pounds. He also says that the largest head from Banff Park which he measured weighed 32 pounds, that the average set of record-class Stone-sheep horns with upper skull would weigh 24 to 26 pounds. A large bighorn head entire with scalp skinned back to the shoulders might well weigh 45 pounds. Some I have carried down steep mountains on my back by holding onto the neck portion of the scalp seemed tiresomely heavy, but at best such a head and scalp, though a welcome burden to the sheep hunter, is a weary one. Best way to carry a ram head down is to tie it to an Alaska pack board. In my younger days I once carried the hind quarter of a large Dall ram and both backstraps down a mountain to camp on a pack board. The head and scalp made a very awkward burden, as in addition to the meat I also had a pair of binoculars, a miniature camera, and a scope-sighted rifle.

Rams are rather belligerent creatures—toward each other, anyway. Valerius Geist says they fight primarily for dominance. They fight at all times of year. Two rams coming together sounds—to me, anyway—like the clicking of billiard balls.

Geist says the mildest form of blow a ram delivers is the butt. He says it is a "downward blow with the head, in which the chin is drawn in and the horns thrown forward and down."

What Geist calls a "clash" is the meeting of two rams. He says the rams try to strike with one horn. The ram rises on his hind legs. Then the ram's body starts to fall down and forward. As in the butt the chin is drawn in and the horns flung down and forward. The technique is to deliver the maximum foot-pounds of energy by utilizing forward and downward motions. It is like the delivery of a baseball pitcher who combines the forward movement of his body, the motion of his arm, and the snap of his wrist to get the maximum speed on the baseball.

From what I have observed I believe it is accidental if rams strike each other with the noses and the bases of their horns. The impact occurs farther up the horn. Often the horns of old rams are broken clear through to the core. This commonly happens with the horns of desert rams, probably because they are so dry. The horns of one old desert head I have is broken through to the core on one horn about 7 inches from the base and at 14 inches from the base. Many times horns are chipped out at the ledge 12 to 14 inches from the base—probably the portion that makes contact in clashes.

I have seen rams stand with their heads lowered and their horns touching. What the function of this ritual is I cannot say.

Once in Sonora on a little "bench" on a hillside I saw where a couple of rams had fought it out. The ground was torn up and there were several chunks of horn that had been broken off. Around the battle area in a circle were the tracks of rams that had apparently been spectators to the fight.

Rams are apt to wham into each other at any time. Geist says it is generally the ram lower on the pecking order who attacks the dominant ram. Rams strike each other with their front feet and also strike at ewes.

Rams also "horn" shrubs and small trees like young jackpines. I have seen horns with fresh pine gum on them. When they run through low brush like willows, dwarf birch, and alpine fir they get sap on their horns. This darkens in the sun and it picks up dust. Often the naturally yellow horns of Dall sheep are fairly dark because of this accumulation of sap and dirt.

The ram's heavy horns are his status symbol, his weapon, and his burden. I have seen old rams lying with their chins on stones or frost hummocks to ease their tired neck muscles.

12
The Grand Slam Caper

One afternoon in August 1946, I was riding along the bottom of a canyon cut into the rolling northern British Columbia tundra by a little creek named after an old trapper named Billy Nevis (pronounced Neeves). With me was my outfitter, the dean of the Stone-sheep guides, the late Frank Golata. Beside me rode a rather plump little doctor of exactly my age who practiced medicine in a small Illinois town called Carlyle.

I've told something about this hunt in the chapter on Stone sheep. I was on my first hunt for Stones. Dr. Wilson L. DuComb, my companion on the trip, was on his second. Doc and I were both sheep-hunting nuts, and like all sheep-hunting nuts we loved sheep, lofty peaks, high ridges, chill breezes, bright skies, and wild country. In those days, most American hunters could take sheep or leave them alone, and we were members of a very small fraternity.

Until that day I had never laid eyes on a Stone sheep, but I was excited because we were beginning a long pack trip that was to take us back into the wilderness country at the heads of the Muskwa and Prophet rivers. Later in the hunt, we pitched our tents in the same spot where L. S. Chadwick had camped in 1936 when he took the world-record Stone, the greatest sheep trophy ever collected in North America and one of the greatest in the world.

Nevis Creek, a noisy, shallow little stream with occasional deep pools full of lazy Dolly Varden trout, fishtailed back and forth from wall to wall of the canyon it had cut. I suppose we had to cross it thirty times that day as we rode downstream toward the Besa River.

We were a long way from mountains then, but sheep like canyons almost as much as mountains and I was half expecting as we rode along to see some Stones. Almost as soon as we had hit the canyon, we had found tracks.

Presently Golata pulled up his horse and pointed. Possibly 225 yards ahead and maybe 250 feet above the creek, seven Stone rams lay on a ledge calmly watching us. In those days, the limit on sheep was two north of the Edmonton–Prince Rupert line of the Canadian National Railroad. If one of these rams was good enough to collect I would assure myself a trophy. I could be more particular on the next one.

I got off my horse to glass them, sat down in the sand with a scope-sighted .270 in my lap. All were typical Stones with gray heads and necks, brown-black saddles, black tails, white rumps. All were old rams. The one that caught my eye was an ancient one with heavy, broomed, and close-curled horns, a type about which I have always been sentimental. He was an excellent ram and on that forty-five-day trip, I saw few better.

Shooting uphill from the sitting position isn't the steadiest way in the world to hold a rifle, but the crosswires looked pretty good when I touched the shot off. All the rams jumped to their feet at the shot and took off down the ledge, but after running maybe 30 or 40 yards, the ram I had shot at tumbled off the ledge and fell with a tremendous splash right into Nevis Creek. He had been hit a bit too far back.

That was my first Stone. Later on in the trip, I got another that was No. 10 in two record books. I didn't know it at the time, but that Nevis Canyon ram had me the fourth or fifth hunter ever to collect all four varieties of North American sheep—bighorn, desert, Stone, and Dall. At the time I had no idea whether I was the fifth or the five hundredth. All that I knew was that I was fascinated by sheep and by sheep hunting.

The term "Grand Slam" was fastened on the feat of collecting all varieties of sheep by my good friend the late Grancel Fitz, New York writer, advertising photographer, big wheel in the Boone & Crockett Club, trophy hunter, record compiler, and student of hunting literature. Around 1949–50, Fitz wrote for *True* magazine an article called "A Grand Slam on Sheep." It concerned a successful hunt he had made for Dall sheep in the mountains surrounding Kusawa Lake in the Yukon. The Dall he secured on that hunt completed his collection of all four varieties of North American sheep. Previously, he had shot a good desert ram in the Cobabai mountains of northern Sonora, a bighorn in Alberta, and a Stone in northern British Columbia on the Prophet River downstream from where L. S. Chadwick shot the No. 1 Stone and from where I later collected the ram that was for a time No. 10. Fitz was a seeker of records. Apparently he was by no means fascinated by sheep hunting. When he got his four varieties, his "Grand Slam," he quit. As far as I know, at the time of his death some years ago he had not ever set foot on another sheep mountain. Another of his ambitions was to collect an example of every species of North American big game. I understand that he accomplished this feat. The idea of collecting one each of every variety of game found in any country or on any continent brings me down with an acute attack of the vapors. I have, for example, about as much desire to bump off a tapir or a musk ox or for that matter a woodland caribou as I have to collect a giant Costa Rican banana-eating fruit bat—if there is such a thing.

In his "Grand Slam" article, Fitz said the legendary Charles Sheldon was the first man to collect specimens of all North American sheep. Sheldon hunted sheep in the Grand Canyon of Arizona and in the Sierra Rosario in Sonora about seventy years ago. Where he got bighorns I cannot say, but he collected many Stones and Dalls in the Yukon and Alaska and, I believe, in British Columbia. He is the author of *The Wilderness of the Upper Yukon,* which I have mentioned several times before. It is the definitive book on the distribution and color variations in the thinhorn sheep. It has long been out of print, difficult to find, and expensive. However, the chart is included in this volume.

The second man to take all varieties of this continent's sheep, Fitz wrote, was Col. Wilson Potter, a wealthy Philadelphian with whom I exchanged a few letters in the last years of his life. The good colonel shot, among other things, the antelope that was for a time the No. 1 pronghorn in the world records and is now tied for No. 2. For those interested in the history of North American big-game hunting, Col. Potter wrote me that he shot this antelope in 1889 in the desert north of Oracle, Arizona, in an area where I have hunted jackrabbits, coyotes, and quail. When I moved from Arizona in 1948, there were still a good many desert mule deer and a few antelope there. Curiously, Potter's great buck was a desert or Sonora antelope, a species which generally does not grow large horns. I know that Potter hunted desert sheep in Sonora, possibly the same year he shot the antelope. He may well have hunted desert sheep in Arizona as well, because in 1899 there were many sheep in most of the mountains around Tucson.

The third man to collect the four species was Dr. Wilson L. DuComb, the general practitioner from Carlyle, Illinois, who was my companion on that hunt for Stone sheep in the Prophet and Muskwa country in 1946. He had hunted in that general area with Golata previously. At that time, he had no idea he was the third man to achieve the Grand Slam. He completed it in Mexico, hunting with the late Charlie Ren some time just before World War II. Through connections in Mexico City, I had obtained his license for him.

The Ernst von Lengerke, a New Yorker who was a partner in a Manhattan sporting-goods store called Von Lengerke & Detmold and which was absorbed by Abercrombie & Fitch, is listed as the fourth person to secure all species. Grancel Fitz listed me as the fifth. Actually, von Lengerke and I completed the slam at almost exactly the same time and may actually have done it the same day, I in British Columbia, he in the Yukon. When Fitz wrote the *True* article which started the whole Grand Slam business, he did not know about Dr. DuComb, but he soon corrected the omission. Fitz himself is No. 6. My old pal the late N. Myles Brown, a pneumatic-tool tycoon of Cleveland, Ohio, and the beloved companion of several fine hunts, was the seventh. He got his desert sheep in the Sierra del Chino in Sonora on a hunt I arranged for him. No. 8 was Herb Klein, who completed the slam with my friend George Parker as a guide in the Sierra Blanca of western Sonora on a license I obtained for him through George Pasquel, member of a famous and influential Mexico City family. I list all this for the sake of the record. The late Red Early went along on that hunt with Herb and became the No. 9 slammer. This was in 1952.

When Grancel Fitz wrote that piece on his Yukon hunt and coined the phrase "Grand Slam," he knew not what he wrought. It struck hundreds of hunters as being the most prestigious caper a big-game hunter could pull off. Various stories and articles in outdoor magazines publicized the Grand Slam. It became the Holy Grail of American hunting, and dozens of people started working toward it. About 260 people claim to have shot all varieties of North American sheep. The term "Grand Slam" and the attendant publicity have made the mountain sheep the most prestigious North American trophy. In my time, I have written a good many stories of sheep hunts and articles on sheep. Some of the boom in sheep hunting may well be laid to my doorstep. I hope that when I arrive at the Pearly Gates, old St. Peter does not hold it against me. He may well do so—and if he does, I shall not argue. I'll simply bow my head, turn around, and go down below where I belong!

Bob Housholder, an Arizona writer and part-time sheep guide, has formed a club with membership restricted to those who have got the Grand Slam. It is practically his private property. He keeps the records and sends out several newsletters a year. Members are entitled to wear a shoulder patch showing the head of a Dall ram and the legend "Grand Slam—North American Sheep." Housholder collects $20 a year from each member. One taxidermy firm has created a gold pin with four sheep heads alleged to represent the various species. Membership in the club is supposed to be a matter of great prestige, and some lads who fell into the clutches of the law for poaching desert sheep gave as an excuse their desire to belong to the club.

To me, all this whoopla is a very sad thing. I wish Grancel Fitz hadn't started it all. The old-timers hunted sheep because they loved sheep, because they loved to be up on those high windswept ridges where they shared the sheep pastures with the sheep, the grizzly, the hoary marmot, the soaring eagle. When they brought back a ram trophy, they were not seeking honor and prestige—they were bringing back memories of icy winds fragrant with fir and balsam, of the smell of sheep beds and arctic willow, of tiny, perfect alpine flowers, gray slide rock, velvet sheep pastures. The old-timers had sheep and sheep country in their blood. In his last years, my old sheep-hunting companion Myles Brown suffered a stroke and could hardly get around. Nevertheless, every year he went to the Yukon mountains he loved so much, hired a pack outfit, set up camp in beautiful sheep country, drank in the smells of willows and water, watched the sheep with binoculars and spotting scope. I know how the old-timers felt because I knew many of them and am one of them myself. I am sure that many young sheep enthusiasts feel the same way.

However, today, alas, many sheep hunters apparently care little for sheep and even less for sheep country. They are after glory and prestige and the sooner they can get the tiresome business over with and slap those ram heads on the wall, the better they like it. In an old issue of the Grand Slam Club's list of those who have made it, I find a proud notation behind one man's name that he collected all four species in eighty-two days. Whoopee! A more recent Grand Slammer who got the big-game-hunting bug late in life, when he was loaded, managed to collect all four species in thirty days! He raced hither and yon, chartered planes and helicopters, bought up guides and outfitters. I understand that every ram cost him over $10,000. He is the Instant Sheep Hunter. It took me well over ten years but I enjoyed every minute of it.

As a staff writer for an outdoor magazine, I got many letters every year from hunters who wanted to undertake the collection of a Grand Slam. I had to discourage most of them. The feat becomes tougher to accomplish—particularly to accomplish honestly—by the year. Permits for the desert and bighorn sheep are difficult to get and in some cases almost impossible.

Back in the days when I was hunting desert sheep, I could always secure a special permit. I had influential Mexican friends, and in Mexico if you know the right people or have a lot of money you can get a permit to do practically anything. I didn't have any money but I did have friends in Mexico and at the University of Arizona who could put in a word for me. I also knew the Sonora sheep country and knew enough Spanish to get by.

I must pause here to tell a story. A wealthy European of my acquaintance found himself in Mexico City some years ago. He decided to see if he could not obtain a sheep permit. He went to the proper office, saw the man who could issue the special permits, and said if the permit were issued he would be glad to donate $500 in American currency to the official's favorite charity. The official indignantly refused the poorly disguised bribe, told the European sportsman that he was an honest man. The European was a man of the world. He sighed, dug down deeper, came up with $2,500, asked the official if a donation of that size would interest him. The official pocketed the 25 C-notes, wrote out the permit. Honesty, like everything else, is something that should be taken in moderation!

For the would-be Grand Slammer, the desert sheep is probably the toughest nut to crack. For the past several years Mexico has held an open season on special permit in certain areas in Lower California. A few legal rams are also taken in Sonora. Permits are very expensive. Arizona has a slowly declining desert-sheep herd that numbers around 2,500 with the animals scattered over dozens of dry, rugged ranges in the state, and a concentration in a couple of federal reserves. In a recent open season, the heaviest ram ever taken in Arizona was shot within sight of Tucson in the Santa Catalina Mountains. However, Arizona issues only a small number of permits and of these nonresidents are eligible for only 10 percent. In 1971, 915 nonresidents applied for the quota of eight permits. However, since Arizona had its first desert-sheep season about twenty years ago, eighty-six nonresidents had surmounted the desert-sheep hurdle there by 1971. Today I understand that the chance of a nonresident drawing a desert-sheep permit in any one year is less than one in one hundred. Nevada has a fair herd of Nelson's desert sheep, but there are many dozens of applicants for each permit. A member of the Arizona game commission told me that every permit for Arizona bighorns could be sold for $5,000!

California has a sizable population of desert sheep, but it has never had an open season. With the anti-hunting sentiment so strong in California, I am sure that the sky would split right open and game department officials would be torn asunder by wild horses if a limited open season were recommended. Utah has some desert sheep and has held limited seasons for a few residents only. New Mexico has taken a few desert sheep from the Hatchet Mountains of the southwestern part of the state and also a few Rocky Mountain bighorns.

All in all, the chances today of any one man being able to collect a desert bighorn are about as good as his chances of being elected president of the United States or winning the Irish Sweepstakes. Actually, an individual probably has more chance of becoming a movie star or inheriting a million dollars.

The bighorn situation is better—but not much. Colorado has a considerable number of bighorns but nonresidents are not permitted to draw for sheep permits. Idaho has somewhere around 2,000 bighorns centered around the Middle Fork of the Salmon River, one of the roughest pieces of country on earth. However, for a good number of years anyone resident or nonresident who had a general hunting license was allowed to hunt sheep on purchasing for a nominal sum a special permit. Rams were badly shot down, total sheep numbers declined, and Idaho has gone back to the limited-permit system. Wyoming has a pretty fair sheep herd with sheep doing well in some areas, and 25 percent of the sheep permits are reserved for nonresidents. I believe the man who must have a bighorn has the best chance of getting a permit and connecting with a ram in Wyoming. The Wyoming sheep country is very lovely and there are excellent sheep outfitters and guides in the state. I have shot only one Wyoming bighorn, but I have seen a good many rams when I was hunting elk there. Once I knocked off a big 6-point bull and two fine rams I had not seen came tearing around a point. The rams and the bull had been bedded down on the same shale slide.

Montana has a few very tough areas where anyone can obtain a permit to hunt sheep and also some areas where trophy rams are reasonably plentiful and permits not too difficult to obtain. However, I am told that 1,640 hunters applied for forty permits in 1973 in the Sun River area. Montana is on the edge of the area in southwestern Alberta and southeastern British Columbia that has produced the largest bighorn heads and the heaviest sheep. An acquaintance of mine who is young, tough, and an experienced sheep hunter shot a 43½-inch bighorn in Montana in a recent year, and I heard of another ram that went 44 inches around the curves and will place in the top ten of the records.

Washington has made successful transplants of California bighorn from British Columbia into various sections where similar sheep were once present but have become extinct. However, the chance of anyone's obtaining a Washington permit is about as good as his chance of hitching a ride on a spaceship to the moon. In 1971 there were 3,500 applicants for seventeen permits to hunt Washington bighorn.

The status of the bighorn in Canada may be better than it is in the United States—but not much. In 1972 for the first time, sheep hunting by nonresidents was prohibited in the southern half of the Alberta Rockies. The species is preserved by the great string of parks along the crest of the Rockies. Beginning with Glacier Park in Montana next to the Canadian border, there is Waterton Park in Alberta, then Banff, and Jasper. The best bighorn trophies taken today are rams that have matured in these parks and are shot around the edges. Elsewhere, the Canadian Rockies are in a frenzy of exploitation—oil exploration, lumbering, grazing. Roads have been thrust back into the mountains, and wherever the automobile and the meat hunter can go, the sheep are shot out and eventually disappear. I have seen many horns of two-, three-, and four-year-old rams tacked up on barns in British Columbia and Alberta. Something over a decade ago, British Columbia lost a large proportion of its bighorn herd because the forestry department leased out the winter bighorn range for grazing. When the snows came, the sheep went down to their traditional range and starved. The man ambitious to take a Grand Slam is going to find a trophy bighorn tougher and tougher to come by.

As we have seen in the chapters on the Stone and the Dall, the thinhorn sheep present fewer problems, as this is written. However, northern British Columbia, the Yukon, and Alaska are developing rapidly. A railroad up the Rocky Mountain trench in British Columbia is under construction—and this is right in the midst of the Stone-sheep country. New roads in northern British Columbia and the Yukon are making new areas accessible to prospectors and automobile hunters. Today most trophy hunters are flown into one of the many lakes in Stone and Dall country. Often they are hunting sheep the day they get in. Many of them, alas, want to get the unpleasant business of hunting in the boondocks over with as soon as possible. Because of the ease of access from the great number of lakes, these northern sheep are vulnerable. The airplane has cheapened and revolutionized sheep hunting. It is against the law to use a plane to scout for game, but I am told the law is commonly ignored. I have heard of many instances where small planes with doughnut tires have landed hunters above the sheep on smooth ridges. Then the guide and hunter hunt down. Later the plane picks men and trophies up. The use of helicopters is even worse. The desire of the instant big-game hunters to knock off a trophy ram and get the hell out as quickly as possible has given rise to the price-tag system of hunting. It is particularly prevalent in Alaska. The outfitter guarantees a ram or a grizzly for a flat fee, usually substantial. Go in, get the trophy, get out. Bingo! Just like buying a can of corn at the supermarket. Price is plainly marked and satisfaction guaranteed.

Seeking the prestige of the Grand Slam has given rise to a tremendous amount of lying, poaching, and cheating in all sheep areas but particularly for the desert bighorn. One year I went to the annual award dinner of the Boone & Crockett Club. One of the prizewinning trophies was a very good set of desert ram horns on a very small scalp that had been stretched to its limits in mounting. The answer, of course, is that the head had been picked up somewhere and mounted on a papier-mâché form with the scalp of an immature ram. How the judges could have been fooled I'll never know. I have seen several such mounts. A prominent taxidermist has told me that a high proportion of desert-sheep trophies sent to him for mounting by various outfitters were picked-up ram horns with scalps from ewes or immature rams.

One famous trophy hunter who has now passed to his reward is listed by Housholder as having more than one Grand Slam. After his death, this man's best friend told me that the man had never shot a desert bighorn, that when he hunted desert sheep he sent his guide up with a rifle and the trophies were brought down for his approval. Desert-sheep hunting is very hard work. Another trophy hunter who was enormously rich and had a beautiful wife spent every night in a luxurious Alaskan hotel. Every morning he and the doll he was married to were flown by float plane to a lake surrounded by sheep mountains, where tents, camp chairs, cold drinks, and cook and guides awaited. There the man held hands with his lovely while he watched sheep and grizzly with a spotting scope. When he saw what he wanted, he sent an Indian guide up for it. In another case an acquaintance of mine told me of two magnificent rams he had taken. He described the hunts in breathtaking detail. Some years later, I chanced to run into the outfitter and guide who had taken him out. I innocently inquired where this mighty hunter had polished off those splendid old rams. They laughed so hard they almost fell off their bar stools. One head, they told me, was a pick-up that had been given to him by an old trapper, and he had bought the other from an Indian who had found the ram where it had been killed by a spring snow slide.

The poaching of desert sheep is widespread. I am told that it is not very common in Arizona now, but back in the 1920s and 1930s, it was routine for the lawless to hunt Arizona sheep for trophies and meat. One Arizona outfitter whom I've mentioned before advertised Mexican sheep hunts but did all his hunting in Arizona. One rather devious citizen of California has bragged that in recent years he has shot several rams in Arizona along the lower Colorado River. Another Grand Slammer who has more than a few dollars to rub one against the other knocked off his desert bighorn in Utah. Even today, Nevada game officials believe poaching by trophy hunters is a significant factor in keeping down the numbers of Nelson's desert bighorn.

A man long in the desert-sheep-poaching business is Hugo Castellanos, a Mexican national who until fairly recently lived in a suburb of San Diego, California. In December 1971, Castellanos was arrested by officers of the Fish & Wildlife Service. An Associated Press story with a December 16 Los Angeles dateline quotes the Service as saying that over the years Castellanos had taken into Lower California 200 sheep-poaching American trophy hunters. The latest word is that Castellanos jumped his bail and is now operating from the Mexican side of the border.

I know one man who completed his Grand Slam with Castellanos. I understand that Castellanos guaranteed every client a trophy. In order to be able to do this, he kept Mexican hunters out in the mountains looking for trophy rams. When they shot them, they brought the heads and scalps to Castellanos, who had a warehouse on the Mexican side. If the client didn't manage to shoot a ram, he took one of these heads home. The fee was $1,000 for the first head. If the client wanted to be a real desert-sheep hunter, he could get a second head for $500 and a third for $250. That's merchandising!

Most famous example of barefaced poaching of desert sheep was the Swanson case in California. Swanson was a California taxidermist who for a high fee took trophy-hungry hunters out to poach rams in the Anza-Borrego State Park and other isolated areas in the California desert. Swanson pleaded guilty. Swanson kept good records and a considerable number of hunters had their desert-sheep heads seized and in addition had to pay fines. One of Swanson's clients was about to receive a prestigious award given to outstanding big-game hunters, but it was learned that state as well as federal authorities were going to put the arm on him at the ceremony. He landed in California, was warned, turned around and went back to the place he had come from.

Some months before I wrote these lines I was approached by a man in the sheep-hunting business who had a keen eye for a buck.

"I've seen pictures of that 44-inch Dall ram your wife shot," he said. "What do you think she'd take for it?"

"Why do you ask?"

"I know a guy who is trying to class up his head collection. He wants to have heads of all four species over 40 inches. The old bastard's loaded. He'd be willing to pay well for it."

"Like what?" I asked.

"Like five G's."

"Hell," I said. "We spent that much on the trip!"

"I think he'll go ten!" he said.

"Will he put a brass plate beside it saying: 'Shot by Eleanor O'Connor and purchased for $10,000'?" I asked.

"Don't make me laugh!" he said. "I've got a cracked lip!"

Bob Housholder, keeper of the records of the Grand Slam, told me in 1971 that over 230 people claimed to have collected all four varieties of North American wild sheep. It is a Big Deal! Several have now had the honor of knocking off all four varieties in one season. I note that seven women had taken the Grand Slam. I heard somewhere that one lad of seventeen or eighteen had done it, all, I believe, in one season. One man says he has collected ten Grand Slams.

I have seen some Grand Slam collections with not a single head that was a trophy—all little rams from five to seven years old that when they were knocked off had useful lives before them.

When most of this chapter came out as an article in *Outdoor Life* I got more mail on it than on any article I had ever done in my thirty-five years with that worthy magazine. Most of the letters I got approved of my sentiments, but I made many of the Instant Hunters sore and a lot of flak went caroming around in sheep-hunting circles. One outfitter wrote me that the majority of his clients wanted to get in, knock off the first fairly respectable ram they saw, and then get home to the Old Salt Mine, the Little Woman, the Kiddies, and the Boys at the Elks' Club. One Grand Slammer quoted in the club newsletter was furious because outfitters wouldn't agree to seven-to-ten-day (boom, boom, in-and-out) sheep hunts.

Since this flak was falling around and the Instant Hunters were moaning and nursing their scars, Bob Housholder has "purified" the membership of the Grand Slam Club. Members who have taken desert rams must prove that they took them over twenty-five years ago when a little fudging did not count or that they shot the rams with legal permits in Mexico, or in Nevada, Arizona, or Utah. The club now has over 150 presumably legal and honest members. Furthermore, old Bob will sell Grand Slammers for a mere five bucks certificates of their honesty and purity. These are suitable for framing.

I love sheep hunting! I love sheep country from the hot, barren mountains of Sonora to slanting sheep pastures far above timberline in northern British Columbia and the Yukon. In the days when hunters packed into wilderness areas, climbed, sweated, looked over enough sheep to get outstanding rams, shot their own, I thought it the greatest field sport in the world. It is still a great sport but the Instant Sheep Hunters out for prestige and the crooked outfitters out for the fast buck are making it stink pretty bad around the edges!

13
The Sheep Hunter's Clothes and Equipment

Some people have odd notions about sheep hunting. One very rich but elderly gentleman wrote that he would like to get a good trophy ram and asked me to recommend an outfitter who would take him into an area where he could hunt from a jeep. Another correspondent likewise wanted an outstanding ram but he disliked living in a tent and wanted a sheep area where he could stay in a steam-heated motel with a tub bath, not a shower.

Others who have seen fanciful sheep-hunting pictures by imaginative artists are convinced that sheep hunting should be undertaken only by alpinists and that sheep occupy country of snow and solid rock that is practically indistinguishable from the summit of Mt. Everest. Sheep hunting usually takes some physical labor and even some discomfort. Now and then a sheep hunter will get himself into situations where he might break a leg or even his neck, but sheep usually inhabit country where though the climbing is tiresome and even exhausting it is not dangerous. A couple of times I have been in situations where there was a possibility that I might injure myself or even get killed, but both times it was in the desert mountains of Sonora where the sheep inhabit more rugged country than they do in the north.

The sheep hunter who is going into the north country should choose his clothes with the knowledge that he will not only encounter changes of temperature in the course of his hunt but may also encounter great change in a single day. He should be equipped for dry weather and wet weather, fairly warm weather and weather that can be bitterly cold.

In 1956 I went on a thirty-day pack trip in the Yukon with Bill Rae and two other hunters. We started out on September 1, with a pack string from Aishishik Lake, which is about four hours' drive by automobile from Whitehorse, and headed for Prospector Mountain in the Dawson Range. The first week or so it was frosty at night and hot at midday, so hot that I was somewhat too warm in long wool underwear, cotton pants, and wool shirt. When we got to the country where we hunted sheep I would start out on horseback in the morning wearing long underwear, wool shirt, pullover sweater, and usually a medium-weight stag shirt. Mornings were frosty, but in the middle of the day in an area sheltered from the wind, I would be comfortable with only the wool shirt. I would usually leave the stag shirt, which I wore over the shirt and sweater, on the horse when we tied them up to begin our climb. Sometimes I would leave the sweater on the horse too.

My guide and I would try to get off the sheep mountain and back to our horses while we still had a half-hour or so of daylight. However, we were usually around two hours from camp on horseback, and by the time we got in it would be dark and I would be wearing everything I had on and still shivering. Later when I went out I would start out with a down jacket instead of the wool stag shirt.

Ten years before, in 1946, I was on a long pack trip to the head of the Muskwa and Prophet rivers in northern British Columbia with Frank Golata as an outfitter. We took horses out of camp to ride to the hunting area only one day. The rest of the time we used what my Kentucky grandfather used to call shanks' mare—our feet. As I have recounted already, I shot an outstanding Stone ram on a high series of rolling uplands known as the Prophet Bench about 3,000 feet above the Prophet River. When we left camp that morning there was heavy frost on the ground. I wore long wool underwear, a fairly heavy wool shirt over a Pendleton wool shirt of medium weight, wool pants, and two pairs of wool socks, one light and one fairly heavy, inside logger boots with hobnails. My hat was a wide-brimmed fur felt job of the 10-gallon type. I carried by a ⅞-inch Whelen-type sling a .270 on an engraved commercial Mauser action barreled by Bill Sukalle and stocked in French walnut by the late Bob Owen. The scope was a Weaver K-4. My binocular was a 9×35 Bausch & Lomb and I carried a Zeiss Contax camera. Golata wore a "Trapper Nelson" packboard and in a sack on it he carried our lunches and a length of light rope to tie the sheep head on with—if I got a sheep. Golata also carried in his packsack an Argus 20× spotting scope and tripod.

When we started out on the long climb there was a heavy frost on the ground and I was uncomfortably cold. The day was bright and clear and from about eleven o'clock until around three-thirty, when we started back with the head and meat of a fine ram, I was uncomfortably warm in my long johns and two shirts. We didn't get off the mountain and on the trail to camp until after dark. When we hit the welcome warmth of the cook tent I was shivering with cold.

On hunts for northern sheep from bighorns to Dalls I have never carried a canteen, as the hunter in the northern mountains can usually count on an icy little stream, a pothole in the tundra above timberline, or the seepage from a snowbank. If the guide is an Indian and if he and the hunter are not in the presence of game, the guide will usually manage to produce a blackened tin can with a wire handle and some tea and sugar in filthy bags. Hot tea tastes pretty good up in those chilly mountains.

The sheep seasons in northern British Columbia and the Yukon open August 1. The hunter can run into some pretty warm weather when he steps off the plane at Watson Lake, Fort St. John, or Whitehorse. If he packs into the sheep country he may be pretty warm on the lowland trails. In camps around timberline he will generally find pleasant days and chilly nights. However, the sheep hunter should be prepared for just about any kind of weather. On an August hunt in the Pelly Mountains near the Northwest Territories in 1949 a very wet and cold July had been followed by a very warm and dry August. I had long wool underwear and wool pants with me but I never wore them. All the time my hunting and traveling uniform was light underwear, wool shirt, cotton khaki pants—the same clothes that I had worn to hunt sheep in the Sonora Desert in November and December. Even in zero weather Charles Sheldon wore gabardine pants and light underwear.

As you have probably gathered by now the weather in the northern sheep country is changeable and unpredictable. From the first of August on the mountain hunter can encounter rain, snow, bright warm days, cold, raw overcast days. He will often run into heavy snow by the middle of August, and if he is hunting after the first of September at least one good snowstorm can be expected and should be planned for.

The last week in September and the first week or so in October can be bitterly cold. On the 1956 trip which I have mentioned and which began on September 1, the last ten days of September were very cold. There was about a foot of snow on the ground and at night the temperature went around zero. The creeks froze so hard that the packhorses could walk across on the ice. At our camp at what was known as Dry Pass our water bucket in the tent froze solid every night. As far as I know no one had ever camped at Dry Pass to hunt sheep. When we were there in 1956 Bill Rae and Fred Huntington were after caribou. Red Cole had gone on over a high mountain pass a couple thousand feet above timberline to hunt for moose in a valley in the Ruby Range. Some years later my wife and I camped at Dry Pass and hunted some promising-looking mountains where no one had ever hunted sheep. My wife knocked over the ancient Dall that won her a Boone & Crockett award. It was not particularly cold up on the mountain the day she shot the sheep, but a wind was blowing and my poor wife almost froze. The "chill factor" must have been formidable!

But to get back to that freezing week in late September 1956. On that trip we had a bumbling, inefficient, drunken cook. When the main camp followed Red Cole and his guide over the high pass to the Ruby Range we didn't get started until ten-thirty and the cook had not put up lunches. When we got to the campsite I was half frozen and starving. Red's guide had just brought off a frying pan full of bannock. I ate a big chunk soggy with butter and drank a cup of hot coffee. Nothing I have ever eaten tasted better.

As I have said in the chapter on hunting desert sheep, the best footwear for hunting in dry rocky Sonora are light shoes with 6- or 8-inch tops and substantial composition soles to protect the feet. In the much wetter country in the northern mountains the sheep hunter needs soles that will dig in more. When I first started hunting in Canada the standard boot worn by the Alberta sheep guides was a modification of the oil-tanned logger boot worn by lumbermen. These boots were generally of somewhat lighter construction and have round-headed Hungarian hobnails instead of the lumberman's calks. The nails stick to the steep, grassy hillsides the hunter has to climb. They also hold well on wet rock because the nails catch in the little bumps and cracks in the rock. The stout soles protect the feet from bruises. Boots for use in the north should have 8-inch tops. Wearing them the hunter can walk through little creeks and rills without shipping water. These boots are not waterproof. If exposed to water or melting snow for a long time they will eventually let water through. But they are extremely water-resistant.

As ordered by lumbermen these boots have rather high heels which most city dwellers find a bit awkward. Best is a compromise between the ordinary low heel on a street shoe and the high heel worn by lumbermen. These boots can be bought ready-made but it is best to order them made to the exact fit by the White Shoe Company of Spokane, Washington, or Pierre Paris, Vancouver, British Columbia. These boots will just about last a lifetime of fall hunting. I have a pair which I purchased from White in 1949. I have used them on many sheep hunts and I even wear them on pheasant hunts in Idaho and Washington when the ground gets frosty. I have had places sewed up where the thread has rotted, otherwise they have needed no repairs. A couple of times each year I heat some neat's-foot oil, warm the boots, and apply the oil with a brush. On a pack trip I take along a bottle of neat's-foot oil or some other dubbin. Once the hunter gets used to the weight of these boots he finds them very comfortable and they support and protect the feet.

Since the 1940s many hunters have been wearing boots with lugged soles. Of these the "Vibram" brand is the best known. I have a pair of light boots with 8-inch tops and Vibram soles which I have found excellent for sheep hunting. I have never used them in wet weather. How they will stick to wet rocks I cannot say. I would not use them in the desert myself, although some hunters do use them. I would prefer a slightly lighter shoe.

For snow I have worn the L. L. Bean "Maine Hunting Boots" with rubber bottoms and 8-inch leather tops. These must be worn with a thick felt insole. Extra felt inner soles should be taken along, so one pair can be drying. For snow something like this is a necessary evil. This boot is slippery and gives no support to the feet. It is all right for level ground but I would hesitate to do any serious climbing when wearing a pair.

Best for keeping the feet dry and fairly warm, and yet enabling the wearer to do some climbing, are probably the silicone-tanned boots insulated by foam rubber between the leather lining and the outer portion of the boot. With lug soles of the Vibram type these boots, though heavy, can be used fairly well for climbing.

For plain cold weather the rubber "insulated boot" is probably the best. They keep cold out pretty well but they also keep moisture in. They are waterpooof but clumsy.

In very cold weather and the "dry" snow in northern British Columbia and the Yukon the Indians and the white trappers wear for use on snowshoes two or three pairs of wool socks and over them smoke-tanned moosehide mukluks.

As a usual thing the weather is not cold enough during the hunting season in the north for insulated boots, but it is not a bad idea to take a pair along just in case. Nor is it so warm that khaki pants are more comfortable than wool. I like wool pants of medium weight "stagged" (meaning cut off a couple inches shorter than street pants) and kept up with suspenders rather than a belt. If a belt is worn it should not be tight. It can be used to carry a case for sunglasses, a small camera, or a leather cartridge box.

I like to take three wool shirts of a neutral color. Like most mammals, sheep are supposed to be colorblind but they see contrast. I can wear two and still have one shirt hanging up to dry. I take three "union suits" of lightweight underwear of Australian lamb's wool. I take six pairs of socks of pure wool, half short socks of the "athletic" type and half long. I will usually wear one pair of short socks and one pair of long ones. I always take a half-dozen large bandana handkerchiefs. In chilly winter weather one around my neck and tucked down into my shirt keeps the cold and wind from my neck.

If the northern hunter goes out from camp on a day that looks even slightly like rain he should tie rain gear on the saddle back of the cantle. When I first started hunting in Canada the standard piece of rain gear was a big yellow saddle slicker that covered the wearer from neck to ankles. Today, the favorite rain outfit consists of a pair of waterproof pants of rubberized fabric and a jacket of the same material. The pants keep the hunter dry but they are bulky, clumsy to walk in, and often scare a skittish horse. On threatening-looking hunting days I simply take the jacket and leave the pants in camp. If I have to make a long ride in the rain with a pack string I take the pants too.

I always wear a broad-brimmed hat to keep the snow and rain off my glasses. Anyone who is dependent on glasses for good vision should take a second pair. Those with eyes sensitive to light should take tinted glasses to wear in case there is a lot of glare on snow. Even during the first two weeks of August nights can get pretty nippy in timberline sheep camps. I like a medium-weight down sleeping bag. With this I take two medium-weight wool blankets. I put one over the air mattress and lay the down bag on top. In case of very cold weather I fold the second blanket, put it inside the bag, and have one thickness over me and one under. An 8-by-8-foot or 8-by-10-foot waterproof canvas tarp should be taken. The tarp is used as a ground cloth in camp. If an outfit is on the trail, camp is often made on wet ground, and such a tarp is indispensable. The outfitter has extra tarps used as pack covers which he will furnish for ground cloths. However, these are usually old and full of holes and are not waterproof. Plastic ground cloths are waterproof but they do not breathe and should never be taken. I learned that the way I learn most things—the hard way. A friend once gave me a nylon ground cloth that was waterproofed with plastic. The moisture from my body did not escape and condensed on the ground cloth. My sleeping bag was wet most of the time. I always take a down pillow and an extra pillowcase. Some like inflatable rubber pillows but they give me the creeps. Down sleeping bag and air mattress should be of good quality. There is really no substitute for down for weather ranging from chilly to bitterly cold. On most trips, as I have said, I take a down bag of medium weight along with a couple of blankets. If I am to be out after September 1, however, I take a heavy-duty 90-by-90-inch robe. I have slept in such a robe in perfect comfort with the temperature below zero. Often I have had heavy frost form where my breath struck the edge of the bag, but inside I was warm.

In the 1970s there are few long pack trips in the sheep country. Instead the hunters fly in to a base camp. Then they go out with a light outfit and camp high near the sheep. There will usually be two guides and two hunters, a tent for the guides and one for the hunters, a saddle horse for each man, and a couple of pack horses. Often a horse wrangler goes along to keep his eye on the pack horses, to do a little cooking perhaps, and to keep grizzlies from raiding the camp. Such camps are no laps of luxury. When I go on a jack camp I generally roll toilet gear, pajamas, camp slippers, and a change of clothing in my bedroll and leave duffle bag or panniers at the main camp.

The Japanese have just about taken over the binocular market. Bausch & Lomb, the big American optical company, bought D. P. Bushnell, an importer of Japanese optical goods, and is no longer manufacturing the excellent and famous line of B&L binoculars. However, B&L is distributing Japanese copies of their fine 9×35 and 7×35 binoculars. Zeiss, the famous optical concern in West Germany, took over Hensoldt, another prestigious German company. Zeiss has discontinued most if not all of the Hensoldt models and has greatly simplified its own line. Zeiss binoculars are imported into this country to a limited extent but they are very expensive. Leitz, the German maker of the great Leica cameras, makes good binoculars of the roof-prism type in 7×, 8×, and 10×. They, too, are very expensive. In the past the British firm of Ross has made excellent binoculars but I do not believe they are now imported into the United States.

The sheep hunter should take with him a fairly light compact binocular that he can carry on his chest with a strap around his neck. He should shorten the strap that comes with the binocular until he can just get it over his head. Then he will wear the glass on his chest tucked under his shirt when it is not in use. To carry like this, my favorite is a Zeiss 8×30B, the model with porro prisms. The "B" means that the glass is made with folding rubber eye cups. The spectacle wearer can fold the rubber eye cups back and get a much wider field of view than he can with eye cups made for those who do not wear spectacles. Zeiss has a beautiful glass known as the 8×50B. Like the 8×30B this has folding rubber eye cups. Looking through this wonderful glass is like looking out of a window at a new, bright, perfect world. The only thing wrong is that the glass is heavy and bulky. The Zeiss 10×50 is no longer made. It is identical to the 8×50 except for power. Until I got the 8×30B for $120 at the Shannon Airport in Ireland in 1962, I used a beautiful Bausch & Lomb 9×35 with shallow eye cups made especially for spectacle wearers. This is a great sheep glass. It has a good field, sufficient illumination, and good definition. I have read many times windy advice on the choice of binoculars by people who do not know what they are talking about. One bit of bum advice is that no one should use a glass of over 7× because the glass cannot be held steady and the wobble will tire the eyes. My answer is that riflemen are used to holding things steady. An 8× or 9× glass enables the hunter to pick up detail he would otherwise have missed with a glass of lower power.

Actually the sheep hunter can use a 10× binocular with profit. The choice of the sheep hunter's glass depends on a compromise of power, bulk, weight. I have also read that the mountain hunter should use a light binocular that he can carry in his pocket. That is like saying the sheep hunter should carry a revolver because it is handy. The idea of the sheep hunter's binocular is to find and size up sheep at long range. He needs definition—to tell bedded sheep from stones, to tell ewes from rams, to tell shootable rams from unshootable ones. The small, light glass like a 6×15 has its place but it isn't in sheep hunting. It lacks definition.

Because the sheep hunter will use a binocular for long stretches, he needs the best quality. A binocular that is slightly out of collimation will give the user a fearful headache after an hour's use. Prisms and lenses should be the best, and prisms should be strongly mounted. If they are not, hard use will knock them out of collimation and the eyes will struggle constantly to pull cockeyed images together.

As a compromise for carrying in the field I know of no glass better than the Bausch & Lomb 9×35. I have used one in many sheep ranges from the Cassiars of British Columbia to the Kopet Daghs in Iran. My one criticism of the glass is that it is a bit on the bulky side. Next to the 9×35 I would put the beautiful and slightly less bulky 8×30 Bausch & Lomb. Neither is available at present. The 8×30B Zeiss is a light, handy, and compact glass, not quite in the same class optically as the Bausch & Lomb 9×35. The 8×32 Hensoldt "Dialyt" roof-prism glass is also light, compact, and a joy to carry and use.

The Leitz "Trinovid" binoculars seem today (1974) to have taken over the market composed of binocular users to whom price is no object. High German wages and devaluation of the dollar in comparison to the West German mark makes the Trinovids very expensive. However, they are good investments for those who can afford them. Zeiss also makes another 8×30B which is called the "Dialyt." In outward appearance it looks about like the Leitz Trinovids. I played with one and was impressed by its wide field of view and great brilliance.

The sheep hunter going north will find that white guides almost always have binoculars, often very good ones such as Ross, Bausch & Lomb, and Zeiss. Indian guides almost never have binoculars but if they do they are some cheapjack and flimsy Japanese make, glasses that are out of alignment and have poor definition. For that reason I always take a second pair for the guide's use. Since the guide does not have to carry a rifle he can carry a fairly heavy and bulky glass. I once had a 12×60 Leitz, a wonderful instrument but heavy. It was great to use when there wasn't time to put up a spotting scope. With it horns and antlers could be plainly seen that could not be made out with an 8× or a 9× glass. My present heavy-duty glass for the guide's use is a Zeiss 10×50. It is heavy, bulky, but a tremendous instrument optically.

The equipment of any serious sheep hunter or for that matter any mountain hunter should include a good prismatic spotting scope. I made up my mind that I would never again be without one when I was in the Yukon in 1945. Several times my guide and I spotted bunches of sheep with my 8×30 Bausch & Lomb, made long and tiresome stalks, only to find that we were afer small and unshootable rams. When I hunted Stone sheep the next year in northern British Columbia I had the now-obsolete Argus 20× spotting scope. I found the Argus to be excellent. Likewise a 25× Unertl. For the most part a 20× or a 25× is all the sheep hunter needs, but occasionally he will want more power. He then has two ways to go. One is to get a variable-power spotting scope. These are available with power changeable to from 15× to 60×. My own feeling is that power over 30× is seldom useful, as the higher the power the more mirage it picks up. The object seen through the scope at 60× looks larger but it doesn't look plainer. The other way to go is to take along an extra eyepiece. At the present I am using a Bushnell with a 20× eyepiece and an extra 32× eyepiece.

On a sheep hunt the guide usually carries the spotting scope. If he has some sort of a pack sack the scope will go in it. However, it is wise for the dude sheep hunter to get some sort of a case made so spotting scope and tripod can be carried together by a strap over the guide's shoulder. When the guide is on horseback he can hang the scope by the strap to a saddle horn.

The spotting scope to be efficient should always be used on a tripod. It should be a good solid one. Today most spotting scopes are threaded for camera tripods. These work very well if they are sturdy. Putting the spotting scope over a rock or a hat simply does not work!

14
Notes on the Sheep Rifle

As I have said, I shot my first ram, a desert bighorn, in the middle 1930s in the Mexican state of Sonora. I used a light 7×57 Mauser with a Lyman 1-A peep sight mounted on the cocking piece of the bolt—a type of sight seldom seen these days. The cartridge was the now-obsolete Western Cartridge Company load of 139-grain open-point bullet at a velocity of about 2,800 foot-seconds in a 22-inch barrel.

Such ballistics sound modest indeed in these days of thundering magnums, but they are certainly adequate for sheep. A friend of mine has just returned from Iran as I write this. He had a successful hunt for red sheep and ibex. The rifle he used was a custom-made 7×57 on a pre-1964 Model 70 action and with a 22-inch barrel, a rifle very much like the one I took my first ram with almost forty years before. The load he used was the Canadian-made Dominion brand with a 139-grain soft-nose bullet at 2,825 foot-seconds in a 22-inch barrel—or at least in the 22-inch barrel of my remodeled and restocked Model 70 Winchester in 7×57 caliber. At any rate my friend pronounced this combination of rifle and cartridge as being the world's finest for mountain hunting.

A wild ram is a rare and valuable animal. Few hunters ever are lucky enough to get a shot at one. The man who does get a shot should make every effort to make that shot as nearly perfect as possible. He should put it in a vital area. One of the ways to do that is for the sheep hunter to use a rifle that he is familiar with, that he is not afraid of, and that he shoots well. I once read some data compiled by the Wyoming game department on the loss of big game by wounding—and wounding comes from poor and careless shooting. It runs in my mind that for every two rams taken one was shot at, wounded, and lost. These horrifying figures come about not because the hunter didn't use a powerful enough rifle, but because he couldn't shoot.

Since I shot that first desert bighorn I have hunted sheep in Wyoming, Alberta, British Columbia, the Yukon, Iran, and in the rugged mountains of the southern Sahara Desert in the Chad Republic of central Africa. I traded off that little old 7×57 Mauser back around 1940, but if I still had it I wouldn't hesitate to take it sheep hunting. The only change I would make would be to put a modern 4× scope on it. That would bring the total weight up to about 8 pounds, the weight of the scope-sighted sheep rifles I have used in recent years. The little 7×57 cartridge is still an excellent all-round cartridge, one with light recoil, excellent accuracy, and with the lighter bullets a trajectory adequately flat for 95 percent of all sheep hunting. The light recoil of the little 7-mm. is of great importance because except for some hairy-chested outdoor writers most of us shoot rifles of light recoil better than we do rifles of heavy recoil and also because the sheep hunter must often shoot from odd and uncomfortable positions from which he may be hurt by heavy recoil. He might even be kicked off a rock ledge.

That first ram of mine, as I now remember it, was shot at around 30 yards (good quail range), certainly not over 50 yards. This short range was by no means exceptional, but the fact that the sheep was running was. Actually most sheep are taken when they are standing or perhaps more often lying in their beds. This short-range business may take some non-sheep hunters by surprise, but I have shot more rams at under 200 yards than I have at over 200. Probably more under 150 yards. The last desert ram I shot was not over 30 yards away, and the best Dall I have ever taken was maybe about 40 yards from the muzzle when it went down. The reason for the close shots is that sheep are often but not always found in rough country where they can be approached from behind ridges. On occasion longer shots must be taken, but the rule by which the sheep hunter should abide is never to take a shot that he is not absolutely certain he can make, be it 30 yards or 300 yards. If he is doubtful of his ability to make the shot and to place the bullet in the right spot he should not shoot. The biggest mistake he can make is to blaze away at long and doubtful range—at best to scare the ram and run it out of the country and at worst to wound and lose a fine trophy.

Now and then some ambitious neophyte sheep hunter drops by my place to show me his notion of a sheep rifle. Usually it has a long barrel, now and then with some dreadful contraption of a muzzle brake, and generally it is chambered for some frighteningly powerful magnum cartridge with which our beginner plans to knock a ram off at 600 yards. Often these monsters weigh from 9 to 10½ pounds and with their 26-inch and sometimes even 28-inch barrels they are about as handy to get around with in the mountains as vaulting poles.

During a brief stretch early in my sheep-hunting career I went the route of the heavy, long-barreled rifle. I was seeing quite a few rams that had seen me first at long range because at the time I had not learned to hunt sheep. I reasoned that if I had a heavy target-type rifle with a high-powered scope I could really pick off those old *machos cimarrones* that had been sneering at me from the tops of ridges 400 and 500 yards away. I acquired a .30/06 target rifle with a 26-inch medium-heavy barrel and fitted a Ziess Zielsechs 6× scope on a side mount. One hunt was enough to cure me. The rifle was about as handy to carry around in the rocks as a grand piano. The weight wore me down and the long barrel was always catching on rocks and the low brush and the little stunted trees of the Sonora sheep mountains. I liquidated my investment at painful loss and went back to more seemly rifles.

There is no law against carrying rifles with long heavy barrels and chambered for magnum cartridges back into the sheep hills. But they only complicate things and are completely unnecessary. If it fills anyone full of bliss, euphoria, joie de vivre, and whatnot to lug around a 12-pound rifle chambered for a .300 Super Magnum cartridge and wearing a barrel as long as the neck of a tall giraffe I am all for him. Hunting is for fun and games anyway. The point is that the hunter does not need such a monster in the first place and is handicapping himself with it in the second.

The sheep rifle should above all things be portable, handy, and relatively light, as the sheep hunter carries a rifle a lot more than he shoots it. On two of my last North American sheep hunts I have fired the grand total of two shots at rams—one at around 100 to 125 yards and the other as near as I could estimate at about 200 yards. Each connected and that was that!

The famous Model 1903 6.5-mm. Mannlicher-Schoenauer carbine made in Austria has an 18-inch barrel stocked to the muzzle in classical Mannlicher style. I have one which I acquired for purely sentimental reasons since I have never shot it in the field. Fitted with a Griffin & Howe side mount and a 4× Leupold scope the carbine weighs slightly over 8 pounds. Ballistics of the 6.5×54 MS are not impressive—a 160-grain bullet at around 2,400 foot-seconds or a 140-grain bullet at 2,580—but for at least three-fourths of the rams I have taken I would not have been handicapped by its use.

The Germans and Austrians used the short Mannlicher-Schoenauers to hunt chamois, the lively little goat-antelopes of the Alps. I have never laid eyes on a chamois in the flesh but from pictures I have seen he looks to me to be about the size of a coyote. I'd guess that anything from a .222 Remington on up would be good chamois medicine.

Britishers stationed in India and hunting the big wild sheep and goats of Cashmere and Tibet in the old days went to heavier rifles and more powerful cartridges. They used rifles built on Mauser actions and even some double rifles as well as single-shots built on the Farquharson action. Barrels were 26 and 28 inches long. However, they always had stooges along to carry the rifles, and it is a well-known law of physics that rifles weigh less when carried by someone else.

When I was a fledgling sheep hunter and outdoor writer back in the 1930s, factory bolt-action big-game rifles ran a good deal heavier than they have in recent years. Put a scope on a 1938 Winchester Model 70 or a Remington Model 30 and you had a rifle that tipped the beam at around 10 pounds. Put a scope on a Model 1903 Springfield sporter that was sold to members of the NRA complete with Lyman 48 receiver sight for as little as $40 and the outfit weighed even more—around 10½ pounds, or a good weight for a .458 Winchester elephant rifle. These muskets were pretty burdensome. Suppose your rifle weighs 2 pounds more than it should and you have to climb 2,000 feet with it. That's equivalent to lifting a couple of tons one foot! Even the good and highly accurate Savage Model 99-R came out when scope-sighted on the heavy side. Barrels were then standard at 24 inches and fairly stiff. Stocks tended to be bulky.

In 1938 I bought from Bill Sukalle, a crack Phoenix, Arizona, barrelmaker and metalsmith, a flat-bolt Mauser action with a 24-inch .270 W.C.F. barrel. This cost me $35. It was during the depression and Bill was probably short of cash. The famous Alvin Linden stocked it for me with a plain but very hard piece of Balkan walnut for all of $75 and I had Frank Pachmayr mount a Noske 2½× scope on a Noske side mount with a special Pachmayr base. Complete the rifle weighed 9 pounds. It was still on the heavy side and the barrel was too long, but I carried it in rough country in Sonora, Wyoming, Alberta, British Columbia, and the Yukon, shot it well, and with it had collected good specimens of most North American game animals as well as all varieties of North American wild sheep by 1946.

However, it was always a bit burdensome and I eventually went to lighter rifles. I now have a pair of .270s with which I do such sheep hunting as I still undertake. Each began life as a pre-1964 Model 70 Winchester. One has the old standard-weight barrel which was cut to 22 inches and turned down by Al Biesen. The other is the regular Winchester Model 70 Featherweight that was introduced in 1952 except that a steel floorplate and trigger guard were substituted for the standard aluminum. Each was stocked in good, hard French walnut by Biesen. One has the old Stith 4× Bear Cub scope, the other a 4× Leupold. Both scopes are mounted by the now-obsolete Tilden mount made in Denver. Each weighs exactly 8 pounds.

As practical, fast-handling, and accurate sheep rifles the matched pair would be difficult to improve upon. On a long trip I take both. The No. 2 rifle has a slightly larger chamber than the No. 1. I take factory-loaded ammunition, reloads with full-length-sized cases, or reloads with cases fired in the No. 1 rifle, so cartridges can be used in either rifle. I have yet to have either of these rifles go out of action but on a long trip a spare rifle in the party has been known to come in handy.

These are not showy rifles. The wood is good but not spectacular. Shaping, inletting, finishing, and checkering on both rifles are beyond compare. Using good 130-grain bullets in front of 62 grains of No. 4831 in Winchester-Western cases, either will put the first three shots into an inch or less if I do my part. The No. 2 rifle is my particular pet. Month after month, year after year, in sunshine and in rain it puts its favorite load with the 130-grain Nosler bullet as I have described it above into a little group 3 inches high at 100 yards. I have used both of these rifles on African safaris as well as on North American mountain hunts and they do just as good a job on the large African antelope such as kudu, gemsbok, and white oryx as they do on sheep, mule deer, and elk. I shot a Barbary ram with the No. 1 rifle on a rough little mountain in the southern Sahara in 1958.

After World War II the big American arms manufacturers put their ear to the ground and started turning out lighter rifles. I do not kid myself that the manufacturers sit around with their tongues hanging out following my every word. I am not quite fat-headed enough for that. Nevertheless, rifles of the weight and barrel length I had been whooping up began to peer out of the bushes. The Remington Model 721, which appeared in 1948, had a 24-inch barrel but it was lighter than its predecessors, the Model 30 and the Model 720. In 1952 Winchester came out with the Model 70 Featherweight, which when fitted with scope and mount weighed about 8 pounds, sometimes a bit less. The Remington Model 725, which was quickly replaced by the current Model 700, was very handy.

Today weights of some factory rifles seem to be edging up a bit. A current (1972) Model 70A Winchester .270 weighs 7 and would weigh about 8 pounds with scope and mount. The standard Model 70 is a bit heavier. A Remington Model ADL in .30/06 weighs 6 pounds 14½ ounces, which would bring it to the good sheep-rifle weight of around 8 pounds or just about right. A Model 700 BDL right off the shelf and in .30/06 scales 7 pounds 6 ounces, and would be a shade heavy as with a scope it would weigh about 8 pounds 6 ounces. A Ruger M77 in .284 caliber weighs 7 pounds 4 ounces with rings but not scope and would come out about an even 8 pounds with scope. Another Ruger, a M77 Magnum in .30/06, weighs precisely 8 pounds with a Weaver K4 on Ruger rings.

I have mentioned my successful Stone-sheep hunt in northern British Columbia in 1971. Jim Rikhoff, one of my companions, was armed with a Winchester Model 70 with the Mannlicher stock and a 19-inch .270 barrel. The little rifle was a shade on the heavy side, since it weighed 7½ pounds without scope and about 8½ pounds with Weaver K4 scope and Weaver top mount. With this rifle my companion took a caribou and a couple of timber wolves with one shot each. He shot his ram twice because after the first shot the ram was kicking convulsively and he was afraid it would kick itself over the cliff.

The guides and wranglers in camp all admired the little Mannlicher-style .270. It was short, handy to carry around in the rocks and in a saddle scabbard, and reasonably light. Two of the guides swore they were going to get rifles just like it. After I returned from the sheep hunt I got a Mannlicher-style Model 70 Winchester in .270. I sent it to Al Biesen, who took off considerable excess wood from the stock, removed the Monte Carlo comb, reduced the circumference of the pistol grip, installed a solid red-rubber recoil pad, refinished and checkered, and installed a Leupold 4× scope. The result is a very handsome little rifle which weighs slightly less than 8¼ pounds.

I doubt if much is to be gained by a barrel of less than 22 inches. With a relatively fast-burning powder like No. 4064 the 19-inch barrel of the short .270 loses about 90 foot-seconds as compared to a 22-inch barrel. If a slow-burning powder like No. 4350 or No. 4831 were used the loss would be considerable and the muzzle blast would be unpleasant. Nevertheless, because slow-burning powders are more suited to the .270 case, No. 4831 gives higher velocity in the 19-inch barrel than No. 4064. The short-barreled rifle has a tendency to be butt-heavy and muzzle-light. However, for those who like short rifles the classic Mannlicher-Schoenauer with its 18½-inch barrel or the short Winchester with the 19-inch barrel are interesting weapons. Jim Rikhoff of Winchester has used his all over the world and he loves it! Still, I think the barrel is an inch or so too short.

Another model that would make an interesting sheep rifle is the Ruger No. 1 single-shot. The fact that the Ruger has no long receiver allows a 26-inch barrel to be used with the same overall length as a bolt-action rifle with a 22-inch barrel. Some may be frightened away from the No. 1 because it is a single-shot, but if a stalk on rams is properly excecuted it is rare that more than one shot is needed. As I look back I would guess that I have taken about nine-tenths of the rams I have collected with one shot. A 7½- or 8-pound scope-equipped No. 1 in 7×57, .270, .280, or .30/06 with a 22- or 24-inch barrel would be an excellent lazy man's sheep rifle. Incidentally, I have a pal who owns a No. 1 single-shot in .270. He says he is getting 3,300 foot-seconds in a 26-inch barrel with the 130-grain bullet in a load that gives 3,140 in my rifles with 22-inch barrels. Modern single-shots like the Ruger and the new Browning offer real possibilities for the sheep hunter who is also a gun nut if the combined weight of rifle and scope is kept to around 8 pounds.

I have never used a pump or an automatic as a sheep rifle and see no need for fast-operating actions, but there is no reason why such a rifle, if of suitable weight, scope-equipped, and chambered for a good cartridge, should not be used. I like a steel buttplate, preferably with a trap for hunting license, possibly a couple of extra cartridges, and maybe a pull-through cleaner. The late Charlie Ren, with whom I used to hunt sheep in Sonora, always put rubber recoil pads on his rifles. He used the rifles as alpenstocks—and they were always beaten up. I never use a rifle butt for support in climbing if I can help it.

I have known sheep hunters to use everything from Model 94 Winchesters in .25/35 to .300 Weatherby Magnums. I'd like a flatter trajectory and more energy than the .25/35 affords, but the .300 Magnums are unnecessarily powerful and rifles for them are too long of barrel and too heavy.

I have taken rams with the .30/06, the 7×57, and the .270 and one each with a .257 Roberts and a .348 Winchester. All of my wife's rams have been shot with a 7×57. Prince Abdorreza Pahlavi of Iran, who is probably the most skillful and experienced of the world's sportsman sheep and wild-goat hunters, used the .300 H&H Magnum when I first knew him. He shifted to the 7×57, then the .270. He has tried the 7-mm. Remington Magnum but has gone back to the .270. He now has four matched pre-1964 Winchester Model 70 .270s, all with scopes, all handsomely engraved, all stocked in French walnut. I now have only three gilt-edged .270s myself. The .280 Remington in a good bolt action is just as good as the .270. I have a lovely one built on a square-bridge commercial Mauser action and stocked by Earl Milliron. I may use it on my next sheep hunt.

I know a good and experienced sheep hunter who is a bit shy of ballistic sophistication. He uses an off-breed 7-mm. Magnum because he is impressed with the published ballistics; then he had the barrel chopped off to 21 inches for handiness. The result is that he gets a muzzle blast that lays the daisies low and a jet of flame on which you can light a cigar 33 feet from the muzzle. Velocity? About what you can get from the much milder. 280 Remington in a barrel of the same length. The same thing happened with the Winchester Model 70 Featherweight for the .264 Winchester Magnum cartridge—a lot of sound and fury but no more velocity than that produced by the .30/06 or .270.

Most shots at rams, as I have said, are short, but now and then a fairly long one must be taken. A few times I have violated my own rule that a shot should not be taken unless the hunter knows just where it is going to land, but I have done so only once in recent years. However, shooting from a rest with a rifle sighted to put the bullet 3 inches high at 100 yards, it is no great trick to knock off an animal as large as a mountain sheep at 300 yards. I can remember by quick recall bouncing a couple of rams at about that distance and one perhaps considerably farther. However, as I have said before, most rams are shot at no great range.

The rifles I use on rams are all equipped with 4× scopes, a power which I consider ideal. However, I have taken at least as many rams with rifles wearing 2½× scopes, and no one is greatly handicapped with the lower power. Some good sheep hunters like variable-power scopes, carry them set at 4× or 5× and turn them up to higher power in the case of a long shot. I have never felt any great need for a variable. Variable-prism scopes are heavier, more complicated, and optically inferior. I do not consider the various rangefinding reticles particularly useful because if a ram is so far away that he cannot be hit solidly with a hold on the top of the shoulders by a rifle of the .270–.280–.30/06 class sighted in for 250 to 275 yards, he is too far away to shoot at.

I have heard some tales by sheep authorities whose hunting experience is very limited about how difficult sheep are to kill. All stuff and nonsense! Sheep are wounded or missed for two reasons. For one, hunters often get wildly excited and miss rams at 50 yards or less. For another, they blast away at long and doubtful range, sometimes wounding but more often missing and scaring the rams out of the country.

I am sure I need not say that the sheep rifle needs a sling put on with quick-detachable swivels. I use slings of the Whelen type with loop adjusted to give me a good steady hold in the sitting position. I don't often use the sling in shooting, but on occasion its use has made a doubtful shot certain.

The sheep hunter should avoid extremes. Rifles with barrels too short and light are difficult to hold steady and shoot accurately. Barrels longer than 22 inches or at the most 24 inches are awkward to carry in rough country. An ultra-light rifle gives a jolting recoil, and a heavy one breaks down your arches. A too-mild cartridge like the .243, while adequate for rams, might be shy of power on grizzlies or moose encountered in a sheep hunt, and the booming, bellowing magnum makes a heavy rifle necessary, doesn't kill any better, and may kick the sheep hunter off a ledge.

The most fascinating and prestigious trophy animal in the world deserves good shooting and good equipment!

15 The Sheep Trophy

Until the years immediately following World War II the classifying of trophy heads in the United States was casual at best. People often said they had "record" heads, but when pressed they were pretty vague about what constituted a "record." Before World War I, sheep heads were generally judged on the size of the base—and bases were sloppily and incorrectly measured.

There were simply no standards. Deer heads were judged by "spread" and by the number of "points." A "point" was considered to be "anything you can hang a ring on." The first list of "Record" North American trophy sheep heads I can find is in *Horn Measurements and Weights of the Great Game of the World: Being a Record for the Use of Sportsmen and Naturalists.* It was compiled and published by Rowland Ward, the London taxidermist. This appeared in 1892 and it is the original record book in English. Copies are rare and are worth a bundle.

In this book the only North American sheep listed are the bighorns. They are ranked by the length of the longest horn. The "record" sheep had a length of 41 inches, a circumference of 17¼ inches, and a tip-to-tip measurement of 26 inches. The head was taken by P. Z. S. Blyth in 1840. No mention is made of the place the ram came from.

Some of the heads listed were from British Columbia, but most were from the United States—Colorado, Montana, California. One that is plainly a desert bighorn is listed as having come from Mexico. It was 37¾ inches around the curl and had a base of 15⅞ inches, and a tip-to-tip measurement of 23 2/4 inches.

By 1914, when the seventh edition of the Rowland Ward record book appeared, it was called Rowland Ward's *Records of Big Game.* By this time Rowland Ward himself had evidently passed to his reward, as the seventh edition was edited by R. Lydekker and J. B. Burlace. In case this information will be handy for anyone's records, editions of *Records* came out in 1892, 1896, 1899, 1903, and 1910, as well as the one in 1914. I once had a 1937 edition, the last published prior to World War II.

The 1914 edition of *Records* lists the Rocky Mountain bighorn, the Stone (Black bighorn), the "Fannin" (Grey bighorn), and the Dall (White bighorn). There is no separate classification for desert sheep. The record bighorn is a Wyoming ram with a curl of 42 inches and a base of 16. It was taken by T. W. H. Clarke, evidently an Englishman because of the three initials. The record Stone came from the Cassiar Mountains of British Columbia and measured 42 and 14½. The tip-to-tip measurement was 28 inches. The record Dall was the famous Dalglish head which I have mentioned in the chapter on the Dall and which was for a long time considered the Yukon record. The measurements were: curl, 47 inches; base, 13¾ inches; tip-to-tip, 28 inches.

The first American book of big-game records was brought out in 1932 by the Boone & Crockett Club. It was edited by Prentiss N. Gray, who was afterward killed in a boating accident in Florida. The book followed the English system of ranking heads by the length of the longest horn or antler. Everyone was broke in 1932. I had a job which paid me $175 a month and I was happy to get $50 each for articles from *Field & Stream.* A very small edition of this first *Records of North American Big Game* was printed. I do not own one and have never seen one. Remington Arms Company, however, as a promotion, published a pamphlet listing the first ten trophy heads for all North American species. This was given away free to those who wrote in for it.

I believe this slender pamphlet marked the beginning of the interest in trophy hunting in the United States, as it was the first readily available publication to give standards. My copy has long since disappeared. When I first got it I was pleased to discover that a buck mule deer I had shot in Arizona in the fall of 1932 would be about No. 10. This was by antler length alone—a poor way to rank a deer head. Actually that was an ugly freakish head. I never had it mounted and it would not have rated nearly so high under a more rational system of classification.

The second edition of the Boone & Crockett Club's record book was called *North American Big Game.* It came out in 1939. It was a rather elaborate book with chapters on the various game animals, suitable rifles, conservation, photography. I contributed the chapter on the Coues (Arizona) whitetail. The late Grancel Fitz was the author of a chapter on the ranking of heads. This, along with a formula worked out by the late James Clark of the American Museum of Natural History, provided the basis for the present system of ranking big-game heads.

However, in this 1939 edition sheep were still ranked by the length of the longest horn. The No. 1 bighorn was the James Simpson head I have mentioned in the chapter on the bighorn. The right horn was 49½, the left 48¼, and the bases 16 and 16⅛. It was listed as having been killed in British Columbia but it was actually poached in a national park in Alberta. The Bovey head, the highest-scoring bighorn head known to be in existence today, is No. 4 in the 1939 book. The longest horn is 46 inches. The No. 1 head in the most recent record book was burned up in a fire.

The famous Chadwick head with its horn length of 51⅝ was the No. 1 Stone in 1939 and is still No. 1 today. The No. 1 Dall had a length of 47½ inches. I mention it in the chapter on Dalls as actually having been on a Stone ram. The desert sheep that was No. 1 was a 44-inch ram from Lower California. The hunter is not listed, but it was a part of the Dr. Henry M. Beck collection. A head of mine which I no longer have is in 35th place.

The first edition of *Records of North American Big Game* to appear after World War II was that of 1952. It was the first to employ the new system of rating—a much more logical business than ranking by horn length alone. Sheep heads were scored by adding the length of both horns taken on the outside edge to the circumference measurements of both bases taken straight around, and the circumference measurement taken at each quarter of both horns. If, for example, the horn is 41 inches around the curl, quarter measurements are taken at 10¼, 20½, and 30¾ inches from the base. These ten figures added to-

OFFICIAL SCORING SYSTEM FOR NORTH AMERICAN BIG GAME TROPHIES

RECORDS OF NORTH AMERICAN BIG GAME COMMITTEE

BOONE AND CROCKETT CLUB

RETURN TO:
N. A. B. G. Awards Program
1600 Rhode Island Ave. N. W
Washington, D. C. 20036

Minimum Score:	Sheep
Bighorn	– 180
Desert	– 168
Stone	– 170
White or Dall	– 170

SHEEP

KIND OF SHEEP

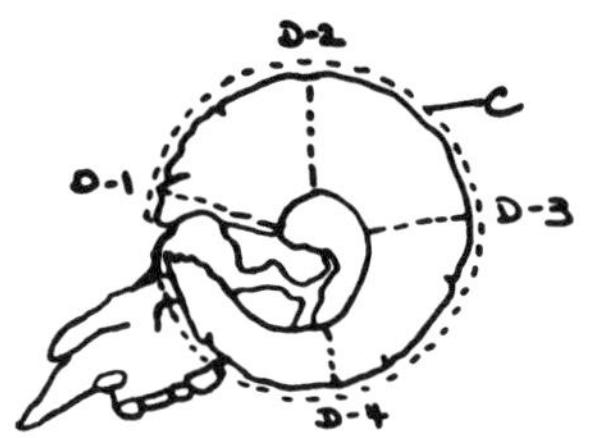

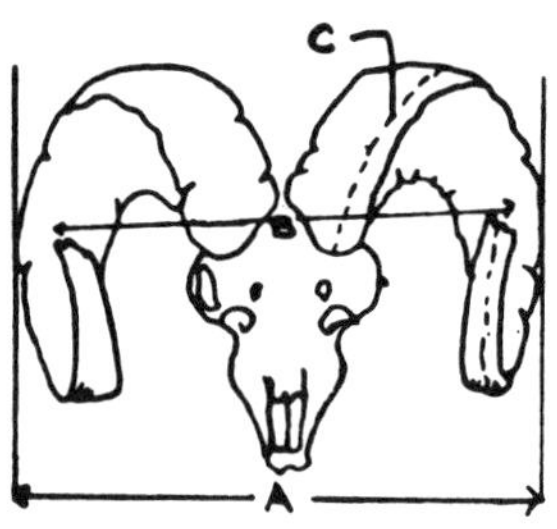

MEASURE TO A POINT IN LINE WITH TIP OF HORN

SEE OTHER SIDE FOR INSTRUCTIONS	Supplementary Data	Column 1	Column 2	Column 3
A. Greatest Spread (Is often Tip to Tip Spread)		Right Horn	Left Horn	Difference
B. Tip to Tip Spread (If Greatest Spread, Enter again here)				
C. Length of Horn				
D-1. Circumference of Base				
D-2. Circumference at First Quarter				
D-3. Circumference at Second Quarter				
D-4. Circumference at Third Quarter				
TOTALS				

ADD	Column 1		Exact locality where killed
	Column 2		Date killed By whom killed
TOTAL			Present owner
SUBTRACT Column 3			Address
FINAL SCORE			Guide's Name and Address
			Remarks: (Mention any abnormalities)

I certify that I have measured the above trophy on 19
at (address) City State
and that these measurements and data are, to the best of my knowledge and belief, made in accordance with the instructions given.

Witness: Signature:

Boone and Crockett Official Measurer

This is the form used to record sheep trophies with the North American Big Game Committee of the Boone & Crockett Club. The total score is determined by both horn

INSTRUCTIONS

All measurements must be made with a flexible steel tape to the nearest one-eighth of an inch. Wherever it is necessary to change direction of measurement, mark a control point and swing tape at this point. To simplify addition, please enter fractional figures in eighths.

Official measurements cannot be taken for at least sixty days after the animal was killed. Please submit photographs of trophy front and sides.

Supplementary Data measurements indicate conformation of the trophy. None of the figures in Lines A and B are to be included in the score. Evaluation of conformation is a matter of personal preference.

A. Greatest Spread measured between perpendiculars at right angles to the center line of the skull.

B. Tip to Tip Spread measured from outer edge of tips of horns.

C. Length of Horn measured from lowest point in front on outer curve to a point in line with tip. DO NOT press tape into depressions. The low point of the outer curve of the horn is considered to be the low point of the frontal portion of the horn, situated above and slightly medial to the eye socket, (not on the outside edge of the horn.)

D-1 Circumference of Base measured at right angles to axis of horn. DO NOT follow irregular edge of horn.

D-2-3-4. Divide measurement C of LONGER horn by four, mark BOTH horns at these quarters even though other horn is shorter, and measure circumferences at these marks.

* * * * * * * * * * * * * *

TROPHIES OBTAINED ONLY BY FAIR CHASE MAY BE ENTERED IN ANY BOONE AND CROCKETT CLUB BIG GAME COMPETITION

To make use of the following methods shall be deemed UNFAIR CHASE and unsportsmanlike, and any trophy obtained by use of such means is disqualified from entry in any Boone and Crockett Club big game competition:

I. Spotting or herding game from the air, followed by landing in its vicinity for pursuit;

II. Herding or pursuing game with motor-powered vehicles;

III. Use of electronic communications for attracting, locating or observing game, or guiding the hunter to such game.

* * * * * * * * * *

I certify that the trophy scored on this chart was not taken in UNFAIR CHASE as defined above by the Boone and Crockett Club.

I certify that it was not spotted or herded by guide or hunter from the air followed by landing in its vicinity for pursuit, nor herded or pursued on the ground by motor-powered vehicles.

I further certify that no electronic communications were used to attract, locate, observe, or guide the hunter to such game; and that it was taken in full compliance with the local game laws or regulations of the state, province or territory.

Date ____________________ Hunter ____________________

length and horn circumference measured at the base and each quarter—a far better system of scoring than simple horn length. (Reproduced by permission.)

gether constitute the score. There is no deduction for unevenness. The Boone & Crockett scoring sheet for sheep shows how it is done.

The Boone & Crockett Club threw a bash in the basement of the American Museum of Natural History in the spring of 1951 to give out the medals for heads taken in 1950. I got second place for a big Dall that year. These award dinners got a good deal of publicity. Outdoor magazines ran pictures of prize-winning heads, and each year interest in trophy hunting increased and more entries came in. The first Weatherby award was presented to Herb Klein in Dallas, Texas, in 1956. I was fingered the next year, and Warren Page, then shooting editor of *Field & Stream,* in 1958. These awards got a lot of publicity.

Soon hunting for trophies became the "in" thing. The idea was to "get one (or more) in the book." Some did not care how they managed to do so. More entries came in to the Boone & Crockett Club. More hunters were in the field. New and unhunted areas were opened up by enterprising outfitters. Excellent sheep heads began to show up from all over. Frank Cooke's area in northern British Columbia was especially productive for Stone sheep.

People began hunting for prestige instead of their enjoyment of freedom, the clean, sweet-scented air, the mountain vistas. Men who shot good trophy rams that did not quite "make the book" were bitterly disappointed. Friends of long standing quarreled bitterly if one man got a slightly better head than the other. Hunters hungry for honors campaigned for the Weatherby Trophy like Nixon running for the presidency. When I became a judge in the annual Weatherby award contest I was deluged with invitations to go on freebie hunting trips, invited to free meals, offered enough free booze to intoxicate a brontosaurus, bombarded with portfolios of 8-by-10 color prints showing the candidates gloating over defunct lions, tigers, elephants, greater kudu, Marco Polo sheep, and whatnot.

As I have told in my chapter called "The Grand Slam Caper," getting a Grand Slam of all varieties of North American sheep became an absolute requirement. If they all "went in the book" so much the better! Some of the candidates seemed to think that if you knocked off all four varieties in thirty days you were practically in. If you could gloat that each of the rams had cost you $20,000 you were just about the Queen of the May. One astounding character who had never hunted before got a Grand Slam in less than thirty days, went through the rest of the world's game noisily, expensively, and as speedily as the laxative is reputed to have gone through the alimentary canal of the fabled widow woman.

The speed with which some of these lads moved getting a ram "in the book" reminds me of a lowbrow friend of mine, a New York ad man from the other side of the tracks. He took his wife to Paris and she wanted to tour the Louvre. He was appalled at the sight of scores of statues, acres of pictures. He pulled the guide he had hired aside.

"How long does this tour take?" he asked.

"Most spend a day," the guide said. "Many spend a week. Some have been known to spend a month!"

"Look, Mac," my pal said, "if you get me out of this son of a bitch in a half-hour there's an extra twenty bucks in it for you!"

To me this hang-up over record-class trophies is a pain in the derrière. Before World War II, people who went sheep hunting did it because they enjoyed being high in beautiful country. They enjoyed seeing interesting animals, making well-executed stalks and clean kills, dreamless sleep that came from tired bodies in chill mountain air. Hunters went out for from thirty to sixty days. They generally planned to collect a moose and a caribou, possibly a grizzly and a goat. The sportsmen tried to take old animals with mature heads, but little attention was paid to "records." These hunters were usually men of substance and of taste.

Even wealthy men didn't go on many hunts, and when they did they were away for considerable time. The first northern sheep I hunted were Dalls. As I described in the chapter on Dalls, I went to Vancouver, B.C., from Tucson, Arizona, by rail, from Vancouver to Skagway, Alaska, by Canadian Pacific Steamship, then from Skagway to Whitehorse, Y.T., by the White Pass and Yukon narrow-gauge railway. From Whitehorse to the Jacquot brothers' trading post and headquarters at Burwash Landing on Kluane Lake was a day by automobile on the Alaska Highway. This was in 1945. The last time I hunted northern sheep was in August 1973. I flew from Lewiston, Idaho, to Vancouver one afternoon and spent the night, flew the next day to Watson Lake, Y.T., and on by chartered plane to Frank Cooke's base camp at Colt Lake in the northern part of the Cassiar Mountains in British Columbia. It may be because I am a reactionary and a mossback but the longer time spent getting into the country that first time contributes to the mood, the atmosphere, and consequently the enjoyment.

All this reminds me of the sad experience of an acquaintance of mine. He left home, managed to fly to Anchorage, Alaska, in one day. He spent the night in an Anchorage hotel, flew by chartered plane to a lake the next morning. The third day away from home a plane landed him and a guide above a fine ram that had been previously located. He shot it. The plane picked him and the trophy up. He was back home less than a week after he had left. No one realized he had been gone.

But I digress. To me the mounted ram head on the wall should bring back memories of beautiful country, solitude, bright adventure, of a good shot and a clean kill on a well-selected ram. If the ram "makes the book" or not is of small importance. If it is larger or smaller than the one taken by my old pal Joe Doaks on the same trip, that is also of small importance.

Any old ram honestly taken is a rare, impressive, and noble trophy, whether the horns are 35 or 45 inches long. No ram head is a decent trophy if it is immature, if it was poached, if the hunter used a helicopter to get it, if he landed above it in a light plane. I speak not of its having been purchased or picked up. If I had wounded a ram and the guide had chased it down and had killed it, much of the value to me would be lost anyway.

I have the mounted head of an old Dall ram. It misses the record book by a mile. The horns are broomed off and are only about 35 inches long. The fact that the ram is a runt fooled me badly. But I value that trophy. When I look at it I think of a day, a tough day of cold and wind near the glaciers at the head of the St. Clair River in the Yukon, of a long, exhausting climb in a snowstorm, of a rush over a shale slide so my momentum would carry me forward. (If I had tried to pick my way I would have slid and fallen a thousand feet.) I remember waiting for the falling snow to thin out, then the one carefully placed shot and the clean, instant kill! Looking at that head brings me back to the days when I was younger, had good lungs and iron legs.

Most guides who take sheep hunters out are good judges of heads, but it is more enjoyable for the hunter to be able to judge them himself. If anyone is interested in sheep trophies I think he should make it a point to observe carefully every mounted sheep head he encounters. He should either ask how it measures or should measure it himself—with the owner's permission, of course.

The sheep hunter often has the opportunity to look rams over carefully through a spotting scope. On the other hand, he may suddenly have to decide which ram to take out of a running band. A very large head always looks very large to a hunter of experience. A small one looks small.

But here are things to look for. In the first place, those clichés of the beginning sheep hunter, the "full curl" and "perfect points," mean next to nothing. Many horns that make a full spiral are on young sheep that should be left to grow up, and, particularly in desert and Rocky Mountain bighorns, perfect points are the sign of immature sheep.

The thing to look for in the sheep head is mass. The really great ram appears to be *all horns.* He looks top-heavy. It makes no difference as to the type of head—close-curl, medium-curl, argali, widespread, or droopy—the great horns look great instantly to the hunter of experience.

However, we don't always see these great heads. In fact, it is possible for a hard-working hunter, earnest and painstaking, to hunt in good country for a lifetime and never see a great trophy head. However, if the hunter sets some minimum requirements for himself he won't be ashamed of the trophy he displays, and by shooting no immature rams he will not only practice conservation but he will eventually probably get a head listed in the record book.

Any ram with horns that look heavy and are broomed well back is an old ram and a good trophy.

If a pair of broomed-off horns come down below the point of the jaw and up to the bridge of the nose, the head is an extra-good one. If the ends of the broomed horns continue above the bridge of the nose the head is a very good one, will probably be in the record book, and is worth considerable pains to collect.

If, on the other hand, the horns look light, curve *above* the point of the jaw, and have perfect points, the ram is a young one and should not be shot—even if the tips of the horns come well above the bridge of the nose.

If the horns have a medium or close curl, go below the point of the jaw and up to the bridge of the nose, are somewhat broomed and look fairly heavy, they will probably measure 37½ to 38½ inches around the curls. Such a head is one no one need be ashamed of. It is from a ram probably ten years old or older. He has pretty well lived his life and discharged his duty to his kind.

The Stone ram I shot in 1971 was such a ram. The head is a very satisfactory trophy that just missed being large enough for inclusion in the record book. The ram was very thin. He was only nine or ten years old but his teeth were in bad shape. I don't see how he could have lived out the winter.

The poorest excuse I can think of for shooting a ram is for a person to be able to say he has shot a ram. A man I know is very proud of his "Grand Slam." He has had the heads mounted and they are displayed in his office. There is not a decent trophy in the lot. All are the spindly horns of immature rams with perfect points and little mass. In fact, a good many of the Grand Slams I have seen have been of this type. The boys who have taken them simply have wanted to say they were Grand Slammers. They got the unpleasant business of knocking off a ram over with as soon as possible!

There is a lot of hanky-panky in collecting sheep trophies. In the chapter called "The Grand Slam Caper" I told about the lads who keep the horns frozen for ninety days so they won't shrink until they can be measured after the official waiting time elapses. I also mentioned putting pick-up horns and skulls on the scalps of immature rams or even of ewes. The buying of heads and then claiming them for one's own is far more common than is generally realized. Yet another caper is having a taxidermist lengthen the horns by fiberglass. One taxidermist told me of this about as follows:

"Sure I know this is dishonest in its way, but I am not the guy who is dishonest. That is the hunter who asks me to make this trophy bigger. I lengthen horns with fiberglass all the time. So do most other taxidermists. Dumb taxidermists build up the points. That is easy to detect by someone looking for hanky-panky. I like to give my customers their money's worth, so I build the horns up at the bases. That looks better, is harder to detect, and people don't examine the bases anyway!"

Some wonderful things can be done with fiberglass. In the bar and lounge of a club of big-game hunters in Madrid hang what appear to be the skull and antlers of a tremendous Spanish red stag killed by General Francisco Franco. It never occurred to me as I admired it that it was anything but genuine. My friends told me that the trophy was a fiberglass copy of a head taken by the general. The original hangs in his country place at El Pardo.

A chap I know wanted an Angola giant sable trophy to complete his African collection. Permits are unobtainable. He secured one pick-up horn of a giant sable killed by a lion, had a mold made by a taxidermist, who then had two casts made. These were then either mounted on the plate of a real sable skull or on a cast plate. The resulting horns and skullplate were put on a papier-mâché form and mounted with the cape of a typical sable. The result is pretty handsome and the owner's tales of his adventures on his Angola sable hunt would impress the most blasé.

I have yet to hear of the same stunt being done with sheep horns, but it is entirely feasible. In fact, I would not drop dead if I found out it had been done already. A taxidermist friend tells me it has been done.

Once a trophy ram has been collected, great care should be taken to see that the scalp is properly skinned out and preserved, and that the scalp is long enough for a shoulder mount. It should be taken off to just back of the forelegs. Eyelids should be carefully skinned out and the cartilage in the ears removed. The ears should be turned inside out and salted. The cape should be salted and then dried in the shade. Most guides want to skin out the heads their dudes take, and generally they do a good job. Nevertheless, the hunter should know enough about it to be able to check their work.

When the trophy is mounted I think the work should be done within the bounds of good sense and good taste. My favorite mount is the shoulder mount with the ram looking straight forward and alert—as if the ram had seen a pack of wolves or a candidate for the Weatherby trophy approaching. Anyone who has several sheep heads and wants some variety can have heads turned one way or the other. A mount I do not care for is the so-called "sneak mount" with the head extended and turned a bit to one side. Taste varies and everyone has a right to name his own poison, but I don't rejoice over "half-mounts," the front half of a ram extending out of the wall. Life-size mounts of the whole ram, tiger, Alaska brown bear, or whatnot absolutely bring me down with chills and fever. Some of my best friends like them but I wouldn't accept such a mount wrapped in hundred-dollar bills or even in pages from the Shakespeare First Folio or the Gutenberg Bible.

Actually the European way of mounting horns or antlers with no scalp at all—simply the bleached skull on a hardwood plaque—looks good. This is the traditional way it is done in Europe. You see antlers and horns so mounted in Scottish castles, in the shops of London gunmakers, and in the homes of Spanish condes. To me this looks pretty classy!

No one who fails to get a ram in the record book should be plunged into despair. It should not be forgotten that Charles Sheldon himself, who hunted in virgin territory and who must have shot at least one hundred rams, never got a 40-inch head, and none of his heads would make the current record book. Record heads are not found behind every briery bush—and that is why they are record heads. The Alaska game department has a record of 5,076 Dall sheep heads and of these only seventeen, or one in 298, made the record book. I had been hunting sheep for over ten years before I even *saw* a 40-inch head. As more big heads are recorded the standards for the record book are raised and some of the smaller heads are dropped out. This is justly so. I think the records can stand further pruning. At one time I had six sheep heads in the book—a Dall, two Stones, a bighorn, and two desert rams. In the last book I had only a Dall, a Stone, and a desert sheep. I did not retreat into sackcloth and ashes. Those trophies that were dropped because others had shot better ones are still good trophies.

Actually the big record heads are largely a matter of luck, and getting one should shed no special glory on the hunter who turns the trick. One of the largest desert sheep heads ever taken was collected by a fat old man whose guides had to haul him up to the top of a little hill where he could shoot it. As I relate in the chapter on Stone sheep, the all-time world-record Stone was wounded by L. S. Chadwick and finished off by one of his guides. The best North American sheep head I have ever taken came largely through luck—with minimal climbing, an easy shot, and on the first day.

The sheep hunter can ensure that he will not return with poor trophies by not shooting small, immature rams. It is no disgrace to return from a sheep hunt without a trophy. I have gone on many sheep hunts and have returned without firing a shot.

The sheep hunter cannot be assured that he is going to see the record head, that dream ram. That is a matter of luck. Generally there is little skill connected with getting the record. Any time I hear of some super hunter, some veritable Leatherstockings who never fails to return with a record head, I generally suspect that some hanky-panky is going on—and generally a little bird sneaks up and whispers in my ear that there is!

16
The Future of the Wild Sheep

In including in this book a chapter on the future of sheep hunting I am sticking my neck out a country mile. Nevertheless I am going to hazard some guesses. Some of them will repeat points I've tried to make in other chapters, but here we go anyway.

I think the prospect for the indefinite continuation of hunting of desert sheep is very bad—even in the limited numbers available today. As I say in the chapters on the desert bighorns, the invasion of habitat by dams, highways, canals, fast-buck land developers, high-tension lines, motorcycles, four-wheel-drive vehicles, campers, and what not is rapidly depriving the desert sheep of the isolation he needs for survival. In the past he has been protected not by high mountains as is the case with the northern sheep but by lack of roads, lack of water, and lack of human population.

Since World War II, human beings have swarmed into the dry, sunny Southwest and have made a playground of desert that was previously almost uninhabited. Barriers to sheep movement like highways, subdivisions, and canals are threatening the sheep as seriously as overgrazing by domestic stock has done in the past.

Now the little old ladies in tennis shoes, whose hearts are filled with kindness but whose heads are filled with duck feathers, have got laws passed to protect feral burros and wild horses on public lands. These animals are heavier and more aggressive than sheep, eat more, and foul water. As they increase, the sheep will inevitably decrease.

The largest herd of desert bighorns in existence, in the United States anyway, is in Southern California. Dr. Loren L. Lutz, who as president of the Society for the Conservation of Bighorn Sheep has devoted many months and much money to the cause of the sheep, says there are about 4,000 bighorns in California, mostly in the desert ranges of southeast California. This was the area where the big poaching scandal of a few years ago took place. Dr. Lutz tells me that he has seen many dozens of fine rams there, rams with massive 38-to-40-inch heads. The season on bighorns has been closed in California for over a century. It will never be reopened. The little old ladies in tennis shoes and other anti-hunting groups have just too much clout. Friends of the Animals and other such organizations are active and well financed. The powerful Sierra Club, an organization which I in the main hold in high regard, is not exactly anti-hunting but it is by no means pro-hunting either. There is evidence that the National Audubon Society is wavering. If it ever swings into the anti-hunting camp, hunting is indeed in trouble.

The Fund for the Animals is hysterically against hunting and is one of the organizations opposed to all hunting on the public lands. The anti-hunters do not mind if cattlemen starve bighorns to death, or if coyotes and wolves pull them down and eat them half alive. In fact, they approve of the predator's rustling his groceries. What throws them is the notion of someone *enjoying* hunting. This thought drives them absolutely mad.

This outfit particularly is great on inventing phony statistics and getting them printed in newspapers, and thus filling the mind of the non-hunting city-dweller with froth. Some years ago an official in an anti-hunting organization wrote a letter to the New York *Times* saying that the Australian kangaroo was in danger of extermination because American sport hunters were shooting it off for the sheer joy of seeing the poor little creatures bleed and quiver. This is pure hogwash. I have never been in Australia but I am an international hunter of a sort and know dozens of international hunters. Among them I have known exactly three who have shot so much as one kangaroo. In reality, the animals are taken by professional Australian hide hunters who shoot the kangaroos, skin them, and export about 1,500,000 hides a year. Apparently the population is stable because the kill varies little from year to year. Yet I am sure many earnest and credulous New Yorkers read the canard in the *Times* and filed it away in their brains under the heading "All Hunters Are Bastards."

In an official statement, the Fund for the Animals says: "Hunters each year cause untold pain and suffering to countless millions of animals. For every bird or animal killed quickly by a hunter's bullet, many more are wounded and escape to die a slow and agonizing death or are crippled for life." This far-fetched and hysterical statement is difficult to prove or to refute. However, this outfit is noisy, well financed, and well organized, and if there is anything a politician is afraid of, it is noise!

God knows the hunter himself is no shining knight in silver armor. All too often he is an ignorant slob who doesn't know how to hunt, who can't shoot, and is too lazy to follow up a wounded animal. The slob hunter fouls his own nest. He strews the landscape with garbage, tin cans, and junk. He wants to ride a gasoline-propelled vehicle instead of walking. His idea of a good hunt is one where he can shoot a bull elk or a buck from the road, back his pickup to it, load it in, and go back to his beer can and his TV set. Because of the prestige involved, many such jerks have become involved in sheep hunting. As I mentioned in the section on desert sheep, one of the finest desert rams ever taken in Arizona was shot by a slob in a pickup and the head was buried. It is yahoos of this type who harass the various game departments, who sneer at the findings of biologists, who howl that any hunt that requires the use of a horse or a guide is a "rich man's hunt."

Today the numbers of such thugs are legion. Since sheep hunting has become almost as prestigious a caper among Nature's Noblemen as a tumble in the bracken with a drum majorette or an assignation in Monte Carlo with an Italian contessa, many of these primates have become sheep hunters. In this windy book I have also already mentioned that one of the finest sheep trophies ever taken in Baja California was shot by a fat old man who literally had to be dragged by his guides 50 feet up a knoll to make the shot.

Some of these slobs are poor. Some are rich. As Sophie Tucker is reputed to have said, "Believe me, honey, rich is best!" But rich or poor, a slob is a slob. A rich slob hires a helicopter to locate sheep, has it land him above them, hunts down. The poor slob poaches rams from his pickup or trail bike. A rich slob shoots five rams in Alaska to get one that will "make the book." The poor slob sticks his rifle out of the window of his pickup and shoots a ram in a game preserve so he can tell his pals about "that ram I shot." At the Northern Bighorn Conference I attended in Great Falls, Montana, a week before I wrote these lines, a biologist told how some slob had shot both rams of a transplanted herd of California bighorns. In Washington a member of the clan shot a ram in the holding pen *before* he could be released.

Another "sportsman" wrote me that he thought hunting desert sheep was very easy. I responded that I didn't find it that way and asked him where he had hunted. He had shot these rams, he wrote, from a boat on Lake Mead when they came down to water. The poachers who knocked off rams from rock blinds at water holes also found them easy, I have no doubt.

In Arizona, Nevada, and Utah there are many thousands of acres of potential habitat for desert sheep. Whenever I drive through Nevada I see many ranges which undoubtedly held sheep at one time and certainly could hold them again. However, most of these ranges, although marginal livestock range, are heavily grazed and would be difficult to pry loose from grazing permitees.

Isolation has protected the desert sheep of Sonora and Baja California, but from what I read and hear, Sonora has been invaded by paved roads, new ranches, mines, and tourists. The Mexican government has plans to put a paved highway from the northern border of Baja California the length of the peninsula to Cabo San Lucas at the tip. Development and desert bighorns do not go well together. I am extremely pessimistic about the future of the desert bighorn—and so are the biologists.

The picture for the Rocky Mountain bighorn is brighter, but not much. Herds in several areas in Idaho and Montana are static or declining through competition with cattle and elk and to some extent with deer. In areas where sheep have been restored and limited hunting is allowed, many hundreds apply for each permit. In a few cases game-department men go along with the lucky permit holder to show him a ram and to keep him from shooting ewes, deer, or cattle.

There is bitter and growing opposition to nonresident hunters in both Alberta and British Columbia. In Alberta, nonresident hunting is now forbidden in the once great sheep country between the Bow River and the American border. Outfitting has thus been killed off in its very birthplace. Dr. Valerius Geist, biologist and author of *Mountain Sheep,* tells me the sight of an outfitter's camp containing an American hunter or two drives the Canadians mad.

As this is written, Alberta has around 4,000 to 5,000 bighorns outside of the national parks, about the same number as Wyoming. Including those in parks there may be as many as 10,000 in Alberta.

For many years most sheep hunting in British Columbia has been done by Americans, but today more Canadians are getting interested in the sport. Canadians are seen even in isolated Stone-sheep country. In the fall of 1973 when my guide and I rode into my favorite bit of northern British Columbia ram country near Colt Lake we saw from the trail a camp that had been set up by backpackers. I sat down on a ridge and located two hunters in my favorite ram basin. Later that day we heard shooting there and a few days after that we saw where a ram had been butchered. The hunters had been flown in by float plane and had backpacked an outfit to within reach of the ram basin. The Canadians and the backpackers bear no love for the outfitters who take out the "rich" Americans.

In Prince George one time I got a much-needed haircut. My barber told me he had been sheep hunting. He and a companion had driven in on a new road that had been built to a mine. They had camped by the road and had then hunted back into the hills. They had not returned with trophies or meat but their trip had not been entirely unsuccessful as they had got some shooting and were quite certain they had "drawn blood" on three different rams.

As roads are developed and country is opened up the automobile hunters move in. Some of these people are good shots, good hunters, and full of ethics; but many, alas, are slobs of the purest ray serene.

It is the native automobile hunter whose heart is full of malice and envy who is the principal opponent of the nonresident trophy hunter. He is found everywhere and wherever he is found he howls for the nonresident's scalp. He sings the same song in Alberta, British Columbia, Idaho, Montana, and Wyoming. He has more votes than the outfitters and consequently more power. He has already thrown the nonresident out of southern Alberta. He has caused a big jump in nonresident license fees in British Columbia and would dearly love to throw the nonresident out altogether.

Collecting a good representative bighorn trophy calls for planning, hardship, and climbing. Today good bighorns are usually taken out of high jack camps, often in inaccessible areas reached by backpacking. Like hunting the desert bighorn, getting a good Rocky Mountain ram is a job for the young and the tough, or for the middle-aged man in fine condition.

From what I can learn, the nonresident probably has a better chance of getting a permit and securing a shot at a good mature ram in Wyoming than anywhere else. Heads run larger in the Sun River country of Montana but I am sure a permit there would be difficult to secure. What I have just written applies in the middle 1970s. It may apply in 1980 and it may not. Tragic sheep die-offs occur with great rapidity and there may be a die-off in the Sun River herd. Furthermore there is gathering opposition to bighorn hunting of any sort.

The Stone sheep of northern British Columbia and the southeastern Yukon are not yet in trouble but they are hunted far harder than they have been in the past. High charges by outfitters have not discouraged American trophy hunters. And as of the fall of 1974 the British Columbia game department has boosted the license for the nonresident to a figure which should give all but the well-heeled considerable pause. My hunch is that other boosts will follow and that a quota system for Stone rams, at least for nonresidents, is not far in the future. The resident British Columbia hunter regards the nonresident as a competitor. He resents his ability to fly to the take-off point by commercial airliner, to charter a plane to go into the sheep country, to hire an outfit and a guide. He votes in British Columbia and the American does not!

At the present time the Dall sheep is by far the most plentiful variety of North American sheep. Estimates of Dalls in Alaska alone vary from 30,000 to 50,000. I have seen estimates of between 20,000 and 30,000 sheep in the Brooks Range alone. As far as I have been able to find out no one has any idea how many sheep there are in the Yukon or the Northwest Territories. My own guess is that there are about as many as there are in Alaska.

Much of the Dall-sheep country is isolated. So far the hand of man has changed it little. The Dalls have been spared the competition of domestic livestock. In much of the Dall range the sheep are on the increase. Indians and Eskimos, who in the past have killed the sheep off badly, are abandoning their traditional hunting life and are moving to town where they can be near the white man's fleshpots, can collect and spend their relief checks, watch TV, and get jobs as truck drivers, automobile mechanics, waitresses, and chambermaids.

However no one should sell short the ingenuity, the persistence, the shortsightedness, and the greed of mankind. The fact that the arctic and the subarctic are isolated and thinly populated today is no guarantee that they will remain so. At best it can be said that the Dalls are in no danger at the present and in no danger in the immediate future. Furthermore the hunt for Dalls is a good tough hunt in some of the most beautiful country in the world. The hunter of white rams in Alaska generally flies into a lake and then takes off on foot or backpacks in from a road. Human nature being what it is, there is some cheating. Hunters are often landed above the sheep on smooth ridges above timberline by light planes with doughnut tires. I have heard reports of sheep being hazed toward hunters by harassing with planes. Locating sheep by planes is illegal, as is harassment, but it is difficult to prevent. Generally, though, the hunter who gets a good Dall trophy earns it!

I am convinced that the future holds more and more propaganda against sheep hunting and pressure to prevent it entirely—particularly in the United States. Most biologists are convinced that the taking of old rams does the sheep no harm. An eleven- or twelve-year-old ram has done most of his breeding and is sexually about as ardent as a seventy-year-old man. No harm is done if someone knocks him off to hang on the wall. Indiscriminate shooting of mature rams is thought by some biologists to be bad, as they believe that if young rams do not learn migration routes from old rams they never learn. Actually there are accessible herds in Alaska where every year all of the "legal" rams—those with three-fourths curls or over—are shot off annually and such herds do just as well as those that are never hunted.

Biologists prefer to keep their options open—so sheep can be hunted or not hunted as they deem best. They look upon mature animals as a harvestable surplus which will be taken by hunger, by age, by cold, or by predators if the hunter does not gather them in. Furthermore, biologists generally view hunting as a valuable management tool—a means to keep sheep from getting so plentiful that they endanger their food supply and as a means to scatter them and to prevent them from lying around in their own dung and infecting each other with disease. And the open season, even if for only a few rams, is a public-relations gesture for the game departments. By permitting hunting they show they are giving the license buyer something for his money. Hunters look sourly on money spent on any animal they stand no chance to hunt. For this reason the open season on sheep is a good idea. The Wyoming game department would not have been able to buy land for the Wind River herd, for example, if the public had no prospect of ever hunting them. If there are elk in country with sheep and the elk can be hunted and the sheep cannot, the public pressure will be to build up the elk at the expense of the sheep.

Nevertheless, open seasons on sheep are fraught with danger. Let us suppose that a few sheep are imported at great expense and a small healthy herd is established. The biologists decide that there are five mature rams that can be spared. Should these sheep be taken or not? Generally the game department proudly announces that there is a surplus of five rams and there will be a public drawing for licenses. Any holder of a big-game license can apply. The game department is swamped with 5,000 applications. It costs nothing to apply. Sheep hunting is a prestigious caper and it might be fun. Many apply who have never shot a big-game animal of any sort. Many apply who have only very vague ideas as to what a sheep looks like. Comes the great day. Five lucky hunters are drawn. One is a thirteen-year-old boy whose father, mother, sisters, uncle, and great grandfather have also applied. Another is a businessman who weighs about 275 pounds on the hoof. Another is a truck driver who has never tasted sheep meat and would like to get some for his freezer. Among those who are not drawn are some who would value a sheep trophy above anything else, who are good shots, good hunters, good climbers.

The 4,995 applicants who do not draw are sore. Three legal rams are taken. One hunter is arrested and fined for bringing in an illegal ram. Two ewes and two legal rams are found dead, and the rancher with a grazing permit on the sheep range announces to the papers that he is missing nine cows and that presumably they have been done in by those damned sheep hunters. The local chapter of the Friends of the Animals chews out the governor and the governor chews out the director of the department of fish and game. In turn the director takes out his frustrations on the biologists who recommended the hunt and on the officer in charge of enforcement.

Because of the prestige connected with sheep hunting and the scarcity of rams the demand for sheep hunting greatly exceeds the supply. My own notion is that sheep hunting should as far as possible be saved for those who value the privilege.

I am going to make some suggestions which I am sure will raise some hackles, will get me hanged in effigy, and which are probably unworkable.

In an effort to eliminate the casual, just-for-the-hell-of-it type of applicant I think a fairly high application fee should be required. I would suggest $100. This would be nonreturnable but it would put the applicant, in case he did not draw the first year, on the list of paid-up applicants for the four succeeding years.

My next notion is that the license itself should be high enough to keep it out of the range of the meat hunters and the just-for-the-hell-of-it hunters but not so high that only fat cats could afford it. I would suggest a resident fee of $200 for the license with a second license for the next year available for $100 if the hunter did not find the ram he wanted or otherwise did not fill on his first try. I would suggest a nonresident license fee of $500 with a $250 license the next season if the license holder did not fill.

In the case of a rare species like the desert sheep of Arizona a successful sheep hunter should be barred from further participation for ten years. If a license holder wounds a ram his license should be considered filled. If he is caught in any game-law violation his license is immediately forfeited and he would not be permitted to draw for ten years.

It is my feeling that the hiring of guides familiar with the country, with sheep, and with sheep habits should be encouraged if indeed not made mandatory. This notion is probably not practical as it would make the slob hunters howl like goosed gorillas. These citizens don't mind providing themselves with cases of canned beer, thick steaks, and flagons of ancient sour-mash bourbon for their hunting trips but it is a point of honor with them that game and hunting should be just about free. If a guide conducts the hunt he should be held responsible for the conduct of his client.

If there is no guide requirement every hunter who draws a permit should be required to attend an indoctrination course. He should learn to be able to tell a ewe from a ram, a young ram from an old one, a trophy ram from an indifferent one. The would-be hunter should also be taught something about the realities of sheep hunting. Much writing on sheep hunting has been done by one-trip experts. Too much malarky has been written about "long-range shooting on sheep and goats." The tendency of the beginner is to blaze away at the first thing he sees which he thinks is a "legal ram" even if it is several hundred yards away.

I recall with considerable choler a story in one of the Big Three outdoor magazines some years ago. Actually it was a "cover story" in that the great event was depicted by the reproduction of a painting on the cover. This showed a hunter carrying what looked like a 46-to-47-inch bighorn head on a packboard. I opened the magazine. The photograph showed this great ram to have been a three-year-old which by no stretch of imagination could have been called "legal." The story itself told of a typical slob performance by a couple of resident Wyoming sheep hunters who had backpacked in, had opened up wildly at long range, and had finally messily whittled the poor little ram down.

I remember other tales which have raised my hackles. One professional outdoor writer shot what he called a "mighty ram" in Wyoming. I doubt if the horns were 30 inches long and the ram was maybe five or six years old. Yet another outdoor writer went on his first sheep hunt in Alberta a good many years ago. He got a barely legal ram with perhaps horns of 32 or 33 inches around the curl. He processed that ram through about seven outdoor magazines and he must have worn the hair off the carcass moving it around to take pictures of it. Then after he had sold the story of the hunt several times he started turning out articles on how to hunt sheep, how to cook sheep meat, how to mount your own sheep head, and on useful things that can be done with sheep feet. It is from tales like these that beginners get their wild ideas of sheep hunting.

Nevada requires an indoctrination course of all those who draw bighorn permits. A legal ram in Nevada regulations is an old ram with horns that score well by Boone & Crockett standards. The bighorn, either desert or Rocky Mountain, is a trophy animal and it should be managed as a trophy animal. Its hunting must be necessarily restricted, not only because the animals are rare but because large numbers of hunters open the herds to harassment, wild shooting, and illegal kills. In the days when any license holder with ten bucks in his pocket could obtain a license to hunt sheep in the Middle Fork area of the Salmon River, as many as 600 hunters were in there at one time. Some were good hunters honestly looking for trophies, some had secured competent guides, but many, alas, were ignorant and irresponsible meat hunters and thrill seekers.

I know a young man of twenty-six. He is a schoolteacher without much money. He is a very tough and self-reliant guy. Every day he runs 8 miles to keep in shape. In the fall of 1973 he backpacked into an area in Montana that is so rough the game department feels restrictions on permits are unnecessary. He had a little tent, a light sleeping bag, dehydrated food, a good binocular, a light scope-sighted rifle. He had read everything he could about bighorns and tactics for hunting bighorns. He was out alone for three weeks. He passed up some fair "legal" rams. When he finally found seven old large rams with trophy heads he knew that he must wait until they bedded down for their middle-of-the-day rest. Then he made a long circuitous stalk, came on them from above and behind. He shot a fine record-book ram at 35 yards! He skinned out the head himself, packed head, scalp, and meat to camp and then out to a road on a packboard.

That's the kind of a guy who deserves the rams!

Index